Fr

NIAGARA

to

MONTAUK

From Niagara to Montauk

The Scenic Pleasures of New York State

C R Roseberry

With the cooperation of the
New York State Geological Survey

State University of New York Press
ALBANY

Published by
State University of New York Press, Albany

Printed in the United States of America

For information, address State University of New York
Press, State University Plaza, Albany, N.Y., 12246

Library of Congress Cataloging in Publication Data

Roseberry, Cecil R.
  From Niagara to Montauk.

  Includes index.
  1. Geology—New York (State)—Guide-books.
2. New York (State)—Description and travel—Guide-
books. I. New York State Museum and Science Service.
Geological Survey. II. Title.
QE145.R67   917.47′0443   81-5640
ISBN 0-87395-496-3   AACR2
ISBN 0-87395-497-1 (pbk.)

10 9 8 7 6 5 4 3

CONTENTS

FOREWORD

New York's landscape owes its form to the presence of diverse rock types and deposits, in a wide variety of structures and attitudes, each responding in its own way to weather and erosion. Geology, the study of earth materials, attempts to explain how features such as Niagara Falls, the Palisades cliff, and Fire Island dunes were formed. Study of New York's socioeconomic history reveals that the variation in geological features across the State has influenced the pattern of human occupation, affecting the location of Indian trails, cities, agricultural regions, and mining districts. In short, New York's geologic diversity has produced a scenic wonderland and has been a principal factor in the State's economic and political history.

Visitors and residents alike, sensing the relationship between scenery and rock formation, or the interplay between geology and history, ask questions such as: How old is Niagara Falls? What caused the vast field of elliptical hills, called drumlins, in central New York, of which the Mormons' Hill Cumorah is most famous? How were the Finger Lakes formed? Which is the highest mountain in the State? Where is the oldest rock? Where can one collect unusual rocks, minerals, and fossils? Why is it said that geology influenced the outcome of the American Revolution? C.R. (Tip) Roseberry has filled a need for such information in a style that is nontechnical, easy to read, and yet geologically correct. No other popular-style book has yet explained so fully the historical consequences or the physiographic grandeur resulting from our geological heritage.

To make the book as current as possible, Tip Roseberry refers to geological processes that are thought to result from "plate tectonics." The plate tectonics theory is based upon the rapidly collecting evidence that the earth's crust is broken into a series of rigid blocks, or plates, that drift independently over the globe's surface, buoyed up by softer material of the interior. Throughout the past, these plates have pulled apart to form rifts, collided to form mountain ranges, or rubbed past one another to form long fault zones. As yet, however, the details of these processes are incompletely understood. Such phenomena as the modern, rapid rising of the Adirondack Mountains, or the occurrence of earthquakes in the New York City region, are not fully explained. Thus the reader must realize that the interpretations presented here are based upon the newest evidence available, but that these will be modified and refined as geological investigations continue.

In this volume, Tip Roseberry has, like a master winemaker, concocted an elegant mix of history, folk tales, and geologic descriptions worth savoring. His talent as a journalist, combined with his love of New York's history and geology, have created a blend of historical anecdotes and geological information that I highly recommend to both casual visitor and serious student.

Dr. Robert H. Fakundiny
State Geologist of New York
Albany, New York

PREFACE

Not everyone is a devotee of the fine arts, but almost any sentient being enjoys scenery. The emotional response to panoramic landscapes, tall mountains, lakes, rivers, and seashores is something deeply ingrained in the psyche; a heritage, perhaps, from remote, less civilized ancestors who lived in closer communion with their natural environment than does modern, sophisticated, and urban society. Spontaneous as this reaction may be, it is possible to enrich and intensify the pleasure derived from such spectacles with increased knowledge about them.

It is a truism that full appreciation of a fine painting, a noble piece of sculpture, a symphony or a ballet, depends in large measure upon some understanding of the artistic frame of reference, techniques, genre, and derivation of the work. The same generality applies, in a real sense, to the scenery around us.

In a foreword to the book *Art Tours and Detours in New York State* (S. Lane Faison, Jr., Random House, 1964), Dr. Louis C. Jones, executive director of the New York State Historical Association, spoke of seeing "with your whole mind, not just with your eye." He urged the reader, using the volume as a handbook, to look thoughtfully at the art—"Then, going from museum to museum, let your eye wander across the countryside and think about that, too. God was good to us even before the artists arrived."

From Niagara to Montauk is a successor to *Art Tours and Detours* in that it was sponsored by the State Board of Regents as a book that, in their estimation, needed doing. It aims to achieve what Faison's book did in relation to gallery art. The motive is to point up the principal scenic gems of the state, to depict and illuminate them, and to interpret them in terms of how they happen to be where they are and what they mean geologically. It is written by a nongeologist, and the last thing in the world it intends to be is a textbook.

Geology is a science that has gained greatly in appeal for the lay public. Everyday people avidly collect rocks, minerals, gem stones, and fossils. They have stood patiently in long queues to behold chunks of rock brought back from the moon. They have read with keen interest popular magazine articles, or watched television programs, about the revolutionary new concept of plate tectonics—of continental drift and periodic long-term "collisions" between continents. This breakthrough in comprehension of our planet lends fresh and dramatic nuances to any viewing of the Hudson Highlands, the Taconics, or even Manhattan Island.

The author, a geological hobbyist since his delighted exposure to the subject as a Cornell undergraduate, had tried his hand at writing popularized geology on a regional basis for newspaper series and, in one instance, a minor book. This background led to discussions with Dr. Hugh M. Flick when he was Associate Commissioner for Cultural Education in the State Education Department, and Dr. John G. Broughton, state geologist and subsequently Flick's successor as Associate Commissioner. Both had the idea that the diversified geology of New York State might somehow be made interesting for the general reading and traveling public. As an outgrowth of these talks, the writer was contracted by the Board of Regents to research and write this book.

A succession of field trips to all corners of the state ensued, in which the author was frequently accompanied by one or another geologist from the State Geological Survey. The bulk of the indoor research was pursued in State Museum bulletins, handbooks, and reports. The writing was done in a close working relationship with members of the Survey staff, according to their specialized areas of expertise. There were also many consultations with leading geologists of various universities around the state as to their most recent findings.

For such cooperation, the author wishes specifically to express gratitude to the following individuals: Dr. John G. Broughton, now retired as Associate Commissioner for Cultural Education, State Education Department, and former State Geologist; Dr. Hugh M. Flick, the previous Associate Commissioner; Dr. Hugo A. Jamnback, Jr., director, State Science Service; Dr. James F. Davis, former State Geologist of New York, now State Geologist of California; Dr. Donald Fisher, State Paleontologist; Dr. Yngvar W. Isachsen, specialist in igneous and metamorphic rocks; Dr. Lawrence V. Rickard, specialist in sedimentary rocks and particularly the Catskill Mountains; Dr. Robert H. Fakundiny, the present State Geologist, formerly associate scientist for environmental geology; Dr. M. Raymond Buyce, former curator of mineralogy, New York State Musuem, now of Denver, Colorado; and Robert J. Dineen, specialist in glacial geology. Apart from the State Museum and Science Service, valuable assistance was also given by these persons: Dr. Parker E. Calkin of the State University of New York at Buffalo; Dr. Ernest H. Muller of Syracuse University; Dr. Robert Le Fleur of Rensselaer Polytechnic Institute; and Dr. Maynard M. Nichols of the School of Marine Science, College of William and Mary, at Gloucester Point, Virginia, who guided the author on a tour of Long Island as an authority on the geology of that island.

Aerial view of Niagara: American Falls at left, Horseshoe (Canadian) Falls at right, separated by Goat Island.

NIAGARA
A Roar of Erosion

Somewhere around the year 1300 A.D., a short but rampant river in the unbroken North American wilderness split in two, creating a dual cataract which the Indians who witnessed the dramatic event named Niagara—"thunder of the waters." The rumble of the falls could be heard from a great distance.

At that hour the nations of Europe stood on the threshold of the Renaissance. Edward I sat on the English throne and had just annexed Wales to his kingdom; he was trying with vain and bloody results to subdue the fierce Highlanders of Scotland. In Florence, Italy, Dante began writing his *Divine Comedy*. Marco Polo, a Venetian merchant, had lately returned from a lengthy sojourn at the court of Kublai Khan in the Mongol capital of Pekin, where he was told of Cipangu (Japan). Polo's book of *Travels* was enormously popular among the literate of the time, stimulating explorations that eventually led to the discovery of the New World.

In due time French explorers found Niagara Falls by having to portage around it. Probably the first white man of consequence to view the mighty spectacle was Cavelier de LaSalle in his expedition of 1669-1670. Quebec fur traders had been using the Ottawa River route from Montreal to the upper Great Lakes, bypassing Lake Erie. LaSalle set forth to find both the Ohio and the Mississippi rivers, of which the Indians had informed him. In that quest he was guided up the Niagara River from Lake Ontario, broke a trail from Lake Erie to the Allegheny River in Pennsylvania and thence to the Ohio. His chaplain, Louis Hennepin, a Belgian friar, became the first man to describe

Niagara in print, in 1678. He pictured the falls as 600 feet high!

The previously single waterfall, eroding its backward way at the head of a majestic canyon, neared a place where the upper river made a sharp right-angle bend. An offshoot of the impatient current jumped the inside bank about 700 years ago to take a shortcut across the angle. This diagonal branch rejoined the parent river just below the main falls by pouring over the east wall of the gorge. The new cataract thus born became the American Falls, while the senior one kept on doing the principal share of the erosion, gradually assuming a bow-shaped curve as it began rounding the bend. The Horseshoe (or Canadian) Falls now carries 90 percent of the river's volume and has retreated 3,000 feet since the separation, whereas the American Falls has cut back less than 200 feet.

The elongated rock hummock around which the stream divided is Goat Island, so named because a pioneer farmer pastured sheep and goats there in the summer; a stray goat was marooned alone on the island for an entire winter and survived. Goat Island, between two great cataracts, has been called "the most exciting spot in America." It is composed of the same durable Lockport dolostone (a variety of limestone) as the lips of the falls and the caprock—that is, the hard top layer—of the whole gorge.

The dolostone overlay, 80 feet thick at the falls, rests upon 61 feet of weak Rochester shales. As the shales crumble from beneath with spray, frost, and water seepage, the resistant caprock loses its support and topples away in huge blocks. The American Falls lacks the force to clear away these blocks from its base, as the more powerful Horseshoe Falls does. Hence the American side allows them to pile up as a talus (fallen stone) slope reaching midway up the face of the cliff. Less than a century ago, this cataract still boasted a full vertical drop. Now it turns into white foam when the water hits the talus. The Canadian Falls, by contrast, has a very deep plunge basin.

Many waterfalls in the United States are higher—one in New York State (Taughannock)—but no other pours so awesome a volume. The Niagara River conveys the combined discharge of the four upper Great Lakes—Erie, Huron, Michigan, and

Superior. About half of this outflow, however, is diverted before reaching the falls for the Welland Ship Canal and hydroelectric turbines on both sides of the border. These diversions slow the rate of erosion yet do not markedly diminish the beauty.

More than 10 million people come annually to take in the splendor of the falls. Too many make the error of believing they have "seen Niagara" once they have seen the two cataracts. The gorge beyond is a mighty spectacle in its own right, warranting a full day's exploration that is made easy by the fine parkways that flank the clifftops.

The seven-mile gorge, emerging on a line between Lewiston, New York, and Queenston, Ontario, is the diary kept by the falls during their rearward march. For this reason it is a valuable key to the latter-day development of the Great Lakes. Variations in the width of the chasm, for instance, record periods of fluctuation in the volume of the river. The narrow lower gorge tells of the earliest stage when only the water from Lake Erie's predecessor came over the precipice. Again, the Upper Great Gorge—the two miles between today's falls and the Whirlpool Rapids—represents the 4,000 years since the Great Lakes settled into their present basins.

These lakes had their beginnings some 20,000 years ago during the final withdrawal of the Wisconsin Ice Sheet. The depressions containing them probably originated as preglacial stream valleys tributary to the Mississippi drainage system. Recurrent advances of mile-thick ice from the northeast scooped the valleys wider and deeper. The glacier finally left a chain of terminal moraine deposits across the Midwest, blocking off southerly escape for the postglacial drainage of the area.

The receding ice front stood like a colossal dam against which meltwater and normal drainage from the liberated land collected as marginal lakes. Whenever the waning front cleared lower divides, the ponded waters coalesced into ever larger and longer lakes. For some time these lakes used an outlet at Chicago into the Mississippi. When the ice at length retreated into Canada, the three upper Great Lakes—Superior, Michigan, and Huron—established an escape route from Georgian Bay down the

Trent River channel into the future Lake Ontario basin; this outlet in turn gave way to a vent through the passage now held by Lake Nipissing into the Ottawa River. Eventually the northern land, so long depressed under the enormous weight of ice, "rebounded" (in a process known as isostasy), tilting the lake basins like platters toward the south, so that the St. Clair River exit past Detroit finally prevailed. Lake Erie now received the full outflow.

Meanwhile a sensational series of events had set Niagara Falls going. The melting ice front uncovered the Finger Lakes region and central New York, inviting marginal waters from the Midwest to creep eastward until they spilled across a sequence of north–south rock ridges at Syracuse, slicing one short gorge after another. A grand waterfall at Jamesville, much like the present Horseshoe Falls, was a lineal forerunner of Niagara, though 150 miles distant. (Its dry crescent at the Clark Reservation, a state park, will be visited later in these pages.) The torrent rushed on, plunging over additional falls, to discover a still lower escape at Rome into the Mohawk valley and thence into the Hudson.

With the floodgates opened at Rome, the surface level of the pent-up lake waters fell 400 feet, whereupon glacial Lake Iroquois came into existence. Lake Iroquois, the larger and higher antecedent of Lake Ontario, tossed its icy waves 200 feet below the escarpment of Lockport dolostone. The ancestral Lake Erie now seized its opportunity to spread out over the limestone platform, dropping down the edge at various locations before finally settling upon the Lewiston–Queenston position. At first it probably fell directly into Lake Iroquois. That infant cataract was nowhere near the size of the present falls, since the three upper lakes then had their outlet across Ontario.

There had actually been an earlier edition of Niagara Falls about 15,000 years ago, tumbling over the Lockport cliff three miles further west at the site of St. David's, Ontario, during an interglacial period of ice withdrawal. That previous waterfall cut its gorge two miles southward to the present location of the Whirlpool, which spins its vortex in the plunge pool of the older cataract. (An estimated 2,000 years were consumed in hewing that gorge). The glacier readvanced, completely refilled the gorge with its debris, and pushed further to the south before the climate warmed again. The new falls, starting from Lewiston, eroded their way headward until they intersected the old buried gorge at the Whirlpool, partially reexcavating that portion. In so doing they created a right-angle elbow for the present flow of the river.

Speculation as to the age of Niagara Falls became serious after Louis Agassiz, the great Swiss naturalist, proclaimed his glacial hypothesis in the mid-1800s. In view of this breakthrough, some American geologists began to wonder if the Niagara gorge might serve as a yardstick of postglacial time. Since a military survey by the British in 1746, the average annual recession of the falls had been four feet, eight inches. By applying this rate to the seven miles of gorge, could the age of the falls be calculated, and thus the approximate date when the ice left that region? It was not all that simple, scientists appreciated, because many variables were involved, such as fluctuations in the volume of the river. Still they arrived at a loose figure of 25,000 to 30,000 years, which was cited to geology classes, and Niagara was hailed as the Time Clock of the Ages.

But alas, the clockworks were sadly out of kilter. More recent scientific findings have set the age of the falls in the neighborhood of 12,000 years. This figure is supported by radiocarbon datings of organic material from the beaches of glacial Lake Iroquois.

Second to the falls themselves, the most awesome feature at Niagara is the Whirlpool, three miles down the gorge. Here the chasm abruptly widens into a highwalled amphitheater where the raging current, after chuting the mile-long Whirlpool Rapids, rotates in a fearful gyration, finally diving beneath itself to exit at a right angle. This remarkable feature takes the form of a swollen elbow between the upper and lower gorges. The river has reexcavated the head section of the buried St. David's gorge, which extends straight ahead in line with the Whirlpool Rapids. Borings in the fill have shown the older gorge to have been much deeper than the present one, its rock bottom being 200 feet lower than the floor of Lake Ontario. Fragments of spruce wood brought up from a deep test drilling were submitted to the radiocarbon (Carbon 14) dating process, which placed their age at around 14,000 years—2,000 years before the birth of the present Niagara Falls.

The Whirlpool is an exciting spectacle from any viewpoint, but the truly thrilling way of beholding it is a trip on the Spanish Aero Car, which operates from the Canadian side only. The 40-passenger open cable car, so named because it was modeled by a Spanish engineer after a tramway he had built in Spain, passes to and fro 250 feet directly above the swirling vortex; it is not for acrophobes. The sight is also well viewed from solid rock in the Whirlpool State Park on the American rim.

The advent of railroad travel in the nineteenth century opened Niagara to tourist invasion. The fringe areas nearest the falls, then privately owned, deteriorated shamefully under commercial exploitation. Tawdriness and vice prevailed. A mutual crusade to redeem them sprang up on both sides of the international boundary. In 1883 the New York legislature passed an act creating the Niagara Falls Reservation. Its purpose was to "preserve the scenery of the falls of Niagara and to restore the said scenery to its natural condition." This act set a precedent in the United States for governmental condemning of private property, by right of eminent domain, in order to protect and preserve natural scenery. Within two years the Province of Ontario followed suit by expropriating the shabby strip then notorious as "The Front" for conversion into the Queen Victoria Park.

Another battle remained to be fought against wholesale diversion of water by hydroelectric companies. By 1905 the New York legislature had authorized nine power franchises. In Ontario, power rentals had financed the development of Queen Victoria Park. Public clamor culminated in the Boundary Waters Treaty of 1909 to regulate the amount of water that could be diverted from the falls. In 1950 a new Niagara Diversion Treaty was negotiated, ensuring a minimum flow of 100,000 cubic feet per second over the falls during tourist season. (The total flow from Lake Erie is twice that quantity.) The great penstocks of the two power authorities are man-made prodigies of the lower gorge.

The Niagara Falls Reservation became the original state park of New York, and it remains the focal point for visitors on the American fringe. It is one of 10 New York State parks strung along the river, interconnected by the Robert Moses Parkway. The observation tower, rising 282 feet from the cliffside bottom of the gorge, commands the American Falls from above and below. Elevators from a promenade deck descend to the base, where visitors may venture into the thick spray of the cataract on the one hand or board the tourist boat, *Maid of the Mist*, on the other. The Reservation takes in Prospect Point and Goat Island. Although Terrapin Point was closed at this writing because of dangerous cracks in the rock, a fairly close acquaintance with the Horseshoe Falls may be gained from that side of Goat Island. The old Cave of the Winds no longer exists, as a result of repeated rockfalls, but its elevators give access to the Gorge Walk along the foot of the Goat Island cliff between the two cataracts. The preferred method of getting around Goat Island is by Viewmobile, miniature trains that allow stopovers at the major points of interest. For the more venturesome, helicopter flights over the falls may be engaged at the upstream end of the island.

The *Maid of the Mist* cruise is the most exhilarating experience to be had at Niagara. In reality there are two *Maids of the Mist* which carry on an alternating shuttle between dock landings on both shores. With passengers zipped up in waterproof gear, the sturdy vessels plow stubbornly ahead as far as they can go into the very throat of the Horseshoe Falls. The boiling foam is so aerated that the boat rides a foot deeper than in normal water. The mist finally closes off all visibility, and foredeck passengers are buffeted by spume and powerful air currents. The name *Maid of the Mist* was derived from an Indian legend about a chief's daughter who was sent over the falls in a canoe piled with gifts to propitiate the Thunder God, who lived behind the curtain of water and reached out to save her.

The Robert Moses Parkway follows the east rim of the gorge. The first stop going north should be the Schoellkopf Geological Museum, housed in a circular stone building of ultramodern design, which presents the story of Niagara with theatrical flair, including a documentary movie.

Further along, the Whirlpool State Park offers fine outlooks on both the Whirlpool and the furious rapids that lead into it. The Spanish Aero Car may be seen making its dizzy crossings. The next state park is Devil's Hole, a deep, craggy cleft in the side of the gorge, once the location of a lateral waterfall that may have been a tributary from the east or a detouring branch of the Niagara River from upstream finding its way back home. Stairs and a pathway descend into the notch, where can be found a cave made by water undercutting the capstone. The trail goes on down to lead alongside the Devil's Hole Rapids, into which Seneca Indians in 1763 pitched a British supply train—men, horses, and all.

Although the gorge ends at Lewiston, a tour of the American side is hardly complete without driving the few extra miles north to Old Fort Niagara via the continuing Robert Moses Parkway. This is one of the most ideally restored colonial fortifications on the continent (ranking with Ticonderoga,) first built by the French at the mouth of the Niagara River on Lake Ontario, later enlarged by the British, and winding up in American possession. The broad, smooth-flowing river, placid in contrast with its upstream paroxysms, lies under the silent guns of the rejuvenated fortress. The best scenic viewpoint is the raised stone platform of the Rush-Bagot Memorial on the northern bluff beside the French Castle, gazing into the blue infinity of Lake Ontario.

There is no gainsaying that the Canadian side holds the supremacy, not only for panoramic vistas of both falls but for the striking and geologically significant features along the gorge. It is also notable for its imaginative horticulture. The writer's favorite approach to the falls is from the Ontario direction, crossing the Peace Bridge at Buffalo and following the riverside Niagara Parkway. That way one experiences a gradual buildup of the drama—from the smooth, navigable upper river to the increasingly tempestuous rapids, seeing the mist of the Horseshoe Falls in the distance, finally beginning to hear its roar, and then emerging suddenly upon the full spectacle.

Excepting only the *Maid of the Mist* adventure, one gets the "feel" of the Canadian Falls best from the esplanade railing near the Table Rock House. The spray is so thick that spectators who wish to move in close should be prepared with raincoats. A popular novelty at this point is the Table Rock Scenic Tunnel, which bores some distance into the rock face behind the cataract. Patrons of this concession are required to don rubber boots and waterproof attire before entering the tunnel. Short side tunnels end at open windows looking into opaque curtains of plunging water—though one gets rudely splashed in the face for the privilege.

The Niagara Parkway is the pleasant rimrock route on the Ontario side. Its first turnoff is for the Great Gorge trip. Lowered by elevator, visitors reach a boardwalk 1,000 feet long, close beside the galloping Whirlpool Rapids. The gorge is quite narrow at this stretch, with the river as little as 250 feet across, and the diversely hued sedimentary rock strata of the opposite wall stand forth clearly. This segment of the gorge was eroded by a reduced volume of drainage from a smaller Lake Erie. Then, suddenly, the upper three lakes began to pour through the Detroit–Windsor channel, greatly increasing the erosive power of the falls. It was then, 4,000 years ago, that the hewing of the Upper Great Gorge began.

Not far beyond the Whirlpool and its Aero Car, still going north on the Niagara Parkway, is Wintergreen Terrace, a broad platform of Lockport dolostone that was scoured by an earlier version of Niagara Falls. While that cataract was booming, it was somewhat like a duplicate in reverse of the present situation; that is, it was split in two by a lesser Goat Island, and the second (or "American") falls was on the Canadian side. From the edge of Wintergreen Terrace, huge blocks of tumbled dolostone are seen down the slope. Below them is Niagara Glen, a dry section of gorge in whose floor ambitious hikers may follow a wooded pathway to the riverside.

A roundtrip of both sides of the Niagara gorge is easily accomplished by crossing the bridge between Lewiston and Queenston.

In the 1960s an outbreak of commercial rivalry gone to extremes produced the three tall observation towers that dominate the skyline of Niagara Falls, Ontario. These are the

Seagram's Tower, the Skylon Tower, and the Oneida Tower, each of which affords a slightly different perspective on the falls. The Seagram's Tower is nearest to the Canadian Falls. The Skylon is the most pretentious of the trio, with a revolving restaurant at its top that gives diners a changing view while they eat.

During the tourist season of 1969, the American Falls was dewatered (dried up) by means of a cofferdam at the upper end of Goat Island, for the purpose of an engineering study by the Army Corps of Engineers to decide what might be done toward preserving and restoring the beauty of those falls, and indirectly of the Horseshoe. The American Falls is in danger of committing suicide by the continued accumulation of talus up the face of the cliff. The final report on the study was issued in 1974 by the American Falls International Board. Its principal conclusion was that the "guiding policy should be to accept the process of change as a dynamic part of the natural condition of the Falls, and that the process of erosion and recession should not be interrupted." In other words, let nature take its course.

That was not quite the whole story, however. The board did favor removal of some of the talus material and raising the level of the so-called *Maid of the Mist* Pool, which has been lowered some 20 feet by diversion for power purposes.

One discovery that emerged from the dewatering was the surprising extent of fissuring in the dolostone ledge by solution. Another was that fish accustomed to living in the aerated foam below the falls died from deprival of the excess oxygen.

Niagara Falls is speedily accessible via the Niagara spur of the New York State Thruway (Interstate I-90). For the American side, leave the expressway immediately after crossing the northern Grand Island bridge (Exit N-21) and get onto the Robert Moses Parkway. If aiming for the Canadian side first, turn off the Thruway spur (I-190) and follow signs for the Peace Bridge in Buffalo. After checking through customs, turn into the Niagara Parkway beside the river. Alternatively, one may keep straight ahead on the Queen Elizabeth Way to a right turn on Ontario Provincial Route 20 for Niagara Falls, Ontario.

THE RIDGE ROAD
Beach of a Glacial Lake

In 1810 DeWitt Clinton, then mayor of New York, was one of a group of seven State Canal Commissioners who set forth from Albany to reconnoiter a route for a canal to link the Hudson River with the Great Lakes. The future governor kept a journal of the trip, which still makes good reading. He was impressed by a bold embankment—"a stupendous natural turnpike," as he described it—along whose crest their hired wagons jogged from Rochester to the Niagara frontier.

"Shortly after leaving the Genesee river," wrote Clinton, "we entered a remarkable road called the Ridge Road, extending from that river to Lewiston, 78 miles. The general elevation of the ridge is from 10 to 30 feet, and its width varies. . . . Its general distance from Lake Ontario is 10 miles. . . . The indications on the ridge show that it was originally the bank of the lake."

Clinton was partially right in his supposition, but mistaken in thinking the ridge was washed up by a higher edition of Lake Ontario. In reality, the body of water that made the shoreline was Lake Iroquois, a glacially dammed antecedent of Ontario. This is more than a mere equivocation. The two lakes at different levels had separate reasons for existence and altogether different outlets. Lake Iroquois occupied a large part of the same basin as Ontario, but was considerably more extensive, overflowing by way of the Mohawk valley.

An important point that Clinton could not have surmised was that the vanished Lake Iroquois would strongly influence the route of the Erie Canal (with which his own name was to be indelibly united in history). Many years would elapse before the exit channels of Lake Iroquois through central New York were

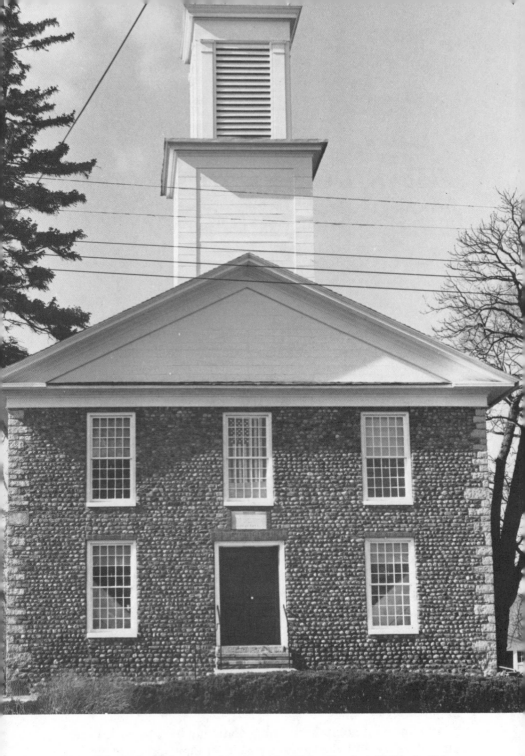

The celebrated cobblestone church on the Ridge Road at Childs, built in 1834. A museum of cobblestone architecture is maintained in this structure.

deciphered, but the canal engineers took advantage of these without the benefit of such knowledge.

Ordinarily a highway does not rank as a tourist attraction in and of itself, but because of its unique interest, if not glamor, the Ridge Road is an exception. It would be misleading to imply that it has any true scenic merit, as its only outlook is upon the level Ontario plain cloaked with spreading vineyards and fruit orchards. Yet it has a certain mild charm, offering a pleasant digression from the monotonous grind of the expressways.

The particular reason, however, for including a chapter on the subject is its significance to an understanding of the geography/geology of this portion of New York State. In effect, the Ridge Road is a postscript to Niagara, although its genesis was contemporary with the birth of the falls. It is very much a fact of life in the counties bordering on Lake Ontario. The Ridge, as it is locally known, is the longest, best-identified shoreline of an extinct glacial lake in the United States. For imaginative travelers, the drive along such a natural parapet may conjure up a vision of the pounding surf and drifting icebergs of glacial Lake Iroquois.

Moccasined feet trod the Ridge for centuries because it afforded a fine, dry trail, and Indians passed the word on to whites. On the average six to eight miles inland from what Walt Whitman called "blue Ontario's shore," it draws a line nearly 200 feet higher. Its nature was so manifest that pioneer farmers recognized it as an abandoned beach and guessed that a much larger Lake Ontario has shrunk away from it. Mollusk shells and driftwood were brought up from wells dug into the embankment. Travel gazetteers of the nineteenth century gave the Ridge Road an alternative name—the Alluvial Way—and one of them observed: "It presents the appearance of a ridge composed of beach sand and gravel stones, apparently worn smooth by the action of water."

Lake Iroquois was the most enduring of all the series of ancestral Great Lakes, a fact that helps to explain the magnitude and well-marked appearance of its shorelines. The "fossil beach" can be traced around the east side of Lake Ontario nearly to

Watertown, and around the western end to the vicinity of Toronto. A hypothetical line between those two extremities represents the approximate position of the ice front during the prolonged period when it was damming up Lake Iroquois.

The Ridge Road offers a handy alternative route between Niagara and Rochester, especially for motorists who have explored down the length of the Niagara gorge to Lewiston and wish to travel east. Pleasant little towns with names like Ridgewood and Ridgeway are spaced along it like beads on a necklace. The early miles going east from Lewiston are rather disappointing, giving little evidence of a ridge or beach. Midway to Rochester, however, the beachlike appearance becomes prominent as the ridge slopes decidedly off on the north. In some long stretches, it takes the form of a wide railroad embankment, dropping off dramatically on both sides. In such instances, the ridge once served as an offshore barrier beach akin to those that border the south shore of Long Island (e.g., Jones Beach and Fire Island), with bays enclosed behind. Marshy places that are vestiges of those embayments can be found just south of the Ridge Road.

Through the north section of Rochester the Ridge Road becomes a street retaining that name, then it continues on eastward through Sodus and as far as Oswego. A newer version of Route 104 has been built east of Rochester which is off the Ridge but more or less parallels it. The old Ridge Road may still be traveled, however, through its old villages. East from Rochester, on the route to Sodus, the shoreline is even more emphatic than toward the west, its slope steep enough in some places that children use if for winter coasting.

Cobblestone houses are a diverting novelty of the Ridge Road. They exemplify an unusual style of architecture that flourished in the nineteenth century because of the abundance of cobbles wave-rounded by rolling on the desolate beaches of Lake Iroquois. The glacier smuggled the original stones out of Canada. Early builders on the Ridge made thrifty use of the materials at hand, mortaring the round cobbles into a medley of patterns in the external walls of their homes as well as schools and churches. Incidentally, this type of construction afforded sturdier protection than frame houses against the wintry blasts that come in from Lakes Erie and Ontario. Some miles west of Rochester there is a tall, square-steepled church built with cobbles that is especially noteworthy.   Cobblestone houses are today much admired as historic keepsakes under the heading of structural Americana. One Rochester connoisseur of the genre published a book entitled *Cobblestone Architecture*. There is a Cobblestone Society, based in the Town of Gaines in Orleans County, which takes particular pride in the church and a schoolhouse at Childs, a village on the Ridge Road.

The Ridge Road is generally synonymous with U.S. Route 104 between Lewiston and Rochester. Eastward from Rochester, a reconstructed Route 104 departs from the Ridge but roughly parallels it on the north; the old Ridge Road may, however, still be driven. In the Province of Ontario, Canada Route 8 follows the crest of the Ridge to Hamilton.

An alleyway in the Rock City Park. Note the quartz pebbles characteristic of the Olean conglomerate rocks.

THE ROCK CITIES
Debris from Far-Off Mountains

The southwest corner of the state, which consists mainly of
Cattaraugus and Chautauqua counties, displays a number of
massive ledges of coarse, pebbly stone that are split off at their
frontal margins into gigantic blocks. Because the fissures between
the blocks vaguely resemble streets and alleys, these features are
popularly referred to as "rock cities." They are unique in
America, and no other such extravagant spreads of quartz-pebble
conglomerate are known to exist in the world. Residents of the
region have sometimes called the rock "puddingstone."

The rock cities have great appeal for sightseers and hold a
special fascination for children, who delight in exploring their
narrow, intricate corridors. Two of them, Rock City Park and the
Panama Rocks, are of such magnitude as to be commercially
exploited, and in earlier time supported resort hotels. A third, the
Salamanca Rock City, lies on state-owned land and therefore is
not managed for profit, but may be conveniently reached on
wheels. Each rock city has a personality all its own, despite their
general similarity.

Aside from the overall novelty of the scenes, the conglomerate
rocks themselves interest visitors with their marked ingredient of
milkwhite quartz pebbles. The rawest amateur will sense that the
content of the great rectangular blocks is secondhand material. It
was once gravel, pebbles, and sand of the kind swept along by
rivers. The question asks itself: Where did such enormous
quantities of gravel come from and by what means was it
delivered at this destination?

Dr. James Hall, who carried out the first state geological survey

of western New York in the late 1830s, wrote that he had been
assured by the countryfolk that these rocks had been dropped on
hilltops by "immense icebergs, which have been stranded, and
subsequently melted away." Dismissing this theory out of hand,
Hall correctly speculated that the rock cities were remnants of
once continuous layers that have been dissected by erosion of the
intervening valleys.

The conglomerate beds (or lentils) outcrop at varying levels in
the wooded landscape, sandwiched amid thick stacks of shales
and sandstones comprising the hills of the Allegheny Plateau.* In
the Allegany State Park* area, they are responsible for flat-topped
mountain spurs, pockets, and amphitheaters in valley heads. The
lentils are of disparate ages, on the order of 300 to 350 million
years, according to elevation—the higher the younger.

The material of these conglomerates, at least the older ones,
originated from lofty mountain ranges in the general region of
New England and the maritime provinces of Canada. The latest
geological thinking, however, has been revised as to the possible
source of the upper and youngest of the layers, the Olean
conglomerate, due to its markedly coarser sand and larger quartz
pebbles. This obviously fresher material may have been
transported from the southeast, across Pennsylvania, by rivers
rejuvenated in a much later renewed upfolding of the
Appalachian ranges, occasioned by continental collision with
Africa.

There was as yet little vegetation on Earth to hold back deluges
of rainwater on those barren heights. Stupendous rivers poured
down the steep flanks into a shallow inland Paleozoic Sea that
covered much of New York State and the Midwest, building its
shoreline ever outward and depositing their sediments layer upon
layer on the sea bottom, which sank progressively to receive
them. In this way the great Catskill Delta was built. The vast
heap of sedimentary strata comprising the Catskills was
accumulated by the action of coalescing river deltas from those
New England highlands, and it gradually fanned out westward

* The variance in spelling as between "Allegany" and "Allegheny" is explained in the
chapter on the Allegheny Reservoir (page 43).

across the state. By the time the front of the spreading delta encroached on westernmost New York, it is likely that periods of excessive rainfall occurred in the eastern mountains. The swollen rivers consequently began bringing quantities of clean, coarse gravel and sand eroded from the rocks (instead of fine-grain sand and silt) and spewing it forth into the shallows. A major constituent of this material was quartz pebbles, rounded by rolling over and over in the long journey.

Conspicuous in the rock cities are frequent interlayers of crossbedding (diagonally slanted strata), which contrast sharply with the enveloping horizontal layers. Gravel being strewn forth from the shore became underwater delta levels, and fresh influxes often slumped over the frontal slopes of these terraces, later to be overtopped and sealed off by fresh deposits.

With the passage of time, the conglomerate strata along with those sandwiching them in were uplifted to become the Allegheny Plateau, stretching level behind the crumpled Appalachian Mountains. Percolating water that held silicates in solution cemented the pebbles and sand into a solid new stone. Stresses during the crustal movements caused joint-plane fracturing in the rocks. Weathering has widened the cracks into fissures—hence the rectangular blocks of the "cities."

ROCK CITY PARK

The most impressive and popular of the make-believe municipalities is the Olean Rock City, whose business title is Rock City Park. At 2,350 feet above sea level (1,000 feet higher than the city of Olean), this broken ledge caps the highest area in a broad region near the Pennsylvania boundary. The sweeping panorama of mountainous terrain would make a visit worthwhile even without the interesting rocks. The conglomerate platform is one of the best viewpoints from which to scan the peneplain effect so characteristic of the Allegheny Plateau. The forested ridges marching off to the horizon are all practically on the same level, as they constitute the remains of a flat plain to which the ancient land surface had been shaved down by the elements before a horizontal uplift took place.

The specific rock found here is the Olean conglomerate, the most visually entertaining of the lot because it is studded with the largest white pebbles, ranging in size from a pea to a tennis ball. These are smoothly rounded, often egg-shaped knobs that show clear evidence of having been tumbled in the stony bed of a vigorous stream. These pebbles spent no time shuffling back and forth on any beach. There is no sign among them of the small red jasper pebbles that are seen in the older Salamanca and Panama Rocks conglomerates—another suggestion of different origin.

The Olean conglomerate is the youngest rock bed of the immensely thick Paleozoic sedimentary series in this state, whose bottom layer rests against the base of the Adirondacks. Other leftovers of this distinctive rock appear elsewhere in a few high localities of the region, notably at the Thunder Rocks in the Allegany State Park. It is of Pennsylvanian age, whereas the Salamanca and Panama conglomerates are of late Devonian vintage. More than 35 million years elapsed between the Devonian and the Pennsylvanian, indicating that the waters of the Paleozoic Sea were withdrawn during that period before the Olean conglomerate swept in from a new source.

A visitor enters Rock City Park by walking out upon its "rooftops," where the rectangular nature of the joint-plane fissuring is at once apparent. Short footbridges span the deepest crevices. Breaking away from the parent ledge, mammoth blocks migrate down the slope, moving by soil creep. The conglomerate lentil here is 64 feet thick. The largest of the migrants is Signal Rock, whose weight has carried it farthest from the ledge; this block is said to have been used by Indians for signal fires. The "trademark" feature of the park is a sort of natural bridge named the Sisters, but also known as the Arch. One block is perched across two others.

Early in this century the Olean Rock City was under lease by the Western New York and Pennsylvania Traction Company, an electric trolley line running over the hills between Olean and Bradford, Pennsylvania. Adjacent to the rock city at the summit, that company maintained the celebrated Bon Air Hotel to which it operated summer excursions.

The Olean conglomerate dips gently toward the south into Pennsylvania, whose boundary is only two miles from the rock city. In the northern part of that state, farther east, it underlies the coal measures. Miners used to call it the Farewell Rock because they knew that no coal was to be found beneath it. In all probability the coal deposits once extended northward into New York State but have been eroded—rather than mined—away.

The coal has vanished but petroleum lingers on. A side show at Rock City Park is the pumping of crude oil on the premises. The first artificial object to meet the eye on the rock platform inside the entrance is a pumpjack in action. Ten wells are pumped on a part-time basis into wooden storage tanks. The scenic property, in fact, is leased from an oil company. Deep underground lies a portion of the once great Bradford Pool of oil, and Rock City Hill was the setting for one of the earliest petroleum frenzies. A boomtown popped up overnight within a half-mile of the rock city, and a pipeline carried the crude to Buffalo for refining and shipping. Today the trail winds among greasy black pumprods moving uncannily to and fro amid the towering rocks. A pumphouse engine throbs in the woods; there is a strong smell of attar of petroleum.

Rock City Park is entered from Route 16—the Olean–Bradford highway—by a turnoff six miles south of Olean at the hillcrest.

SALAMANCA ROCK CITY

Underlying the Olean conglomerate by 500 feet is a kindred though dissimilar layer of pebbled rock known as the Salamanca conglomerate. The type location of its outcroppings is the Salamanca Rock City.* Here nobody sells tickets at the gate, there is no hot-dog stand, and nothing has a sign saying "Fat Man's Misery." Yet the trail following the base of the fractured

* A type location is a place where a given rock formation occurs so conspicuously as to have given its name to that kind of rock wherever else it appears in the world.

ledge is well trodden. The place is wrapped in woods, a quiet and shady retreat.

Although this location is not officially publicized, many residents of western New York seek it out through word-of-mouth advertising. Regionally it has been called the "little rock city," evidently to distinguish it from the "big rock city" near Olean. The separated blocks are smaller, the ledge itself being only some 20 feet thick. The blocks migrate down the hillslope similarly to those of the Olean Rock City, creating fissures and alleyways.

During the great Depression, a Civilian Conservation Corps camp for jobless young men improved and lengthened an old lumbering tote road to the ridgetop site, and what resulted is kept in shape by the State Department of Environmental Conservation. Although primarily intended for warden and forest-fire patrol, this well-preserved road is available for tourist use. It terminates in a traffic circle behind the conglomerate ledge, and there are picnic fireplaces around.

This rock differs from the Olean conglomerate chiefly in that it contains smaller white quartz pebbles that are flattened and discoidal (disclike) rather than round. The gravel ingredients obviously traveled a great distance and were longer on the way, thereby undergoing more thorough abrasion. Their source was the high New England mountain ranges and they were distributed by way of the Catskill Delta. The relative flatness of the pebbles is the result of having been shuffled on beaches by wave action. Because of the finer materials, no doubt, the Salamanca formation is more compact and resistant to weathering than the Olean.

Another significant difference is a sprinkling of small red jasper pebbles among the numerous white quartz ones. This presents a complication, since the jasper—so far as is known—could not have come from those eastern mountains of the Taconic folding. The nearest demonstrable source of red jasper is far to the westward, where it is a constituent of the iron-ore ranges around Lake Superior. Taking this for a clue, geologists speculate that the northern shoreline of the Paleozoic Sea at that time extended roughly along the axis of the present Great Lakes. If this detective work is valid, fragments of jasper worked slowly eastward along the beaches, driven by the prevailing west winds. During the long journey the jasper was ground into small, flattened pebbles that ultimately came to mingle with the white quartz pebbles from the east.

Since the Salamanca Rock City is not soliciting tourists, the access route is rather poorly marked. From Route 17, the Southern Tier Expressway, one leaves at the city of Salamanca, branching north on Route 353 toward Little Valley. After crossing the Allegany River at West Salamanca, drive north four miles; take a right turn at a sign saying "Whig Street." Follow Whig Street three miles to another right at an inconspicuous "Rock City" arrow. After a steep rise of one mile on an unpaved road, turn right again to the rocks.

PANAMA ROCKS

Chautauqua County has its own rock city, but the name of it is borrowed from Central America. The story goes that an aged man, known simply as Panama Joe, attached himself to the locality in early days when it was a stagecoach station supporting three taverns. He discoursed to all who would listen about a period he once spent in Panama. The spill of conglomerate rocks at the brow of the hill reminded him of a type of stone he had encountered "down in Panama." Thus the man christened both the rocky outcrop and the village of Panama which grew up in the valley below.

The Panama Rocks are spread over an area of 25 acres along the crest of a low bluff in a woodland setting where varied ferns grow in dank profusion. Aerial tree roots entwine grotesquely around rock masses, sometimes prying them apart. One serpentine example of the exposed roots is aptly labeled "The Python." The trail for paying customers is lengthier and more labyrinthine than at the other rock cities, leading through and into odd crevices and mysterious crannies.

Found at a lower elevation than the Olean and Salamanca

beds, the Panama conglomerate is considered to be older than both. It closely resembles the Salamanca type, having flattened white quartz pebbles as well as a smattering of the same red jasper trinkets. These ingredients indicate a similar dual origin from currents both east and west. The ledge averages 20 to 30 feet thick.

The Panama Rocks are haunted by colorful legends. Situated on a historic overland route between Lake Erie and a loop of the Allegheny River at Warren, Pennsylvania, they are said to have provided shelter for Indian war parties. Many Indian artifacts were formerly collected among the rocks, and an occasional arrowhead still turns up. A recess beneath a cliff is placarded as the Indian Fireplace. There is an Ice Cave, chilly in midsummer, where Indians stored venison according to the lore.

The claim that the Panama Rocks served as a "depot" on the Underground Railway during Civil War time is logical, as they would have afforded good hiding places for runaway slaves. A favored route for smuggling the runaways into Canada was across the narrow east end of Lake Erie. Yarns about bandits, smugglers, and counterfeiters who used the rocks for hideouts may be more fancy than fact. Incautious visitors may bark their shins peering into a so-called Counterfeiters' Den. It is averred that many counterfeit coins and homemade dies were once discovered in this gloomy hole.

True or not, such tales lend a flavor of romance and mystery to the inanimate rocks.

The Panama Rocks are within the village bounds of Panama. From the State Thruway, Exit 61 leads to Route 76 at Ripley. Then, south on that highway, follow a five-mile easterly jog on Route 74. From the Route 17 Southern Tier Expressway at Jamestown, it is 12 miles to Panama via Routes 17J and 74.

ALLEGANY STATE PARK
Untouched by Glacial Ice

With its 94.5 square miles, Allegany is the largest of New York's state parks. Admirers value it for a simple wilderness charm rather than any dramatic spectacle. Hardwood second-growth forests clothe the hills, which are not quite tall enough to rank as mountains—unless in the eyes of people fresh from the plains. Wildlife flourishes almost to the verge of domesticity. In few public recreation areas is nature quite so idyllic.

This park has one quality that sets it apart in a special way. It is the only region of New York State that was never invaded by the continental glaciers of the Pleistocene. The complete absence of glaciation is more than an academic technicality. It is manifest in the character of the landscape and even, to some degree, in the kind of vegetation. In the final analysis, it was the deciding factor in the choice of this great tract for a state park, as it makes the scenery what it is.

The park realm is snared in the noose of the Allegany River where it arches north out of Pennsylvania. The southward advance of the ice sheet halted just outside the bounds of this loop, while pushing onward into Pennsylvania on both sides of it. The Allegany took on the role of a marginal river shaped to fit the ice front, gulping all its meltwater and then flowing south to join the Mississippi drainage system. The valley floor of the river was deeply filled with outwash gravel, high-level remnants of which are noticeable today as prominent terraces paralleling the park boundaries. They are often used for gravel pits.

The contrast in landscape between the two sides of the river is striking. Inside the state park the terrain is angular. Streams and

Wooded landscape of the Allegany State Park, as seen from the Stone Tower summit. The even horizon is an ideal example of the peneplain effect so typical of the Allegheny Plateau.

the elements have been working on it for millions of years without interruption by ice. The hills throw out sharp-spined ridges. The valleys are V-shaped and have none of the dimpled mounds in their bottoms left by local glaciers.

On the glaciated (north) side of the river, the contours of the hills are gentler, smoothed and rounded by the passage of ice. Their skylines exhibit a slightly lower profile than those inside the park. The valleys are wider and tend to be U-shaped, the larger ones often strewn with the knobby hillocks of glacial debris. The terminal moraine, heaped by the ice sheet at its utmost front, festoons the farming countryside a few miles back from the river.

Natural lakes are nearly always of glacial origin. Anyone familar with this basic fact may be surprised to learn that Allegany State Park has three pleasant lakes. When the authorities decided that the unglaciated park would be incomplete without some lakes, engineers flung a dam across Red House Creek and two across Quaker Run Creek.

This almost entirely wooded park is a haven for campers, hikers, picnickers, and nature lovers in general. In prehistoric time, it was a hunting domain of Seneca Indians, descendants of whom still live on nearby reservations. Because of its special characteristics, its forested drives are well worth side excursions by tourists passing through on the Southern Tier Expressway. For a newcomer, the most effective introduction is by way of the Scenic Road (ASP 1) southward out of Salamanca. In a series of rising curves, this highway climbs to a hilltop divide at 2,300 feet, beyond which lies (in summer) a green panorama. (This park is also a well-known skiing center in winter). A right turn at the summit guard-station takes one onto a mile-long gravel road leading to a stone lookout tower that affords the best scenic vista of the park attainable by automobile. In a semicircular sweep, the view looks down upon Red House Lake at the one extreme and a segment of the Allegany River valley at the other. The tree-covered hillcrests recede into the distance at a uniform level—the peneplain effect already seen at the Olean Rock City.

The descent down the other side of MacIntosh Hill leads to Red House Lake, which offers a bathing beach, canoeing, and fishing.

This lake is overlooked by the park Administration Building where it is worthwhile to pause, inspect a nature museum, and pick up a park map. Highly recommended is a circuit of the well-kept park roads (ASP 2 and ASP 3) from the Red House nucleus to Quaker Run whose exit leads back to Route 17 and also to the Allegheny Reservoir.

Among the assets of this park are two minor rock cities. Thunder Rocks is the suggestive name given to a score of scattered blocks of Olean conglomerate on the high crest of Limestone Hill. The Bear Cave Rocks are a fractured ledge of Salamanca conglomerate on a hillslope above the Frecks Recreation Area at the head of Quaker Run. The so-called Bear Cave is a roofed crevice penetrating 75 feet into the ledge. No bears are currently in residence, but they are plentiful in the park area along with other wildlife such as raccoons and deer.

Route 17 (the Southern Tier Expressway) is the principal feeder to the Allegany State Park, and the city of Salamanca is the gateway. Besides the over-the-hill Scenic Road from Salamanca—entered near where Route 17 bridges the Allegany River—the park may also be approached via Route 280 further down the river. There is a direct concrete road out of Bradford, Pennsylvania.

ALLEGHENY RESERVOIR
A Restored Glacial Lake

It is time to deal with a bothersome discrepancy in spelling. A reader can hardly be blamed for asking: "Which is it—Allegany or Allegheny?" The equivocal reply has to be: Both.

The official usage of New York State is Allegany. That spelling is entrenched in law by the statute that created Allegany State Park. It is bulwarked by the Allegany Indian Reservation, Allegany County, and the village of Allegany.

On the other hand, Pennsylvania adheres to Allegheny, and this spelling is supported by the U.S. Board of Geographic Names. That state contains the Allegheny National Forest, which borders on the Allegany State Park. The river, most of whose course is in Pennsylvania, is therefore the Allegheny, and the U.S. Geological Survey so maps it on the portion that flows into New York. The stylebooks of Buffalo newspapers call for Allegheny when applied to the river, but only to the river. To further befuddle the issue, there is a village of Port Allegany in northern Pennsylvania.

The Allegheny Resevoir is spelled that way throughout its 27-mile length, roughly half of which extends north into New York. This artificial body of water—a unit in the Mississippi flood control program—is markedly attractive because of its precipitous wooded mountain walls. The spectacle may be enjoyed from excellent highways notched into both flanks on the New York side. Motorboats and sailing craft enliven the dark surface.

The reservoir is, in effect, an interstate section of the Allegany River dammed up. Geologically speaking, an interesting thing to know is that it reproduces an extinct glacial lake. More precisely, the Kinzua Dam has restored the former lake at one of its reduced levels—not in its original full extent.

Water sport on the Allegheny Reservoir. The uniformly wooded hills are typical of the shorelines throughout the length of this man-made lake.

Before the Ice Age, the Allegany River did not curve back into Pennsylvania as it now does. Instead, after passing Salamanca it veered off northwest to join a trunkline stream in the depression now occupied by Lake Erie. Just beyond Salamanca it picked up a north-flowing tributary out of Pennsylvania, which arose from a rock divide at Kinzua (pronounced Kin-zoo).

The ice sheet buried the part of the Allegany River west of Salamanca (past Randolph and Jamestown), but halted along the line of the present boundary of the Allegany State Park. The tributary from Kinzua, cut off from its outlet into the Allegany, was backed up as an elongated lake. The floods of glacial meltwater could not have taken long to fill the tributary valley, and when that was done the lake poured over the Kinzua divide, the outflow finding its way southward into the Mississippi. A high waterfall or steep rapids chopped through the divide, creating a narrow gorge. When the ice retreated, it left the preglacial course toward Lake Erie choked with moraine heaps of glacial rubbish. Deprived of its former route northwestward, the river took over, in reverse, the channel of its previous Kinzua tributary through the narrow gorge and thereby joined the Ohio-Mississippi system.

The Army Corps of Engineers found the deep cleft at Kinzua made to order for a dam with which to hold back flood stages of the upper Allegany. Their plans, however, touched off a legal and emotional controversy over the fact that the revival of the old Kinzua lake would drown out much of the Allegany Indian Reservation. By treaty, the Seneca Nation of the Iroquois owned the bottomlands of the river valley from the Pennsylvania line upstream past Salamanca. The Indians finally bowed to the march of progress and settled instead for some parcels of higher land and modern homes built for them by the Great White Father.

Although the original Kinzua gorge was 800 feet deep, the Kinzua Dam rises to a height of only 179 feet. In normal times the impounded water backs up to within six miles of Salamanca, but a large area of vacant ground is provided at the head to take care of any super-floods. The reservoir protects Pittsburgh and the Ohio valley from ravaging. At the same time it bestows a scenic-recreational dividend upon New York State. Even the displaced Senecas have not been loath to profit by its presence, deriving income from the souvenir and Indian Museum trade.

The Southern Tier Expressway (Route 17) crosses the northern reach of the Allegheny Reservoir. Perimeter roads branch from it on either side by which the lake may be followed to the state boundary.

LETCHWORTH STATE PARK
Grand Canyon of the Genesee

Browsing the public landscapes of a state famed for its scenic diversity, one begins to realize how many of its vaunted beauty spots owe their preservation to the foresight of wealthy individuals. A considerable number of the state parks have originated in this fashion.

The earliest large-scale example of such territorial philanthropy in New York State was that of William Pryor Letchworth, a gentle Quaker industrialist who made and gave away a great deal of money. Whatever his primary motive when, shortly before the Civil War, this man took to buying and restoring the charm of parcels of land bordering the upper chasms and cataracts of the Genesee River, this pursuit became his magnificent obsession.

The publicity that has often portrayed Letchworth State Park as the Grand Canyon of the East may strike Westerners as provincial braggadocio. Still, when allowance is made for the vast difference in scale, certain analogies may be drawn. This is particularly the case with the two High Banks sections of the river at Letchworth, where the castellated gorge walls, with long talus slopes, flare widely toward the top while the stream winds like a ribbon at the bottom. The massive piles of Devonian sedimentary rocks through which the Genesee slashes its way loom as high as 550 feet above the river. The grayish shales and sandstones cannot pretend to compete with the colorful rocks of the Grand Canyon of the Colorado for pigmentation—but why should they?

The fact is that Letchworth Park has so many unique qualities of its own that there is no reason to compare it with anything else in the world. Its wonders are of manageable proportions,

Mount Morris High Banks of the Genesee, lowest of the three gorge segments.

allowing a visitor to grasp the scene with some feeling of intimacy. The rapids of the Colorado River may churn a full mile below, but the Genesee's lovely waterfalls are close enough to hear the splash and feel the spray.

Originating in Pennsylvania, the Genesee River runs north into Lake Ontario. It is the only river that flows entirely across a part of New York State. About midway through the transit, after behaving as a placid and conventional stream in a maturely broad valley, it pitches abruptly into a narrow gorge at Portageville. Within a tortuous two miles it drops over three picturesque cataracts whose combined descent is 272 feet, exceeding Niagara's single plunge by more than 100 feet. These two miles constitute the first, or Portage, gorge—the segment that was purchased and reclaimed by William Letchworth, and named by him Glen Iris. In later years the state park of which he was termed the "good genius" expanded northward to include two lower gorges—lower in the sense of being downstream, but much deeper as well. These are the Portage High Banks and the Mount Morris High Banks. The three interconnected chasms give the park an overall length of 17 miles.

Attractive as they are to modern eyes, the falls and rapids were a nuisance to the Indians. They barred the Genesee from being a continuous waterway for their canoes from Rochester into Pennsylvania, forcing the drudgery of a long carry. The Senecas, to whom the Genesee valley was home, were in early contact with the Canadian French, and so adopted their word "portage"— hence the Portage gorge and its two adjacent villages, Portage and Portageville.

The cataracts of the Portage gorge were given simple names: the Upper, the Middle, and the Lower Falls. In this writer's estimate, the Middle Falls at Letchworth are the most aesthetically perfect waterfall in the state. The grace and relative symmetry of its whitewater profile, as seen from any angle, defy a camera buff to snap a poor picture. The sunlight keeps the colors of the spectrum constantly shimmering in the mist—an effect that prompted the former proprietor to call his private gorge Glen Iris, for the Greek goddess of the rainbow and messenger of the gods.

A rural boyhood in the Finger Lakes region left its imprint on William Letchworth. Finding himself, at 35, a partner in a lucrative carriage-hardware and malleable-iron industry in Buffalo, he yearned for a pleasant country estate for weekend refuge from the busy city that had entrapped him. He was thinking of a place on the Niagara River when a friend told him about the neglected gorge of the Genesee, whose beauty had been sorely marred by lumbering.

The Buffalo Division of the Erie Railroad was constructed in the 1850s, spanning the upstream end of the Portage gorge on a dizzy log trestle 234 feet above the riverbed. The bridge was acclaimed as an engineering marvel, and trains halted to let daring passengers venture out upon it where they could gape down over the foaming brink of the Upper Falls. William Letchworth took an excursion train from Buffalo but did not limit his survey to the celebrated trestle. He explored the west rim of the gorge as far as the Middle Falls, picking his way disgustedly among the stumps of what had been a beautiful stand of virgin timber. An ugly sawmill crowded in against the very shoulder of the waterfall, stealing power from its current. A sordid village of workmen's shacks sprawled nearby. Depressed as he was by the spectacle, Letchworth decided he had found a classic site for his summer home, if only he could repair its beauty. Fortunately the lumbering was nearly played out. His purchases of the ruined land began in 1859 and continued until he owned the whole Portage Gorge, while repeatedly fighting off the efforts of power companies to move in and build dams. It took a long time, but a vigorous program of reforestation and landscaping brought back the loveliness.

A substantial frame building, hitherto used as a tavern, stood on a rock plateau overlooking the Middle Falls. Letchworth enlarged and improved that structure, converting it into a white-pillared Victorian mansion amid handsome grounds. A lifelong bachelor, he entertained guests there and, after retiring from business at age 50, made it his year-round home. The house survives as the Glen Iris Inn, serving as the park restaurant and a focal point for visitors to enjoy its matchless view of the Middle Falls.

The squire of Glen Iris also developed an ardent interest in the Indian lore of the Genesee valley. Tangible results of that hobby are among the assets of Letchworth Park. Close at hand is the Pioneer and Indian Museum containing his extensive collections of artifacts. Further back on a terrace beneath pine trees are the Indian Council Grounds, to which Letchworth moved a deserted Seneca council house. Here, too, he brought and reburied the mortal remains of Mary Jemison, the noted "White Woman of the Genesee." To mark the grave, he erected an idealized statue of Mary, a white girl captured by the Indians as a child, who lived out her days as an adopted member of the Seneca Nation.

In his declining years, Letchworth made a practice of opening his parklike estate to the public on specified days. In 1907 he deeded the property to the State of New York for safekeeping. Accepting the gift, the legislature voted to name it Letchworth Park "to commemorate the humane and noble work in private and public charities to which his life has been devoted, and in recognition of his eminent services to the people of the state." (Letchworth Village, a state institution for mental defectives in Rockland County, is also a memorial to Letchworth's benefactions.)

Subsequent acquisitions by the state have increased the park's acreage to 14,337. Its best prospects are to be viewed from turnouts along the main park drive, which skirts the west rims of all three gorges (there is no counterpart of this road on the east side). The two High Banks sections have no waterfalls—only the impressive canyons. Resistant sandstone layers which produce the falls in the Portage gorge are absent in the others.

The fact that Letchworth has three distinct gorges strung on the thread of the river demands geological explanation. The preglacial route of the Genesee was several miles east of the present chasms, in the wide valley now inhabited by the villages of Nunda, Tuscarora, and Sonyea. The glacier left that valley blockaded by voluminous gravel deposits. The reviving postglacial river was forced into a westerly detour over the undisturbed beds of sedimentary rock and went to work carving the Portage gorge. The bedrock upland formed the west wall of the older valley and was cut into by ravines made by east-flowing

tributaries of the preglacial river. As the towering ice front
retreated, it uncovered one after another of those ravines, at the
same time hemming in marginal glacial lakes along the valley's
sidewall, each lower than the last.

Upon opening a channel through the Portage Gorge section, the
river hit the first cross-ravine and seized that outlet into the
marginal lake. The lake filled and joined the river in cutting a
continuing channel across the next segment of bedrock, which
became the Portage High Banks, ending where a second
cross-ravine was met and the process repeated. This time the river
and the marginal lake combined to go to work on the Mount
Morris High Banks section. When the ice cleared the final exit at
the village of Mount Morris, the river was then able to reoccupy
its preglacial valley as far as Rochester, where it was again
compelled by interfering glacial deposits to cut another gorge in
order to reach Lake Ontario.

Another peculiarity of the Letchworth gorges remains to be
explained—namely, their twisting, S-shaped channels, resembling
meanders. A river deeply entrenched in solid rock obviously
cannot meander. The glacier left a thick layer of ground deposit
(drift) spread on the surface of the upland bedrock. The reborn
river's first task was to channel through the drift deposit. It dug
into this loose material long enough to create several meanders.
These curves then acted like a stencil, so that the lowering stream
incised them into the weak shales when they were reached and
continued on in that erratic course.

Letchworth Park is the world's type location of the Portage
Group of sedimentary rocks, an important component of the
Devonian system. The Genesee was kind to geologists in slicing a
complete cross-section of the Devonian rocks, top to bottom, from
the Pennsylvania border to Rochester.

Of the three cataracts in the Portage Gorge, the Lower Falls is
the least picturesque, but it has a novelty of its own. William
Letchworth made a pathway down to it, which still serves. A
visitor walks out upon Table Rock, a wide floor of ripple-marked
sandstone that was formerly the lip of the falls. Over against the
east wall of the gorge the entire volume of the river now forces

itself through the Flume, a narrow cleft 65 feet deep. The Lower
Falls proper has migrated a few-score feet further upstream,
leaving the abandoned platform dry. Out ahead of Table Rock,
in splendid isolation, rises a conical pillar, flat at the pinnacle,
called Cathedral Rock. This is the remnant of a natural stone
arch. The fierce current spouting from the Flume acted as a drill,
boring through a rectangular projection of the right sidewall to
form a high archway. At length the arch caved in, leaving its
outer support standing as Cathedral Rock.

*The simple way of seeing Letchworth Park is to motor the excellent
park drive on the west side, north or south. Thirteen outlook points
permit good views of the park's principal beauties. The main
highways approaching from the north are Routes 36 and 39; from
the south, Routes 19 and 19-A. The park has four gateways: the
Mount Morris Entrance, the Perry Entrance, the Castile Entrance,
and the Portageville Entrance.*

Peering downward from the crest of an esker, the camera catches magic
glimpses of the Devil's Bathtub at the Mendon Ponds Park. This lakelet
is a good example of a glacial kettle-pond.

MENDON PONDS PARK
Landscaping by Ice

Rounded, rolling, knobby, and dimpled hillocks with gentle contours are common in New York, nowhere more abundantly than in the central and western regions. They lend a sculptural touch to landscapes that, lacking them, would be humdrum. They are a gift from the Wisconsin Ice Sheet. Too often, where these attractive knolls occur in clusters, they have been preempted by golf courses or real estate developments.

Fortunately, one of the finest displays of such glacial topography in the state has been preserved in the Mendon Ponds Park, 10 miles southeast of Rochester. With its four square miles this park is the largest unit in Monroe County's exceptional park system.

The glacial features on display are kames, eskers, and kettle-holes. A number of the kettles contain water—hence the Mendon Ponds. The largest of these lakelets is Hundred Acre Pond. Apart from the land forms, this park also contains many exotic and rare plant species. It is rather generally wooded, the only hindrance to viewing its glacial aspects in full scope.

So near to a populous city, the Mendon Ponds preserve would almost certainly have undergone "development" if embattled nature lovers had not rescued it by getting it made a county park in 1928. Before that it had been farm and pasture land. More recently the U.S. Department of the Interior has designated the park as a Natural History Landmark, thereby formally endowing it with "national significance."

The glacial debris that comprises the various forms was deposited underwater in a fairly deep lake. When the ice sheet was in its last recession phase, its front stood across the Mendon Ponds vicinity for perhaps several hundred years. The series of ancestral Great Lakes impounded by the gigantic ice dam had lowered to the stage identified by glaciologists as Lake Warren, which spread across western New York as a narrow belt of water marginal to the ice front. The Mendon kames heaped up during that period now rise in striking contrast to the fairly level meadowlands on either side, suggesting an especially debris-laden portion of the ice front at this particular location.

A great deal of meltwater from the waning ice sheet flowed into Lake Warren, carrying a burden of gravel that the glacier had plucked from the ground it passed over, probably some of it from the basin of Lake Ontario. Rivers developed on top of the ice, cutting into its surface and dislodging embedded debris. The gravel discharged from these surface streams piled up as conical mounds underwater, which settled into rounded knolls, or kames, when the lake drained off. Since the tops of the higher kames stand as much as 170 feet above the surrounding country, the depth of the water into which the gravel was dumped was certainly greater than that.

Much of the meltwater ran in subsurface tunnels within the ice, and these hidden stream beds collected gravel to a considerable depth. As the containing ice melted away, the gravel slumped into sinuous ridges known as eskers. Such ridges—which may be considered fossil stream beds—are sometimes miles in length. They often resemble railroad embankments.

Icebergs broke away from the glacial front—as they do in Greenland and Antarctica today—and drifted off in the marginal lake. Not infrequently a large block of ice was buried in gravel before it was fully detached. In that case it was insulated and might take hundreds of years to melt. As the ice disappeared, the enveloping earth caved in, leaving a depression known as a kettle; when such pits hold water they are called kettle-ponds. These formed the basins of the Mendon Ponds, although many of the kettles in this park have remained dry.

The kames of Mendon Ponds Park are generally distributed along the lines of two parallel eskers, both of which are more than two miles long. Hiking trails follow the spines of the eskers. The eastern ridge pursues a serpentine course and is one of the outstanding examples of its form in the state. The pathway along the ridge of the western esker is part of a much-used prehistoric Indian trail which led from Lake Ontario into the Finger Lakes region. Indians frequented the Mendon Ponds for fishing, and charcoal left from their ancient campfires has been excavated along the shores.

Just inside the park entrance there is a Visitor Information and Nature Center. Although a simple network of roads winds among the kames, the footpaths and bridle trails offer the best means of exploring the area.

The direct approach from the city of Rochester is Clover Street (Route 65), which passes the main park entrance. The northern boundary of the park is within a half-mile of the State Thruway. Drivers who wish to make the short detour should leave the Thruway at Exit 46, turn abruptly north on Route 15 for one mile, thence east on Route 253 for five miles, and finally south on Route 65 to the park.

A striking aerial view of Cayuga Lake, with the campus of Cornell University sprawled on its hilltop in the foreground. The zigzag aspect of the lake suggests the river valley that preceded it.

THE FINGER LAKES
Imprints of the Great Spirit

The floors of Seneca and Cayuga lakes are considerably below sea level. The maximal sounding of Seneca is 634 feet, that of Cayuga 420 feet. These figures do not represent the lakes' true rock-bottom depths because an unreckoned thickness of glacial fill, topped by more recent lacustrine sediments, blankets the bedrock.

Statistics of this kind are an appropriate introduction to the 11 Finger Lakes strung across west-central New York. The astonishing depth, in proportion to width, of the two largest applies in lesser degree to the rest. Their basins all were reamed and overdeepened by tongues of glacial ice grinding south in what had previously been river valleys. The grooving action was repeated and intensified in at least three or four readvances of the ice sheet, after periodic withdrawals, during the million-plus years of the Pleistocene epoch. These are the most remarkable series of linear, roughly parallel lake valleys known anywhere in the world.

According to Indian mythology, the grooves were made by the Great Spirit pressing his outspread fingers upon the chosen land of the Iroquois tribes. This theory is logical enough if the Divinity used but one hand to create the five eastern lakes of the series—Seneca, Cayuga, Owasco, Skaneateles, and Otisco. The six western lakes are smaller and less regular, both in shape and spacing—Conesus, Hemlock, Canadice, Honeoye, Canandaigua, and Keuka. Except for Hemlock Lake, they all bear Indian names, and two of them, Seneca and Cayuga, the names of Iroquois nations.

The 11 beautiful lakes aligned in sequence midway between

Lake Ontario and the Pennsylvania boundary strongly influenced
the pioneer settlement and growth of western New York. Because
of the obstacles they posed, the main cross-state travel
routes—turnpikes and railroads—were laid out to the north and
south of the array of lakes. After the Erie Canal was opened,
Cayuga, Seneca, and Keuka were tied into the state canal system;
Cayuga and Seneca still are today.

With their steeply pitched sidewalls, these lakes do not meekly
lend themselves to tourist embraces. Only in rare instances does
a highway hug a lakeshore, and the lean beaches are uniformly
shingle—that is, fragmented shale. The narrow shores in
proximity to a city or village are nearly always usurped by private
cottages. The exceptions are five state parks which possess good
water frontages: Cayuga Lake State Park, Taughannock Falls,
Sampson, Seneca Lake Park, and Keuka Lake Park. A scattered
few municipal parks also afford public access to the cool waves.

Before the glaciers came along, these valleys, all at greatly
higher elevation, carried streams that drained into the presumed
Ontarian River in the original depression of Lake Ontario. The
master river of the Finger Lakes occupied the valley that
antedated Seneca Lake, partially accounting for the fact that
Seneca became the deepest of the lakes. This was the ancestral
Susquehanna River, which in those times flowed north (one
geologist proposed the blend name of Susqueseneca to identify
it). The notch of Sodus Bay, indenting the south shore of Lake
Ontario, is a remnant of that Susqueseneca valley. The Cayuga
River, nearly as large, is believed to have become a tributary of
the Susqueseneca somewhere to the northward.

The ponderous creeping ice from Canada encountered an
unusual set of circumstances to shape the Finger Lakes. The
Appalachian Plateau extends north into New York State almost to
the Thruway, presenting a clearly defined escarpment. The
glacier met this rampart head-on and bulldozed its way into the
north-sloping river valleys which were like embayments. The
enormous pressure of perhaps 3,000 feet of moving ice was thus
concentrated in these valleys, making them generally U-shaped,
like fjords. The through valleys that continue on southward

beyond the heads of the Finger Lakes testify to the driving force of the ice. Scattered across central and western New York are a number of such through valleys that do not at present contain lakes but look as if they should. Most of them did in their earlier careers. One of these is the celebrated Tully valley, south of Syracuse, which held a forerunner of Onondaga Lake.

Even more characteristic of the Finger Lakes country are the hanging valleys. In no other part of the United States are hanging valleys so abundant, or so dramatic in their scenic effects. These were originally the routes of lateral tributary streams joining the main north-flowing rivers at grade. The glacial tongues gouged the central valleys so deep that their tributaries were left stranded—or hanging. The lips of these hanging valleys are generally around 600 feet higher than the present lake levels. Streams debouching from them have to find their way down to the lakes, and this accounts for the countless waterfalls and gorges all over the region. Five enchanting state parks are centered around the gorges descending from hanging valleys: Watkins Glen, Enfield Glen (Robert H. Treman), Buttermilk Falls, Taughannock Falls, and Fillmore Glen. The shoulders of every Finger Lake are gashed by dark ravines, many of them nameless, marking the courses of streams climbing down off their high shelves.

Still another gift from the glacier is the Valley Heads Moraine, which was responsible for damming up the lakes. During the glacial withdrawal period, the ice front halted for at least several hundred years along a wavering line a few miles south of the major lakes. High-level lakes were dammed by the ice front in the heads of the valleys. Meltwater streams on the surface of the glacial tongues poured their burdens of gravel into these deep standing lakes, and it was heaped into kame-moraine mounds that were left behind when the lakes drained to lower levels. The display of kame-moraine hillocks in the Cayuga Inlet valley south of Ithaca is especially striking. The shapely, dimpled knolls clutter the valley for 10 miles, and may be well observed by driving Route 13 out of Ithaca toward Elmira, or Route 34 to Spencer (Spencer Lake is a kettle-pond left by the melting of a

buried ice block). Probably the bulk of their material is
rock-rubbish scooped out of the basin of Cayuga Lake.

Such obstructions in every valley forbade any southward outlet
for the Finger Lakes, so that their drainage is all to the north, as it
was for the preglacial rivers. By the same token, the Susquehanna
River, while the ice stood in its way, was compelled to locate an
alternative outlet south across Pennsylvania into Chesapeake
Bay. Afterward, having become well entrenched, and with its
previous Seneca Lake route blockaded by the Valley Heads
Moraine, the Susquehanna retained its southerly course through
the Appalachian range.

Cayuga Lake, 40 miles long, is the largest of the Finger Lakes,
as well as the most widely known because the city of Ithaca, with
its Cornell University and Ithaca College, is at its head. As all
mankind knows, Cornell's Alma Mater opens with the words "Far
above Cayuga's waters, with its waves of blue." It would not have
been there except for glaciation. The bottom of the preglacial
Cayuga River valley is believed to have been at approximately the
present level of the main quadrangle (Arts Campus) of Cornell,
receiving Fall Creek there as a tributary from the east. The Baker
Laboratory of Chemistry stands on a high "fossil" delta which
Fall Creek built in glacial Lake Ithaca. Such delta terraces, like
steps, are common at the mouths of Finger Lakes gorges, and
these are often quarried for sand and gravel.

The city of Ithaca maintains Stewart Park at the head of
Cayuga Lake, reached by an exit from arterial Route 13. Early in
the century this was known as Renwick Park and came near to
being the first "Hollywood" of America, with movie studios going
full tilt and exploiting the Finger Lakes scenery. It was here that
Pearl White filmed her famous serial *Perils of Pauline.*

Among other public parks offering direct contact with the
water, Taughannock Falls State Park has most to recommend it.
The hewing of the cavernous Taughannock gorge has built a
large, symmetrical delta thrusting a quarter-mile into Cayuga
Lake from the west shore at one of its deeper parts. The facilities
include a bathing beach and a marina.

Cayuga Lake State Park is near the north end of the lake, not far from Seneca Falls on Route 89. The prime asset of this park is an extensive, sandy bathing beach—as distinguished from the usual shingle beaches. Naturally, the sand has to be "imported."

The city of Geneva prides itself on a straight two-mile frontage across the foot of Seneca Lake. This corridor has long been a municipal park, but a section of it at the northeast corner of the lake was transferred to the state in 1958 to become the Seneca Lake State Park. These adjoining state and city parks are handiest of any for a traveler to reach because the confluent Routes 5 and 20 pass directly through them.

Down the east side of Seneca Lake, a mere 12 miles from Geneva, is the much larger Sampson State Park with its three miles of waterfront and 1,522 acres of land. Tent and trailer sites are available here, with a sweeping view across the lake near its maximum width. This popular park is a sequel to the noted inland Sampson Naval Training Station of World War II. After the war it was converted into an Air Force training base. The Finger Lakes State Parks Commission acquired the premises from the federal government in 1960.

Keuka Lake merits separate treatment, not only for its beauty and the unusual sapphire hue of its water, but because it is a maverick among Finger Lakes—an exception to the rule. Instead of being linear, it is shaped like a boy's slingshot. Hammondsport nestles at the base of the handle, while the crotch of the fork is held apart by a singularly handsome promontory, Bluff Point, its contours smoothed by ice. It was from the surface of Keuka Lake that Glenn H. Curtiss, the pioneer aviator, first lifted his invention, the flying boat, and appropriately enough there is a Glenn Curtiss Museum in Hammondsport. The museum competes for attention with several wine cellars and a wine museum. Keuka Lake State Park borders on the West Branch of the lake, and no visitor thereof should omit the short drive, amid vineyards, down to the headland of Bluff Point for its breathtaking outlook on the lake.

The explanation for Keuka's peculiar shape is the fact that the preglacial river in this instance flowed south instead of north; the West Branch of the lake represents what was a tributary of that river. The other Finger Lakes west of Seneca also originated as south-flowing river valleys. Their direction of flow was only tentative, since they were tributaries of a large preglacial Dansville River which traveled northwest into the Ontarian River.

Perhaps the pleasantest of the municipal lakefront parks is that of Skaneateles, which fringes the north end of Skaneateles Lake. This immaculately kept park extends along the main street of the village, which in turn coincides with Route 20, the Cherry Valley Turnpike. It was the gift of a beneficent resident of the village. Motorists who pause there, enchanted by the marvelous vista up the sail-studded lake, are reported at times to outnumber the inhabitants of the town.

The same Route 20 is equivalent to the main thoroughfare of Canandaigua. Although it does not quite border the water, it irresistibly invites a viewing of Canandaigua Lake. Lovely lengthwise views are easily had from the village's own Kershaw Park, with public bathing beach, at the foot of the lake, and also from the adjacent amusement attraction, Roseland Park. A high viewpoint of this exquisite, 17-mile-long lake is the crest of Bare Hill, about midway up the lake on the east side, a turnoff from Route 364. A spectacular view from the west side, opposite Bare Hill, may be had from Seneca Point, off Route 21.

Route 20 skirts the northern ends of Canandaigua, Seneca, Cayuga, and Skaneateles lakes, and crosses the Montezuma Marshes, a wildlife refuge that is actually an extension of Cayuga Lake. Route 17, the Southern Tier Expressway, is within easy range of the south ends of the major Finger Lakes. Principal cross-routes between the lakes are Routes 96 and 96-A, Geneva to Ithaca; and Route 14, Geneva to Watkins Glen. The best approach to Keuka Lake is Route 54, between Bath and Penn Yan, which ties into Route 14 south of Geneva. Route 54-A, north out of Hammondsport, is that rarity, a highway that closely hugs the lakeshore.

HARRIS HILL
Soaring Capital of America

The National Soaring Museum, focal point for the Soaring
Society of America, is found near the summit of an unusal hill
that was developed as the home grounds of that society two years
after its organization in 1932. The place is called Harris Hill in
commemoration of the first person to fly a glider from its field.
That man was Lieutenant Henry B. Harris, a flight instructor for
the Massachusetts Institute of Technology's Aeronautical Society
and key member of the MIT Soaring Club.

The museum, claiming to have the most significant exhibits of
sailplanes and historic gliders in the world, fronts upon runways
from which motorless aircraft, towed by powered planes or
automobiles, take to the air. Both national and regional soaring
competitions are held here, and the field is in use by individual
hobbyists much of the time, in season. Since 1978 the Soaring
Museum has been housed in a slick new building, with 16,000
square feet of exhibit space, for which a good share of the funds
were raised among soaring people nation-wide. The structure was
designed by a distinguished architect, Eliot Noyes, himself a
sailplane buff.

A sailplane is a graceful, long-winged bird that rides thermal
updrafts—even thunderheads—to great heights, and makes
cross-country distance flights by hopping from one cloud to the
next. The sophisticated metal sailplanes now in use, with cabins
and instrument panels, evolved out of the primitive
wood-and-fabric gliders of early days.

Harris Hill, five miles as the crow flies from Elmira's business
district, is part of a dissected buttress of the Allegheny Plateau.

The gliderport on the crest of Harris Hill. The white structure alongside
is the National Soaring Museum. Silhouetted against the wooded slope in
foreground is a small airplane with a sailplane in tow.

Taking a cue from ardent soaring activities which sprang up in
Germany during the 1920's, a National Glider Association was
formed in this country. Its leaders set out in search of what was
then regarded as a primary requirement—a reasonably horizontal
hilltop with a steep flank neighboring a valley that produces
updrafts of wind. The quest ended with a clump of plateau-like
hills northwest of Elmira, overlooking the wide Big Flats section
of the Chemung River valley whose floor is level as a prairie. The
initial glider flights and contests were launched, not from Harris
Hill, but from the cleared top of its neighbor, South Mountain.
The first national glider meet in the United States was held there
in 1930, and Elmira grew excited at seeing the noiseless craft
sailing over the city. The location was adopted for annual gliding
tournaments, but simple gliders were going out of fashion.

German soaring experts came over for these meets, endorsed
the site, and fired up the Americans' enthusiasm for sailplanes.
The Soaring Society of America replaced the Glider Association
in 1932. Meanwhile the present Harris Hill had been spotted as a
better location, although the summit space consisted of wooded
fields and stone fences. Leases were obtained, clearing and
grading were hurriedly done, and the 1934 meet of the Soaring
Society was scheduled there. The new hilltop was referred to at
the time simply as the "headquarters ridge."

In preliminary testing of the site, Lieutenant Harris of MIT was
first in the air, remaining aloft two and one-half hours.
Tragically, one week before the meet was to open, Harris was
killed when a tow-car he was driving for someone else's takeoff
overturned with a broken wheel. The Soaring Society voted to
name the new center Harris Hill in his memory.

A traveler on the Southern Tier Expressway (Route 17) need
not be a soaring devotee to make the uphill detour to Harris Hill a
rewarding experience. The scene is worth it, and so is a visit to
the museum. As a matter of fact, one may purchase a flight in a
sailplane while there. The hilltop commands a striking panorama
of the Big Flats valley. At the brow of the hill, an outlook point is
provided, 800 feet above the flatland, which accommodates the
Chemung County Airport.

Sailplanes are nearly always in the air, weather permitting. If not soaring from the hill itself, they will have taken off from the airport, a portion of which is used by the Schweizer Aircraft Corporation and its associated Schweizer Soaring School. The Schweizer plant, which pioneered the manufacture of metal sailplanes, is located near the airport. Besides training pilots for soaring, the company purveys passenger flights in two-place sailplanes.

The Big Flats valley is an outstanding example of a one-time glacial lake basin. Reference has been made elsewhere to the so-called Susqueseneca River—that is, the preglacial Susquehanna River which flowed northward in the valley today holding Seneca Lake. In those days the Chemung River was a major tributary of that river from the west, eroding the ancestral valley of the Big Flats. During the Ice Age an offshoot of the glacial tongue gouging the deep trough of Seneca Lake pushed westward in the Chemung River valley, making it wider and steepening its walls.

While the ice sheet was withdrawing, the durable tongue in the Seneca Lake valley still protruded southward, acting as a high dam to block off the eastern end of the Chemung valley in the vicinity of Horseheads. The Chemung River, greatly swollen, filled that valley to create glacial Lake Elmira. Meltwater from the receding ice front swept into this temporary lake, strewing gravel and sand deeply on the lake bed. That thick deposit accounts for the Big Flats.

Meanwhile, Lake Elmira, filled to the brim, found its spillway by cutting diagonally across the buttress of the Allegheny Plateau that includes Harris Hill. The gushing outflow rapidly carved the seven-mile gorge now followed by Route 17-E southeast from Route 17 into Elmira. By this means the pent-up water of Lake Elmira was enabled to join the south-flowing Susquehanna River east of Elmira. When the last ice disappeared, the reviving Chemung River, headed off from its old route by the thick lake-bottom fill in the Big Flats valley, adopted the new gorge route past Elmira and thus became a feeder to Chesapeake Bay.

These rather complex happenings helped to make Harris Hill the right sort of headquarters for the Soaring Society of America.

Almost the entire crown of the hill, including the soaring center and the museum, is embraced in Harris Hill Park, a general recreation area maintained by Chemung County. The approach highway to the Soaring Museum winds through the well-kept park, which affords picnic tables and grills, a five-hole free golf course, a golf driving range, swimming pool, playfields, and a small amusement park especially for children.

The Harris Hill soaring establishment is reached by a circuitous blacktop road, quite steep in places. This highway turns south off Route 17 at Exit 51, near the Chemung County Airport, about five miles west of Horseheads. Follow signs for Harris Hill Park and the National Soaring Museum.

Looking up the gorge of Watkins Glen. A series of pothole borings are seen in the near foreground. The curtain of Rainbow Falls slips over the rock wall at left.

WATKINS GLEN
The Poetry of Potholes

N.Y. State Commerce Dept.

Local people used to refer to Watkins Glen disparagingly as the Big Gully. They called the stream brawling down its intricate corridor Mill Creek because of the sawmills and gristmills utilizing its hydraulic power. Present-day visitors find it hard to believe that dams were built above the lovely cataracts inside the gorge, and that the tunnels through which people now walk were blasted in order to sluice water to mill wheels. In the wake of the Civil War, the name Watkins Glen became a household phrase and sightseers flocked there by rail and steamboat. Hotels, competing with resorts at Niagara Falls, the Catskills, and the White Mountains, soon flourished around Watkins Glen. Morvalden Ells, a small-town newspaper editor, wrought this miracle many years before public relations achieved the status of a profession.

Although typical of hundreds of gorges in the Finger Lakes region, in some respects Watkins Glen is unique. Its front entrance, like the lobby of a theater, opens directly off the main street of a village. A former New York druggist, Dr. Samuel Watkins, laid out and mapped the village and further developed the mills started by an older brother. Dr. Watkins first christened the town Salubria, then Jefferson, but after his death in 1851 the state legislature renamed it in tribute to him.

In 1856 Morvalden Ells moved from Elmira to purchase the Watkins *Republican*. Exploring the Big Gully thoroughly, he gave scenic features fanciful names such as Pluto Falls and Artist's Dream, still in use today. Some wooden walks and stairs had already been installed to enable workmen to reach a mill. The editor obtained permission for their public use, and charged for admission. Watkins Glen officially opened as a tourist mecca July 4, 1863, at the height of the Civil War. Ells sold his newspaper to devote full time to promotion of the area. His articles singing its praises appeared in papers throughout the country. Prominent authors including Mark Twain added their descriptions to Ells's press releases, and noted artists traveled to the Glen to paint the views.

In his wildest flights of fancy, Morvalden Ells could not have imagined a publicity stunt for the Glen as effective as the one supplied by a frightened deer in 1933. One morning a seven-point buck, probably chased by dogs, was found stranded in the gorge on a narrow ledge with a sheer drop of 180 feet. A doe had lost her footing and lay dead in the stream bed beneath.

Food and water were lowered to the animal. A bridge was flung across the gorge to the ledge, but the skittish deer refused to use it. Day by day, the suspense of the situation bloomed into a page-1 newspaper thriller. Motorists drove long distances just to see the deer; 100,000 visitors walked up the gorge over the Labor Day weekend; 350,000 were counted in a period of 11 days. Park officials would not allow anyone too near lest the animal leap to its death. On the twelfth day the deer solved the problem. He picked his way gingerly along the cliffside at dawn, waded the stream, climbed the other side, and went on his way.

As a result of Mr. Ells's activity, a Watkins Glen Improvement Company was formed to make the gorge more accessible. After that, it was sold and resold to financiers, who at some time removed the mills and dams. Wooden walks, steps, and railings gave way to more modern developments such as concrete walkways with outlooks and iron guardrails. Many nature-lovers disliked these so-called improvements as too artificial.

The State of New York purchased Watkins Glen in 1906 for $46,512 as a state reservation, later making it a state park. Today Watkins Glen, the best known of the Finger Lakes parks, is the most highly developed and attracts the most visitors.

In 1935, a Southern Tier cloudburst played havoc with all the Finger Lakes gorges, but especially with Watkins where damage exceeded $1 million. In a way, the flood was a blessing in disguise. It demolished the iron railings, concrete stairways, and walks. In restoring this and other park gorges, the Finger Lakes State Parks Commission made installations more naturalistic by using native stone masonry. If some vestiges of artificiality remain, they are unobtrusive. Who will quibble about a concrete lip needed to prevent self-destruction of a beautiful waterfall?

As New York State's finest example of the pothole type of gorge, Watkins Glen has great appeal to camera buffs. Potholes are borings made by swirling currents in rapidly descending streams. The rotary scouring action of stones and gravel caught in the holes enlarges them into round, deep kettles in the bedrock, where long, narrow series of passages present one pothole after another. Often the potholes break through partitions and merge, giving the stream channel an effect resembling a string of hourglasses. This accounts in large part for the constant novelty of the scenes. A tour through Watkins Glen is a visit to an art gallery of nature, each picture to be savored individually before moving on to the next.

In comparison with other gorges in the Finger Lakes region, Watkins's tortuous and writhing mile-long bed is remarkably narrow in many places. At times the channel squeezes into a flume that is scarcely larger than a groove. Glen Creek splashes over 19 waterfalls of striking diversity, ranging from straight drops to twisted chutes in which the rock has been polished to the texture of mahogany. Frequent layers of resistant sandstone interleaved with weaker Devonian shales created waterfalls. In two instances the trail passes behind the falls. Full of surprises, Watkins Glen relies on an intimate, focused kind of charm rather than stupendous grandeur. The lower portion is floodlighted for viewing at night.

Visitors to Watkins Glen generally follow a tourist trail that ends just below a high railroad trestle. Upstream from that bridge, the channel widens into a section of much larger gorge. This is part of an interglacial gorge carved many thousands of years earlier during a long period of ice withdrawal. Its floor is 500 feet higher than the elevation of the village. This gorge was

filled again when the glacier readvanced. The loose material has
been cleaned out in postglacial time.

Since the Glen has lower and upper entrance facilities, it may
be toured in either direction. Most visitors hike both ways. The
roughly 500-foot climb up is good exercise. The easier method,
however, is to start at the top and saunter down to the front exit.
To accommodate parties lacking a spare driver for this gambit, a
commercial taxicab service is available at the main-entrance
parking lot. The road to the upper entrance (Route 329) is on the
north side of the gorge, off the main street of the town.

*Watkins Glen, the village and park, is located at the head of Seneca
Lake. Route 14, the north–south highway between Thruway Exit
42 and the Southern Tier Expressway (Route 17), is the best
approach. Alternatives are Route 414 from Corning, or Routes 13
and 224 from Ithaca.*

ENFIELD GLEN
An Architectural Gorge

As Watkins Glen is basically a pothole type of gorge, so Enfield Glen is a classic instance of a gorge whose erosion has been governed largely by joint planes in the rock beds.

The entrance sign, five miles south of Ithaca, reads "Robert H. Treman State Park," but residents of the locality cling to the older name. Mr. Treman was an Ithaca banker with a passion for the natural beauties of the Finger Lakes region. He systematically bought up farmlands surrounding the gorge of Enfield Creek and hired a landscape architect to lay out pathways and build stone bridges in harmony with the environment. In 1920 he and his wife donated the property to the state and it became Enfield Glen State Park. He repeated the process with Buttermilk Falls State Park, three miles nearer the city.

Mr. Treman was the first chairman of the Finger Lakes State Park Commission. After his death in 1937, the Enfield Glen park was officially renamed in his honor.

Rectangular joint planes are especially marked in Enfield Glen. Weathering frequently widens them into fissures. The corridors of the gorge typically present smooth, sheer walls and square corners that are almost architectural in appearance. Here and there the water glides along smoothly in straight-hewn troughs like millraces. In consequence of the precedent established by Mr. Treman's landscape architect, the stairways, parapets, and bridges are constructed with native stone, making them blend beautifully with the natural setting.

The overall length of Enfield Glen is three miles, but only a confirmed hiker and nature buff is advised to walk the full distance. Enfield is a triple gorge. The upper and lower sections are the relatively narrow and spectacular postglacial gorges. The

Lucifer Falls at Enfield Glen (officially known as Robert H. Treman State Park).

lengthy middle section is a wide, slope-sided interglacial gorge: that is, it was carved during a long period while the ice was withdrawn. When the glacier recurred it filled up this gorge with debris. The reborn postglacial stream cleared out a portion of the prior gorge while hewing the new one. Every Finger Lakes glen has a buried interglacial gorge alongside, and in several instances parts of the hidden gorge have been similarly reexcavated. The trip through the interglacial gorge segment at Enfield is a pleasant woodland hike but not necessary.

The upper gorge is the dramatic part with most appeal to the average visitor. It is a half-mile walk down to the base of Lucifer Falls, which is the best cataract. This waterfall has a total descent of 115 feet, but, while fascinating, it is not vertical. It is the means by which the stream debouches into the abruptly wider interglacial gorge. Lucifer Falls may be defined as a joint-plane waterfall. Because of the control of erosion by joint-plane fissuring, the creek tumbles sidewise into a deep corridor in which it turns immediately to the left. The alcove of the plunge basin is called the Devil's Kitchen, where, it is said, boisterous rural barbecues were held in pioneer days. No doubt there is a connection between the names Lucifer Falls and Devil's Kitchen.

A visitor with no inclination for the nature walk of the middle gorge will turn back from Lucifer Falls and retrace his steps. The lower gorge, once part of the tour, has not been open to the public since the 1935 cloudburst in the Southern Tier wiped out walkways so completely that they could not be restored.

The lower-entrance area is primarily recreational, its feature attraction being a dammed-up swimming pool. This excellent pool receives the foaming water of the Lower Falls, a picturesque cataract of the jutting "pulpit" (or bastion) type so common in Finger Lakes gorges. The form results from the even weathering of shale beds without a strong capstone, the spray wearing them back at the sides to give the falls a convex, crescent shape.

The front entrance to Robert H. Treman State Park is from Route 13, five miles southwest of Ithaca. The upper entrance is reached by driving west on Route 327.

Taughannock Falls, 215 feet high, as seen from upper outlook.

TAUGHANNOCK FALLS
Highest in the Northeast

Of all the Finger Lakes gorges, that of Taughannock comes nearest to being a canyon. In a length of just over a mile, its floor is practically level between precipices as high as 400 feet. The beautiful waterfall at its head plunges 215 feet in a straight drop.

Taughannock has long been publicized as the highest sheer (that is, unbroken) falls east of the Mississippi, or highest east of the Rockies. Neither claim is justified. Tennessee has a Fall Creek Falls State Park whose feature is a magnificent cataract that makes a vertical dive of 256 feet.

In any case, Taughannock is the highest perpendicular waterfall in the northeastern United States. It is preserved in the Taughannock Falls State Park on the west side of Cayuga Lake. The remarkable delta, thrusting into the lake at one of its deepest parts, indicates the mass of rock material that the stream has excavated from the spacious gorge. The delta is the main recreation area of the park, with bathing beach, a marina basin, and playfields.

The foot of the falls is reached by an easy stroll up the gorge, and its height is best appreciated by looking up. The long drop creates a good deal of the bridal veil effect, and the spray has weathered the shale beds into a rounded amphitheater. The plunge pool is 30 feet deep. A parkway on the north shoulder of the gorge provides access to the Falls View Overlook with its pictorial perspective that is the delight of photographers.

The shape of the falls—a recessed right angle at the brink—is part of its charm. Until 1894, the water came over a projecting right angle. In that year, guests in the resort hotels which then did a thriving business near the top were awakened by a fierce electric storm. After an ear-shattering clap of thunder, they heard a loud roar that shook the buildings. Next morning early risers going out to look at the falls found its profile reversed. A square block of the hard sandstone had tumbled from the lip of the falls, and guests were convinced that it had been blasted loose by lightning.

The height of the falls is the result of a special geological circumstance, in which 200 feet of weak shales are sandwiched between two layers of highly resistant rock. The cataract itself spills over a thick ledge of Sherburne flagstone. The gorge is floored by an even tougher layer of Tully limestone, and the soft overlying shale weathers fast. The limestone, which is quarried on the opposite shore of the lake for Portland cement, has produced a low fall near the mouth of the gorge.

The name Taughannock is a variation of an Indian word supposed to have meant "great fall in the woods." It takes another form in the eastern part of the state where it is applied to the Taconic mountains and the Taconic Parkway. Tunkhannock is a town in Pennsylvania.

The park entrance is on Taughannock Boulevard (Route 89) about 12 miles north of Ithaca. An alternative approach road branches from Route 96 a mile south of Trumansburg. Headquarters offices of the Finger Lakes State Park Commission are maintained at this park.

ITHACA COLLEGE CAMPUS
A Notch in the Hill

The old Ithaca Conservatory of Music was cooped up in a cluster
of made-over dwellings in downtown Ithaca. Within recent years
it graduated to the status of an endowed college and moved up in
the world both scholastically and geographically. Now, at an
elevation of near 1,000 feet, it is farther above Cayuga's waters
than its Ivy League neighbor, Cornell University. Its view of that
Finger Lake is fuller, although distant.

Ithaca College is oriented to music and other arts, not to
science. It has no geology course in its curriculum, which is rather
a shame. Students should have the chance to understand the
reason for the shelf in the nose of South Hill upon which their
sightly campus is laid out.

South Hill rises steeply out of the city, and valleys branch off
either side of its beak. The great through valley of the Cayuga
Inlet lies on the west, that of Six-Mile Creek (a hanging valley) on
the east. Both of these valleys were filled by high-level glacial
lakes draining southward from their overflows into the
Susquehanna River. The two lakes, with icebergs afloat, were
held in those basins until the ice front retreated away from the
nose of South Hill. The western lake stood 60 feet higher than the
eastern, as revealed by their overflow channels.

One day the ice resting against South Hill melted just enough to
allow a trickle of water from the higher lake into the lower. The
trickle grew into a gush, the gush into a torrent. A waterfall
quickly developed and lasted long enough to cut a temporary
gorge, of which the ice made one wall, bedrock of the hill the
other. The bottom of this channel was beveled to a flat shelf in

The outlook from the Tower Club of Ithaca College commands this sweeping panorama over the city of Ithaca, with Cayuga Lake in the far distance. The campus in the foreground is at an elevation of more than 800 feet above the lake, and higher than that of Cornell University, seen dimly beyond the right-hand post.

the rock. When the glacier withdrew, it left a clear-cut notch in the profile of South Hill. The backdrop of the campus is the weathered rock wall of the short-lived gorge.

With further retreat of the ice, the two glacial lakes merged into a single two-pronged body of water with South Hill projecting into it as a promontory. This was Lake Ithaca, and it persisted until the water found a crosscut outlet near Interlaken into Seneca Lake.

And so, because of that glacial episode, Ithaca College looks down upon its long-time rival, Cornell, from an advantage of 400 feet.

From the intersection of State and Aurora Streets in the business center of Ithaca, it is two miles up a stiff grade to Ithaca College on Route 968.

Two parallel drumlins in the Weedsport area of central New York are nicely profiled in this aerial picture.

MORMON HILL
The Sacred Drumlin

To members of the Church of Jesus Christ of Latter-day Saints, Hill Cumorah is a hallowed spot where their creed had its origin. Mormons make long pilgrimages to visit it. They flock in large numbers for yearly pageants retelling the story of their Book of Mormon.

For travelers of whatever faith, cult, or philosophy Hill Cumorah is a singular and pleasant scene. The Mormons, who own and preserve it as a quasi-shrine, are hospitable to all comers. At the foot of the hill on the entrance road is a visitors' center and information bureau, with free guide service available.

Hill Cumorah—secularly better known as Mormon Hill—is a nearly perfect specimen of that novel glacial form, a drumlin. By no means is it an isolated sample. It belongs to a colony which is the most lavish array of drumlins in the world. Approximately 10,000 of them strew the plain between the Finger Lakes and Lake Ontario. Almost every hill along the road from Rochester to Syracuse is a drumlin. The railways of Amtrak and Conrail, the State Thruway, and the Barge Canal cut through drumlins, which make the terrain interesting when looked down upon from airliners on the Albany–Buffalo run.

Drumlin is a Celtic word for "little hill." It entered the scientific vocabulary because a large spread of them in Ireland were the first to be studied. Rural folk living amid the New York cluster used to call them hoddy-doddies. They attract notice because of their peculiar shape in profile view—that of an elongated oval, or half a boiled egg sliced lengthwise, or, as often averred, a dolphin's back. A typical drumlin is smoothly contoured, measures anywhere from a few hundred feet to over a mile long, and stands from 200 to more than 500 feet high. Their soil is richly fertile, so that they invite cultivation. With their gentle slopes, they are tempting sites for farmhouses and real estate subdivisions. Where road cuts bisect them, as the Thruway does in several places, it can be seen that they almost never have a bedrock core.

The Book of Mormon relates how the aged prophet, Mormon, engraved the history of his doomed people, the Nephites, on a set of gold tablets and concealed them "up in the hill Cumorah," entrusting their custody to his son, Moroni. Soon after that, the Nephites were annihilated by the Lamanites in a fearful battle. Moroni was the sole survivor of the massacre, and he completed the written record, adding the Book of Moroni to the golden plates. After a lapse of 1,400 years (as the Mormons believe), Joseph Smith, a farmer youth living near the Hill Cumorah, received a strange visit from a heavenly messenger who materialized from a glow of light. The herald was the Angel Moroni, who confided to Joseph Smith the secret of the plates. In the year 1827 Moroni came again and permitted Joseph to remove the tablets from a stone crypt in the side of the hill, along with a key by which to translate their inscriptions. When Smith had completed the task for which he was chosen, the Angel Moroni returned and took away the gold plates. Smith's translation became the Mormon scriptures and he the founder of a new religion. The migration of the persecuted Mormons from place to place until they reached Great Salt Lake is a stirring epic of American history.

Because of its religious significance, Hill Cumorah is the best-groomed of the 10,000 drumlins. The Mormon church keeps it immaculately landscaped and horticultured. A broad pathway follows the crest of the ridge to a gilded statue of the Angel Moroni on a tall monument. One question to which the information bureau does not supply an answer is: What is a drumlin?

The process by which drumlins are created was long a moot point among geologists. It is all but impossible to investigate the sole of a currently active glacier. Consequently the explanation has been arrived at by rational guesswork. A drumlin is composed of concentric layers—gravel with an excess of clay for a binding material. These layers have the look of being plastered on and rubbed down, as a sculptor might work on a clay model. It is commonly agreed that drumlins were built by accretion as the ice moved over and around them. The condition for their formation appears to have been a thinning advance margin of the ice sheet on a fairly level surface during a late stage of the recession.

Specifically: A reduced lobe of ice occupied the future basin of Lake Ontario, radiating out over the adjacent lowland. The principal burden of this ice was pulverized shale from the lake basin—hence the high content of clay. The thin margin was not exerting so great a pressure on the land as before. With a thrust from behind (a slight readvance), the ice tended to slip, or slide, over the ground without digging in. Where it passed over a slight obstruction, the clay at the bottom adhered and was added to, layer by layer. The obstacle may have been a heap of glacial till, a gob of clay, or a small protrusion of bedrock.

It is characteristic of the drumlin form that the stoss, or up-ice end, is steepened because the ice rammed against it. Then it tapers off gradually and gracefully toward the lee, or down-ice end. The long axis of the drumlins indicates the direction of ice movement, which in the case of Mormon Hill and its near neighbors was from north to south.

These were things which Joseph Smith did not know when he wonderingly lifted the gold plates from the flank of Hill Cumorah. Geology was then almost as unknown a science as Mormonism was a religion. The glacial hypothesis was as yet unrealized.

Mormon Hill is about four miles due south of Palmyra. It is easily reached from the Thruway by leaving at Exit 43 and driving two miles north on Route 21.

Chimney Bluffs, the wave-cut remnants of a giant drumlin on the shore of Lake Ontario.

CHIMNEY BLUFFS
Spires by the Lakeside

The shore of Lake Ontario between Rochester and Oswego is notewothry for a succession of wave-cut bluffs reminiscent of those on the northern margin of Long Island.The galaxy of 10,000 drumlins, of which Mormon Hill makes one, spreads northward, and an unknown number of them are submerged in Lake Ontario. The islands in Sodus Bay are drumlins. The cross-sections behind the beaches have given geologists a welcome opportunity to study the internal structure of this rare glacial form.

Two miles east of Sodus Bay an extra large drumlin has received the wave treatment. It evidently contains an extraordinary amount of gummy clay. Its erosional breakdown has left a weird array of spires, like church steeples, extending a good half-mile along the shore. Some are as tall as 100 feet. These are known as the Chimney Bluffs. Their location is marked on highway maps.

The spires look as if a firecracker would cause them to collapse. In reality, they withstand high winds and the lashing of storm waves. Their durability is explained by the high clay quotient, which serves as a cement binding the gravel and cobblestones together.

The Chimney Bluffs are protected under state ownership. They enjoy the status of a state park, although it is as yet undeveloped. This means that they are devoid of public facilities, but are accessible enough if one knows how to find them. A short saunter along a pebble-strewn beach brings them into view. Cameras are optional.

The cobbles and pebbles on the beach are largely the washed-down rubble from the eroded drumlin. They are fascinating samples of the minerals that the glacier rafted in from Canada.

Because of a lacework of rural roads, the approach to Chimney Bluffs requires careful attention. The simplest way is to leave the Thruway at Exit 41 and drive due north on Route 414 past Clyde, Rose, and North Rose. Continue on Lake Bluff Road but not as far as Lake Bluff. Watch for inconspicuous Chimney Bluffs signs trending east. Where the road touches the lakeshore, park immediately and walk westward along the beach.

MONTEZUMA MARSHES
A Haven for Wild Life

Between the Waterloo and Weedsport interchanges, the State
Thruway slices through a broad marshland on a causeway flanked
by high chain-link fences. Waterfowl on the wing can nearly
always be seen. An ideal sanctuary for migrant ducks and geese,
these extensive bogs and ponds are under federal protection
(Department of the Interior) as the Montezuma National Wildlife
Refuge. Within the 6,433 acres of habitat, some 270 species of
birds have been identified.

The Montezuma marshes are pictorially unique, with their wide
expanses of open water fringed by reeds and rushes. This
spectacle may be experienced by leaving the Thruway for a space
and driving a leisurely five-mile circuit of graveled dike road.
Along the route are turnouts and two observation towers which
afford overlooks on what unmolested nature has to offer. Three
miles of hiking trails are also available, as well as four designated
sites for fishing.

The marsh is, in effect, a northerly extension of Cayuga Lake.
The rock bed of the lake trough lies an unknown depth beneath,
having been filled by late glacial debris topped by centuries of
vegetal accumulation. The swamp is largely a product of slack
drainage. The outlet stream of both Seneca and Cayuga Lakes,
the Seneca River, winds sluggishly through on its way to Lake
Ontario. Along the eastern boundary of the swamp, this river
becomes the Cayuga and Seneca Canal, a feeder branch of the
State Barge Canal system.

Earlier known as the Cayuga Marshes and "the paradise of
mosquitoes," this tract was an appalling obstacle to the Erie

A peaceful view across the water and reeds of the Montezuma marshes. In fall and spring this scene comes alive with myriads of migrating geese and ducks.

Canal, which had to cross a two-and-a-half-mile width. Canvass White, one of the canal engineers, reconnoitered it and reported that it was neither land nor water, but "a streaky and unpleasant mixture of both." A labor force of between 2,000 and 3,000 had to work at times in waist-deep muck and water, preyed upon by leeches and tormented by clouds of mosquitoes. Men by the hundreds fell ill with malaria and pneumonia, and a great many died. Despite all, the channel was excavated to a hard clay bed and walled up on the sides.

The morass produced vast quantities of flag, growing as tall as 12 feet, which was commercially harvested for bottoming chairs and weaving baskets. The area was still called the Cayuga Marshes in 1843 when described by Dr. James Hall in his Natural History Survey report on western New York. In that same year the historian William H. Prescott published his famous work, *The Conquest of Mexico*, which first brought to popular attention the story of Montezuma II, the last Aztec emperor of Mexico. Montezuma's world was overthrown by Hernando Cortes, and he died in captivity in 1520. The "halls of Montezuma" gained further renown during the 1840s with the capture of Mexico City by General Winfield Scott in the Mexican War. By the middle of the century a Cayuga County village bore the name of Montezuma, along with the adjacent bogs. Conjecture as to the reason arises from the additional fact that Mexico City was built on a marshy island in the middle of a high lake whose shores were also swampy, and that the Spaniards finished the draining of the marshes which the Aztecs had begun.

In general, the Valley Heads Moraine dammed up the Finger Lakes at their southern ends. A secondary stand of the receding ice front left a line of loosely strung morainal deposits that similarly enclosed the lakes at the north. Curiously, Cayuga is the only major Finger Lake that tapers into a marshy extension at its outlet; the others are squared off by solid glacial ground—notably Seneca Lake, with its long, straight waterfront park at Geneva. The fact that the Cayuga valley held the last lingering southerly arm of glacial Lake Iroquois has a definite bearing on this singularity.

The glacier left the north end of the Cayuga trough less deeply
filled with its debris than it did Seneca and the rest. Then, while
Lake Iroquois was draining lower, its embayment here had a
leveling effect on the region of the Montezuma marshes. A
number of lateral bars across the Cayuga outlet are seen today as
having been shaped by the waves of Lake Iroquois. The land,
released from the tremendous weight of the ice sheet, has
gradually "rebounded," uptilting the surface toward the north,
which was a critical factor in making the northern end of Cayuga
Lake relatively shallow and slowing the drainage of the
Montezuma terrain. The two large feeding ponds, with areas of
1,500 and 1,200 acres, were developed in the late 1930s by a
company of Civilian Conservation Corps (CCC) boys, who built
seven miles of dikes with roads on them as well as spillways to
control the level of the ponds.

The Montezuma National Wildlife Refuge was established in
1938 to provide a nesting, feeding, and resting station for
waterfowl as well as songbirds. It was selected by the federal
Migratory Bird Commission as one of the finest locations on the
Atlantic Coastal Flyway. Its population also includes white-tailed
deer, woodchucks, muskrats, and other small mammals. It
receives one of the largest concentrations of Canada geese in this
country, more than 100,000 at a time. Blue geese and snow geese
are other perodic guests. Spectators of this wildlife panoply, which
is at its best in fall and spring, will be well advised to come
equipped with binoculars for viewing from the observation towers.

Inside the entrance stands the Refuge Headquarters, an
information shelter where a map leaflet may be picked up that
plots the route of the unguided tour. Close to this shelter are
picnic grounds and the first observation tower.

In recent years, Montezuma has been adopted by the State
Department of Environmental Conservation for an eagle-hacking
program as part of its endangered-species activities. ("Hacking"
is a term from falconry, meaning hand rearing of young birds of
prey, now applied to rearing in the wild.) The Montezuma
marshes are historically a bald-eagle habitat, but they harbored
the last native pair in the 1950s. Now eaglets are obtained from

other states and reared to fledgling stage in artificial nests on two nesting platforms 35 feet high, maintained on the far side of the Tschache Pool, away from human disturbance. When able to try their wings, they are let loose. Through 1978, 11 eagles had been released, and the earliest of these had returned the following seasons.

To visit the refuge, one may leave the Thruway at either Exit 40 or 41, and reenter at the other access. From 41, the Waterloo exit, turn south on Route 414, then southeast on 318 to a junction with Route 20; three miles east on Route 20 there is a sign for the marshes. A counterclockwise circle of the tour, on gravel roads, ends at north–south Route 89. Do not omit a northward jog on 89 for the second observation tower. Route 89 south regains Route 20. At option, one may drive east on 20 to Auburn, then north on Route 34 to Thruway Exit 40. These directions may be reversed.

Green Lake fills the former plunge pool of a mighty waterfall that poured over the horseshoe-shaped limestone cliff at Clark Reservation. The partly wooded cliff is 175 feet high. Headquarters building of the Central New York State Park Commission is at the left, city of Syracuse in the distance.

CLARK RESERVATION
Grandsire of Niagara

In the opening chapter, reference was made to a lineal forebear of Niagara 150 miles distant. The "fossil" waterfall is the centerpiece of the Clark Reservation, near Jamesville in the suburban fringes of Syracuse. The reservation is a state park and, in fact, the headquarters of the Central New York State Park Commission.

The rim of the extinct cataract is shaped even more like a horseshoe than the present-day Horseshoe Falls and it probably carried at least as much water. The diameter across the crescent is 1,300 feet and the cliff looms 175 feet above the plunge pool—higher than Niagara. The plunge basin is occupied by Green Lake, a round lakelet 60 feet deep, whose water reflects a greenish hue under blue skies. The capstone is a massive bed of Onondaga limestone. A foot trail follows all the way around the crescent, and a lower pathway encircles the lake.

This park perpetuates the name of Myron H. Clark, who was a Governor of New York in 1855–1856, after being elected by the tiniest majority in state history. A temperance crusader, his chief distinction was pushing a prohibition law through a docile legislature, soon to be ruled unconstitutional by the State Court of Appeals. Disillusioned, Myron Clark went into retirement in Canandaigua and lived until 1892. Years later his daughter, Mrs. Mary Clark Thompson of New York City, a member of the American Scenic and Historic Preservation Society, learned that the state geologist was anxious to have a certain waterless waterfall protected. Quarrymen active in the vicinity were casting covetous eyes on its limestone cliffs. In 1915, Mrs. Thompson

paid $10,000 for a farm that embraced the site and transferred
title to the Board of Regents on the stipulation that it be preserved
as a memorial to her father. After a period of custody by the State
Museum, it was designated a state park.

The southern environs of Syracuse are furrowed with rock
channels slashed by torrents of glacial meltwater seeking an
escape route which they finally found into the Mohawk valley.
Such a channel gives passageway to the Amtrak railway. The
abandoned gorges indicate a complex series of glacial rivers
parallel to the receding ice front, producing waterfalls when they
dropped over north–south ridges. The rivers shifted north in pace
with the ice front's retreat. Also scattered in the uneven terrain
east and southeast of Syracuse are a dozen or so small, deep lakes
which are unrelated to the local drainage system. They are all
cupped in the plunge basins of short-lived waterfalls, and their
waters tend to reflect a greenish hue.

Long before the Niagara escarpment was cleared, the marginal
lakes working eastward along the ice front had backed up into the
Finger Lakes valleys. Finally the great Onondaga valley was
filled with water which escaped through a southern vent at Tully.
With further retreat of the ice, glacial Lake Onondaga began
finding newer outlets across rock ridges to the east, hewing the
Syracuse gorges one by one. A tremendous waterfall burst into
the valley of Butternut Creek at Jamesville, rapidly eroding its
way backward a mile and a half before going dry because the next
lower outlet, Rock Cut, had been found. The Rock Cut borders
Clark Reservation on the north, and is utilized by the
Erie-Lackawanna Railroad for its entry into south Syracuse.

The best viewpoints for the limestone arc and the plunge-pool
lake below are along a railinged cliff reached by walking up the
lawn slope east of the parking lot. A leftward trail leads to Table
Rock and around the crescent to the opposite point of the
horseshoe, with a bit of rough footing en route. The limestone is
deeply waterworn and fissured, mutely telling the force of the
deluge which hurled itself over the brink. Side trails lead into a
network of paths behind the horseshoe where one comes upon
shallow basins and channels made by the tumultuous rapids

rushing to the cataract.

Ten miles northeast of Clark Reservation, near Fayetteville, is the Green Lakes State Park, a geological sequel. (Green Lakes are fairly common in the area). The two lakes in tandem are cupped in plunge pools created by a rapidly receding waterfall which received the onward flow from the Syracuse channels. They are separated by a narrow isthmus of peat, and the upper, or Round Lake, has been left in its wild state. The isthmus, by recent findings, is thought to conceal a rock ridge, indicating that the plunge pools may have been formed in two distinct episodes of escaping glacial waters, at different levels. No "fossil waterfall" is to be seen here, as at Clark Reservation, because the water was plunging over weak shales rather than any strong layer of limestone, which would have been preserved. The Green Lakes Park is primarily recreational, with a bathing beach on the lower lake and an adjacent golf course.

Thruway Exit 34-A gives upon an arterial highway, Route 481, which heads direct to Jamesville. From the village, take Route 173 westward one mile to the entrance of Clark Reservation.

Amid the giant potholes of Moss Island in the Little Falls gorge. The myriad, grotesque array of holes were bored in the tough old rock by a colossal waterfall of the glacial Iro-Mohawk River.

LITTLE FALLS GORGE
Passkey to a Continent

In 1797, having staked out a farm in the upper Mohawk valley, a Revolutionary War veteran wrote to his brother back in New Hampshire. The brother was soon to join him, and was strongly advised to visit the gorge at Little Falls on the way, "because you'll see God's handiwork as you never saw it before." The letter continued:

"What river and what giant waterfall cut through those rocks and left those vast pot-holes above the canal and the Mohawk that flows there today? I've heard the natives say in Little Falls that the Mohawk disproves the story of creation, for no river, they swear, could have cut those rocks in 5000 years."

The pioneer settlers in the valley had at least a glimmering that a much greater river had made this gorge, which played so crucial a role in American history. The canal mentioned in the letter had just been completed by the Western Inland Lock Navigation Company to hoist Mohawk River traffic around the falls. It later became a connecting link for the Erie Canal. Its present-day successor is the celebrated Lock 17 of the State Barge Canal system, the highest lift lock (40 feet) in the United States, often sought out by tourists.

Little Falls was so named by fur traders to distinguish it from the "great falls" of Cohoes, where the Mohawk meets the Hudson. The falls are negligible today, owing to diversion of water for Lock 17. The Cohoes Falls are similarly cheated of water.

As the lowest pass between the Adirondacks and the southern Appalachians, the Little Falls gorge richly earned its historic title, "Gateway to the West." With some portages excepted, it

permitted a continuous waterway to the Great Lakes.
Consequently it was the key to the interior fur trade and travel
routes. The chasm, a mile and a half in length, is like a tight belt
squeezing the Mohawk valley at the waist. The valley bulges out
broadly on either side. The industrial, rather grimy city of Little
Falls, straddling the river, disposes itself mainly in the bottom and
on the north slope of the gorge. Through this pass are threaded
the Mohawk River, the Barge Canal, the Amtrak and Conrail
tracks, and two major highways.

The gorge slices a preglacial divide caused by the westernmost
of a series of gigantic faults crossing the Mohawk valley. The
vertical displacement in the slippage as between the two sides of
the break was about 2,000 feet. The upthrust side, on the west,
brought toward the surface a block of very ancient crystalline rock
overlain by a great thickness of the tough Little Falls dolostone.
Ages of subsequent erosion left the hard upthrust rock layers
facing east as a fault scarp. From the resulting ridge, headwaters
of rivers flowed in both directions. Rising on the east side was a
Mohawk much shorter than it is now. The westward stream, the
Rome River, was a tributary of the master Ontarian River.

It is generally conceded that the Little Falls gorge was not
carved in a single glacial episode. There were at least three
advances and retreats of the Pleistocene ice sheets. The Rome
River would have been bottled up at an early stage as a lake in the
upper Mohawk valley (i.e., west of Little Falls), and this lake
would have spilled over the divide as a tall waterfall. Repetitions
of this act, in the glacial fluctuations, cut the gorge wider and
deeper.

Only the recessional phase of the last (Wisconsin) ice sheet left
direct evidence of this circumstance. When the pre–Great Lakes
waters from the west burst through at Rome into the Mohawk
valley, they made short work of flushing glacial fill out of the
notch at Little Falls and reviving the cataract. At that time Lake
Iroquois came into being at the threshold level of the Rome
escape, and the resulting subsidence of the impounded waters set
Niagara Falls going at roughly the same time. The volume of
water pouring through the Little Falls notch was at least as great

as that carried by the St. Lawrence River today. Lake Iroquois
endured longer than any other of the ancestral Great Lakes. The
river that rampaged down the Mohawk valley from its overflow is
now referred to as the Iro-Mohawk. From its mouth it spewed
forth the Schenectady sand plains—the area of Albany's unique
Pine Bush—as a delta in Lake Albany.

After some thousands of years, Lake Iroquois came to its close
when the receding ice front cleared Covey Hill, a northerly spur
of the Adirondack uplands extending a slight distance across the
Quebec boundary. The water broke through on the sloping north
flank of this hill to join a marine estuary that had brought
saltwater into the Champlain and St. Lawrence valleys, whose
elevation was still much depressed from the long weight of the
glacier. By that time the gorge at Little Falls was chiseled down
so much that the reviving Rome River reversed its preglacial
westward flow to drop over the falls and double the pristine
length of the Mohawk. Another factor in its reversal was a great
accumulation of glacial rubbish that formed a new watershed at
Rome, thereby determining the location of Fort Stanwix in the
Revolutionary War. Subsequent erosion of the gorge has been
minor compared to that during the glacial epoch. But nature has
been abetted in this task by rock blasting for the Erie Canal and
subsequent railroad lines.

Lengthwise down the middle of the gorge is a slender island of
rock, shaped somewhat like a dumbbell, with a bulge at either
end. The eastern bulge of gnarled old crystalline rock is known as
Moss Island, steepsided, its crest accessible by a path alongside
Lock 17. The island is the dividing ridge between the Barge
Canal and the Mohawk River proper. The much-reduced
waterfall tumbles on the north side. There is no more convincing
proof of the terrific beating Moss Island once took from the raging
waters of the Iro-Mohawk River than those "vast potholes" cited in
the letter of that pioneer Yankee farmer in 1797.

For circumference, depth, concentration, and intricacy, these
hydraulic borings are unrivaled elsewhere in the state. They are
fantastic and grotesque, intersecting with one another, and carved
at different levels as the falls wore down their threshold. Literally

scores of the potholes, large and small, many of them only partial as their walls were broken through, are clustered in the west and northwest section of the Moss Island hill. A few are at least 20 feet in circumference, and the deepest hole has been measured at 30 feet to its gravel bottom.

The veritable city of potholes may be found by following a beaten trail some 200 yards from Lock 17, northwest across the hump of the island. Needless to say it is rather dangerous to climb, twist, and skid among them—especially so for children. Visitors who venture to explore them are reminded that they do so at their own risk. Plain signs along the narrow road to Lock 17 read "Not a Public Thoroughfare," absolving the state from blame if mishap befalls those who ignore them. Furthermore, the lock-tender's only duty is to attend to the canal lock, not to go on search missions for careless visitors.

Mainly because of these potholes, Moss Island was declared a Natural History Landmark by the National Park Service, one of 400 spots so designated in the United States for special qualities. This recognition came as the climax of a hot crusade by preservationist groups to prevent the construction of a bridge abutment on the east end of Moss Island and a highway ramp onto the island for park purposes. The State Department of Transportation has added Exit 29-A of the Thruway and has nearly completed a spur into Little Falls, to join Route 5 through the city. This improved access called for a new bridge across the Mohawk just below Lock 17. The campaign to "save" Moss Island compelled the state to alter plans, curving the bridge slightly toward the east and eliminating the island ramp. For that reason, the bridge was still unfinished at this writing, but it soon would be. Meanwhile, Exit 29-A could be used into Little Falls, crossing the river by an old bridge a little further downstream.

Incidentally, an original lock of the Erie Canal is preserved for public viewing just below the modern Lock 17. The antique lock dates from 1825. It may be visited by walking down a long stairway at the east end of Lock 17.

As just stated, direct access into Little Falls from the Thruway, via Exit 29-A (Indian Castle), will be available when the Mohawk bridge is completed. The city is entered from east and west by Route 5. At the business center of town, Route 167 crosses the Mohawk southward by the Ann Street bridge. This bridge also spans the west end of Moss Island, and beyond that the Barge Canal. A quick turn left from the first span of the Ann Street bridge leads down onto Moss Island. Getting onto the narrow service road east to Lock 17 is a bit tricky. Just before a small one-way bridge crossing the Barge Canal, take a fork onto a dirt road where a sign says "Not a Public Thoroughfare." Take it.

Looking west over the city of Little Falls from Moreland Park. The wide section of the Mohawk valley beyond the jaws of the gorge is German Flats.

MORELAND PARK
A Viewpoint for the Mohawk

In common with the Hudson and the St. Lawrence, the Mohawk is one of the most historic rivers of America. Its enchanting valley was the homeland of the Mohawk Indians, keepers of the so-called eastern doorway to the Iroquois Longhouse. It has often been referred to as the "bloodiest cockpit of the Revolution." This river, more than any other factor, made the Erie Canal possible. Walter D. Edmunds's fine historical novel, *Drums Along the Mohawk*, tells the dramatic story of how the pioneer farmers of the rich valley fought and bled against the vicious raids of Tories and Indians.

Pleasant scenes of the river can be glimpsed from highways skirting the river banks, as well as from the windows of Amtrak trains. Many automobile travelers undoubtedly wonder where outlook places may be found for more panoramic vistas of this lovely valley. To its credit, the city of Little Falls has Moreland Park, atop the northern cliff of the gorge. This park has been developed from what was formerly a spacious private estate.

From a one-time summerhouse, now occupied by the park's caretaker, an expansive lawn slopes toward the margin of the rock wall, some 400 feet above the river. Directly below may be seen the long hump of Moss Island, hiding the Barge Canal's Lock 17 behind it. The chasm, that hems in the city, viewed from this perspective, affords a visual understanding of why it was the low-level pass-key for travel to the west. The westward prospect is particularly striking, revealing a section of the broad river valley beyond the gorge. Those German Flats are part of the bottomland left by glacial Lake Iroquois from the time when it was dammed up behind the Little Falls divide.

The property of Moreland Park, comprising 30 acres of lawn and woodland, was bequeathed to the then village of Little Falls by its 19th-century owner, Dudley Burwell, a wealthy industrialist. Burwell had developed it as his personal estate and erected a mansion. Simply enough, the name he gave it meant exactly what it says, "more land." When Burwell died in 1876, his will left the estate to his close friend, William G. Milligan, for his "use and enjoyment during his life," with the stipulation that, upon Milligan's death, the property would revert to Little Falls for a public park. Milligan died in 1904.

The industrialization of Little Falls was foreshadowed by a gristmill taking power from the waterfall in colonial days, serving the Palatine German farmers who were the principal early settlers in the valley. During the final stages of the Revolutionary War, a raiding party of Loyalists and Indians swooped down one dark night and wiped out the hamlet of Little Falls, burning the gristmill.

The difficulties of building canal locks in the narrow defile are manifest from the Moreland outlook. The Western Inland Lock Navigation Company was incorporated in 1792, with General Philip Schuyler as one of its promoters. A canal with five lift locks was constructed beside the falls, much of it laboriously cut through the tough crystalline rock. That short canal permitted river boatmen to get around the Little Falls, and was a precursor of the Erie Canal.

By all odds the most picturesque view of the Mohawk valley to be had from a highway is just outside Little Falls on the Dolgeville Road, Route 167 going north. A convenient turnout with stone parapet is provided. The outlook is eastward where the valley spreads wide after the river passes through the gorge. The stream meanders peacefully through a vast floodplain which was spewed forth by the tumultous glacial Iro-Mohawk River as it exploded out of the gorge.

Half-hidden by lush foliage in the middle foreground stands the red-brick Herkimer homestead fronting on the south bank of the river—a State Historic Site which is decidedly worth a visit. Its builder, General Nicholas Herkimer, led the Mohawk valley militia to the Battle of Oriskany which stalled the invasion led by St. Leger from the west, intended to have joined forces with Burgoyne at Albany. Wounded in a leg, General Herkimer issued commands for the remainder of the battle while sitting in pain against a tree-trunk. Carried on a litter back to his homestead, Herkimer died following amputation of the injured leg. The story of General Herkimer is summed up on a large metal tablet at the scenic turn-out.

Route 5 traffic channels into Main Street of Little Falls. At the intersection of Main with Alexander Street, turn north on Alexander, and follow Moreland Park signs on zigzag uphill streets. Manheim Street becomes the lead-in to Moreland Park. Apart from the outlook slope, the city has developed a picnic and recreation area as adjuncts of the park.

The wildness of Whetstone Gulf, with a vague impression of the height of its walls, is sensed in this view near the mouth of the gorge. The public is not permitted to walk the stream bottom.

WHETSTONE GULF
A Fearsome Abyss

On the road maps there is a large blank space just east of Lake Ontario oddly unmarked by towns or highways. The blue crinkles of streams look anxious to get away from there. This terra incognita is the Tug Hill plateau, sometimes called the Siberia of New York State. The average annual snowfall on its roof is 216 inches (18 feet), said to be the heaviest this side of the Rockies. The snows are dumped by moisture-laden storms moving in from Lake Ontario. Sleet and hail are not uncommon in midsummer. When so fantastic a quantity of snow melts in the spring sun, it is not hard to picture the runoff at the eaves of a high tableland having an area of 1,400 square miles. This accounts for a phenomenon like Whetstone Gulf.

Two or three other chasms in New York State are deeper than Whetstone, but no other is so deep in proportion to width. The flat-floored gorge is two miles long and its walls, almost vertical, rise as much as 350 feet. Yet it is possible to throw a stone across in some places. At its head is a sheer waterfall with a 50-foot drop. Near this fall a man with outstretched arms can touch the sides with his fingertips, but no mere visitor may test this out. The public is not permitted to walk the bottom of the gorge because of the danger from falling rock.

Whetstone Gulf is one of the least known of the state parks. The nearby Turin Ski Center is more noted, as it rarely runs short of snow. The recreation area at the mouth of Whetstone gorge has a swimming pool and campsites, and most customers get no further than that. A hiking trail follows both rims, crossing the creek above the falls for a five-mile round trip; it is not recommended for children or the fainthearted.

The name of this park derives from the presence amid its rock layers of a fine grade of sandstone which used to serve the neighboring farmers as whetstones. The stone may be seen high up in the gorge walls as distinct light-colored bands interleaved with the dark shales.

The Tug Hill upland, 50 miles long on the north–south axis, is an outlying erosion remnant of the same peneplain surface seen in the vast Allegheny Plateau of the Southern Tier. Its sedimentary beds once overlapped on the base of the Adirondacks. Over the aeons these strata have been eroded back some 20 miles, leaving the wide Black River valley between. A major tongue of the glaciers scoured that valley time and again, shaving away an unguessed amount of the Tug Hill frontage which now stands as a 500-foot rampart facing east. As soon as the ice vanished, drainage from the summit spouted waterfalls over the edge. The result is a series of astonishingly deep, forbidding gorges slashed into the frowning bluff. These are locally referred to as gulfs. At least one of them is larger and deeper than Whetstone, but it is so wild and inaccessible that few people have ever explored it.

Tug Hill is not really a hill at all, but a region. It is a jumble of slopes and gullies, some heavily wooded, others rocky and barren. Some parts are remarkably flat, often swampy. Its wildlife, including deer, bear, and bobcats, makes it an excellent hunting territory. A scattered farming population gave up the struggle long since, leaving here and there a weather-beaten, windowless house. Narrow, puddly dirt roads weave through the no-man's-land, which are extremely inadvisable for strangers to venture upon. Natives have a saying: "Tug Hill is a hell of a country to get lost in." In fact, personnel of Whetstone Park have led search parties rounding up unwise motorists.

In its upper reaches Whetstone Gulf, because of its narrow depth, is probably the most fearful chasm in the state. The clifftops have no guardrails, and it is a dizzying experience to peer down into the abyss while holding onto an occasional tree. The park authorities do not encourage public visitation to those parts, and there are no road signs pointing the way. A few persons have fallen over to their deaths.

There is a way to get to the upper gorge by automobile, but utmost care must be exercised by any who go seeking the stark scenery. Outside the park entrance, follow West Road along the foot of the bluff going north; after about two miles take a right-angle left on Corrigan Hill Road, which climbs sharply up the escarpment. This road starts leveling off fairly near the upper section of the gorge, which is hidden from the highway by a thick pine plantation. Park along the road and follow one of the fire lanes straight through the pines. The abyss abruptly yawns at one's feet.

The entrance to Whetstone Gulf State Park is from Route 26 just north of Houseville and about six miles south of Lowville.

The aerial camera scans a dozen of the Thousand Islands. The one in foreground is Heart Island, site of the amazing Boldt Castle, which never was lived in.

THE THOUSAND ISLANDS
Stone Archway to Canada

It is likely that the Comte de Frontenac would have been as
flattered at having his name commemorated in the Frontenac
Arch as by the majestic Chateau Frontenac hotel on the heights of
Quebec. As governor of La Nouvelle France (Canada) three
centuries ago, Frontenac was on intimate terms with the
Thousand Islands, threading his way among them by birchbark
canoe and erecting Fort Frontenac across from where the islands
begin, on the present site of Kingston, Ontario.

Geologically considered, the Thousand Islands of the St.
Lawrence may be likened to a bridge—the scattered remains of a
narrow arch—connecting the ancient Precambrian rocks of the
Adirondack Mountain dome with the great Canadian Shield, the
real oldland of the continent, of which the Adirondacks are an
extension. This bridge of islands is known as the Frontenac
Arch. Much younger rocks of sedimentary (Paleozoic) origin
flank the arch on both sides of the border. These strata were laid
in the Paleozoic sea horizontally across what later became the
Frontenac Arch, as they were across the Adirondack area. The
arch was subsequently pushed up, along with the doming of the
Adirondacks, during the last 10 million years or so. The relatively
thin sediments have since been eroded away, exposing the highly
resistant older rock as projections in the floor of the St. Lawrence
valley.

All of this would have been unintelligible to Count Frontenac,
who was wholly concerned with establishing New France as a
secure and lucrative colony for his sovereign, Louis XIV; and also
with destroying the formidable power of the Iroquois tribes or at

least with alienating them from the British and Dutch in New York.

Thanks to the mighty St. Lawrence River, those intrepid French explorers, missionaries, and *coureurs de bois* staked out the Great Lakes and the Mississippi valley before the British were more than dimly aware of their existence. They dug in their paddles for 50 miles amid an extraordinary maze of islets which they christened Les Milles Isles. These made ideal camping spots, safe from surprise. If a bemused present-day tourist should catch sight of spectral white canoes gliding noiselessly through a Thousand Islands channel, their ghostly paddlers might answer to such names as LaSalle, Joliet, Pere Marquette, Sieur de la Mothe Cadillac, or Graysolon de Luht (Duluth).

The French estimate of the number of islands was more poetic than mathematical. Not until an International Boundary Commission surveyed the frontier between the United States and Canada in the late 1800s was an official count of the islands taken, and then it came out at 1,692—an island being defined as any rock large enough to have a tree growing on it. Since that survey the total has grown to 1,693. Unable to purchase an island, a determined man of wealth built one for his exclusive occupancy, basing it upon what had been a submerged shoal.

At the place where Lake Ontario moves sedately into the river, in the vicinity of Cape Vincent, the outlet funnel is 10 miles wide. The current divides around Wolfe Island, the first and largest of the Thousand Islands, which has cultivated farms. The leisurely flow immediately radiates among islands and does not occupy any one distinct channel. The zone may be pictured as a broad, low, hilly region which has been partially flooded. The islands are elongated ridges trending northeast–southwest. Before glaciation, it is surmised that an ancestor of the St. Lawrence arose from the Frontenac divide and flowed to the sea.

When the Laurentian ice lobe came creeping, the lay of these ridges corresponded with the direction of glacial movement. In repeated advances, the insistent ice accentuated the striking parallelism of the ridges. Forcing itself upon the northeast ends of the island ridges, it rode over them, producing smooth upward

slopes. At the southwest ends a quite different kind of action
known as glacial plucking took place. The ice froze tight against
the rock faces and pulled away blocks and fragments in its
forward movement. As a result, the ends pointing toward Lake
Ontario frequently display steep cliff faces with hackled surfaces,
outlined by joint planes.

These islands, so worked over by glaciation, are relatively free
from debris left behind by the glacier. The absence is explained
by the apparent fact that they were covered with water as the ice
front withdrew. Lake Iroquois was impounded at the time against
the wall of ice, and it submerged any land surface as fast as it was
uncovered. Some minor drumlins, however, appear among the
rock islands.

Postglacial "rebound" of the land surface, when relieved of ice
pressure, was almost sure to lift some point of the old St.
Lawrence valley above water, and this occurred in the vicinity of
Alexandria Bay. The moment when that rock barrier became
effective, Lake Ontario was born. The uptilting is still going on,
and the land has risen 500 feet at the Thousand Islands since the
glacier.

Camera buffs are delighted by the splurges of a bright red rock
that dress up the watersides of many islands, providing a contrast
with the dark-grained rocks of their basic material. The red stone
is Picton granite, so named for Picton Island where it used to be
quarried before the islands came under state protection. More
than a billion years ago, deep underground, this colorful granite
was squeezed as molten magma into the existing sedimentary
rocks.

This charming archipelago of the St. Lawrence is as much an
international attraction, in its own way, as Niagara. The political
boundary between New York and Ontario zigzags to avoid
bisecting any of the islands, and awards two-thirds of their
number to Canadian jurisdiction. The majority remain privately
owned, but happily the two governments have reserved several,
along with pieces of the adjacent shores, for public parks. On the
American side, these properties collectively comprise the
Thousand Islands State Park. North of the border, they are

lumped together as the St. Lawrence Islands National Park.

The New York park areas are located on seven of the islands, in whole or in part, while the headquarters of the Thousand Islands State Park Commission is at Alexandria Bay, the southern terminus of the International Bridge. Wellesley Island, which the bridge road crosses, is the largest within American custody, nine miles long by five miles wide; 20 percent of it is owned by the state. Two of the park entities, Wellesley Island Park and Waterson Point Park, are on this island alone; the small Mary Island Park is subjoined by a bridge. The state also has a park on one of the other large islands, Grindstone. The Wellesley Island Park is biggest of the Thousand Islands parks, with 2,635 acres and a variety of recreations ranging from water sports to golf. A focal attraction is the Minna Anthony Common Nature Center, which offers museum exhibits on the geology, flora, and fauna of the islands, as well as guided trail walks through an adjoining woodland.

The most thorough and satisfying way of viewing the Thousand Islands is to ride on one of the cruise boats that ply from both sides of the river. The tours, with running commentary, weave in and out among some 40 miles of the smaller islands, many of which are adorned with the swank summer abodes of wealthy celebrities and financiers. Far and away the most dazzling item of architecture is the amazing Boldt Castle on Heart Island. This gothic edifice was undertaken by George C. Boldt, a Manhattan hotel magnate, as a gift for his wife. When Mrs. Boldt died before the castle was completed, her griefstricken husband halted construction, so that it was never occupied as a home. Nowadays the cruise boats circle the island for viewing of the palace, and some of them make stopovers for passengers wishing to inspect the grounds and interior of this grandiose monument to one man's blighted dream.

Interstate 81, the North–South Expressway, goes straight to the Thousand Islands International Bridge. For those approaching from the northeast and the St. Lawrence Seaway, Route 37 becomes Route 12 along the south bank of the river, affording views of the islands. Alexandria Bay is the resort center of the islands in New York State. On the Canadian side, the Thousand Islands Parkway borders the river.

Adirondack landscape with a skyline of High Peaks. The view is from Mount Van Hoevenberg, near Lake Placid.

THE ADIRONDACKS
Top of the State

It is an index to the austere ruggedness of the Adirondack
Mountains that they were the last region of New York State to be
systematically explored and surveyed. The true stature of their
aloof peaks was not recognized until near the middle of the
nineteenth century. They had been largely despoiled for lumber
before the public began to develop a real appreciation of their
scenic grandeur.

Scientists have long known that the basic rocks composing these
mountains are of extremely ancient origin—more than a billion
years. Mainly for this reason, the Adirondacks have been
misconstrued until quite recently as being among the oldest
mountains on earth, gnarled and rumpled in their ups and
downs. This notion has now been discarded. Considered simply
as mountains—regardless of the age of their component
rocks—they are now believed to be relatively young in fact;
compared to Rockies, Andes, and Alps, they are juvenile. Of
course, geologists are entitled to change their minds when fresh
findings warrant.

Spafford's *Gazetteer of the State of New York* (1813 edition),
identified the Catskill Mountains as "much the largest and most
extensive in this state." With an air of anticlimax, this travel
guidebook went on to remark:

*. . . It only remains now to notice the Mountainous country around
Lake George and to the W. of Lake Champlain, called the Peruvian
Mountains; which furnish the northern sources of the Hudson. . . .
These mountains were named* Peru *by the early French inhabitants,
in allusion to their supposed mineral treasures. . . .*

N.Y. State Museum photo by Kenneth M. Fay

Doubtless the pioneer Canadian Frenchmen, with a touch of wishful thinking, were inspired by accounts of gold and silver plundered from the Incas by the Spanish conquistadores. As a matter of fact, there was prospecting for silver in the Adirondacks for some years after the publication of Spafford's gazetteers, but it yielded no metals more precious than iron and titanium.

The Catskills were indeed rated as the highest mountains of New York State far into the 1800s. The actual superiority of the "Peruvians" was not generally recognized until after 1837, when Ebenezer Emmons, a Williams College professor, led a climbing expedition as part of the state's first Natural History Survey. Emmons found that Mount Marcy (as he then christened it) is more than a mile high, the tallest peak in the state. In his report to Governor William L. Marcy, its namesake, Emmons wrote: "The cluster of mountains in the neighborhood of the Upper Hudson and Ausable Rivers, I proposed to call the Adirondack Group, a name by which a well known tribe of Indians who once hunted here may be commemorated."

One clue to the supposed tribe mentioned by Emmons once appeared in a publication of the Smithsonian Institution that cited a word in the Huron dialect—"Ati-ront-ak"—as meaning "They of the Rock Clan." The Hurons, related to the Iroquois, controlled a large territory in Ontario embracing Lake Huron and extending as far east as the north bank of the St. Lawrence River. They were divided into three groups, or clans, the easternmost of which was the Rock Clan. It makes sense to suppose that members of the Rock Clan crossed the St. Lawrence to hunt for beaver pelts in the Adirondacks after the French brought the fur trade into Canada. The Hurons were virtually wiped out, since white men came, by their racial kinfolk, the Senecas.

On the other hand, present-day students of the Iroquois vocabularies maintain that "Atirontaks" was a Mohawk word applied to that tribe's traditional enemies, the Canadian Algonkians, as a term of disparagement. It translates by syllables in this way: "Ati" = they; "ront" = tree or log; "ak" = eat. Therefore: "They eat trees" (or bark). "Atirontak", by this interpretation, becomes "tree-eaters"—a term of insult implying that the Algonkians were such inept hunters that they were reduced to gnawing on the bark of trees.

In any case, Emmons intended the name to refer only to a select few of the highest summits around Marcy. In the course of time, it was extended to the entire region, including the foothills.

Regarded as a topographical province, the Adirondacks encompass nearly 11,000 square miles—one-fourth the total area of the state. Within that scope have been identified some 2,500 mountains, using a minimum height of 2,000 feet as the criterion. The distinction between a hill and a mountain is confusingly vague. The dictionary defines a mountain as a landmass "higher than a hill"; and then says that a hill is a landmass "lower than a mountain." Whatever the official census, 43 Adirondacks are at least 4,000 feet high, and two, Marcy and Algonquin, surpass 5,000 feet. The true aristocracy that qualify as the Adirondack High Peaks are confined to 1,200 square miles in the east-central part of the province, and these are the core of the whole. Besides their commanding height, they are distinguished for their chief constituent, anorthosite. This is a type of metamorphosed igneous (originally molten) rock that is relatively rare on Earth, but quite plentiful in the highlands of the moon.

The Adirondack anorthosite was intruded as hot magma among other deep-lying rocks, roughly 25 miles beneath the surface, and slowly hardened in cooling. In subsequent tensions and stresses, it became metamorphosed (altered) along with the surrounding rocks which were initially sedimentary. The anorthosite is a bluish-gray rock comprised mainly of the type of feldspar known as labradorite, whose crystals often gleam iridescent in sunlight. Pebbles of labradorite in its bed account for the name of the Opalescent River, one of the source waters of the Hudson, which is fed by Feldspar Brook.

The pinnacles of the High Peaks are, for the most part, above timberline, looming up as barren, wind-whipped, rocky knobs that confront exhausted climbers with their final, toughest hurdle. The summits are fringed with a hardy, subarctic type of vegetation. The seeds and spores of such stunted plants, shrubs, and lichens were left behind in high places when the glacial ice melted away.

These peaks are a seclusive, remote company, not of easy

acquaintance. Few roads penetrate their fastnesses beyond the outermost margins, and not all their summits are visible to the casual tourist from the periphery. The majority, however, may at least be glimpsed in silhouette from one point or another on the main highways, which encircle the heartland. Only in a single instance does a toll road lead to the apex of a High Peak, and that is Whiteface, set apart from the rest by the Lake Placid–Saranac intervale. It took a statewide referendum to make possible this exception to the "forever wild" clause of the Forest Preserve Act in the state constitution.

Many of these mountains exhibit a distinctive hallmark—light-hued streaks of naked rock on their steep flanks. These are avalanche scars. In a heavy rain the relatively thin soil-cover sometimes gets waterlogged and takes a landslide. It was a major avalanche of this sort that gave Whiteface its name. The off-white shade of these scars is caused by the mineral composition of the rock anorthosite.

Taken as a whole, the Adirondacks are extremely complex mountains, with many aspects not yet clarified by geologists. They are composed of rocks of various types and ages, all commingled in disarray. The summits billow away to an uneven horizon, rather like storm-tossed waves. Except for a few irregular fault-line ranks, they are not laid out in orderly ranges, and are in no sense related to the Appalachians. The fault troughs, resulting from erosion along zones of weakness, trend in northeast–southwest diagonals. Some contain strikingly linear lakes such as Long Lake, the two Ausables, and the twin Cascades.

In essence, the Adirondacks are a domed-up annex of the Canadian Shield, the real oldland of the North American continent, which constitutes much of Quebec, Labrador, and Ontario as well as the rock basin of Hudson Bay. The Thousand Islands sprinkled in the St. Lawrence River represent the connecting link, the Frontenac Arch. The Canadian Shield is the much-eroded floor of an ancient landmass against whose shores lapped the surf of the earliest Paleozoic Sea, which left its record in the sedimentary rock layers spread upon the continental shelf of that dimly imaginable time. In most of its vast extent, the Canadian Shield has a generally low relief. Why, then, is its Adirondack annex so highly domed?

The primeval matrix of the Adirondacks is a tremendous jumble of metasedimentary rocks (that is, originally sedimentary strata that have undergone great metamorphism). Until recently these were loosely distinguished as Grenville rocks, a term now fallen out of favor. They are equated in age with the typical outcrops in the Ontario township of Grenville, and with the Grenville Orogeny which caused their metamorphosis, but it is no longer valid to speak of a Grenville series of rocks as if they were all laid in a common Grenville Ocean. By whatever name, the basic metamorphics of the Adirondacks are some of the oldest rocks visible in New York State—past the billion-year mark. That is just the figure for their metamorphism, which set going their radioactive "clock," by which science now measures the ages of ancient rocks.

The original sediments of Grenville age were first laid on an ocean floor after being washed down from previously existing highlands millions of years older. Thus the earliest known condition of the Adirondack area was level, with a shallow sea washing over it. After an accumulated thickness of some thousands of feet, those shales and sandstones were hardened and uplifted. Still later they were forced—perhaps in some continental collision—as much as 25 miles beneath the surface, where intense heat and pressure produced the metamorphism. At some time during that process the anorthosite was intruded.

Thus it had long been recognized that the basic Adirondack rocks were over a billion years old, and it was presumed that the mountains themselves were the eroded roots of once gargantuan, comparably antique ranges. Not so. Some very recent and inspired work in the New York State Geological Survey has upset that kind of traditional thinking. Regardless of how old the rocks are, the mountains themselves may be a great deal younger—perhaps as little as 10 million years old. This idea, if valid, is revolutionary indeed. It was triggered by indications that the Adirondacks, at least in their core area, may be "growing" at a rate much faster than erosion wears them down. In recent years a remeasurement of old surveyors' benchmarks has shown an average annual rise of approximately three millimeters over a period of 44 years. This is triple the rate at which the Swiss Alps are known to be rising.

The long-held belief that the Adirondacks had stood up as a mountainous island, or at least a promontory, in the Paleozoic Sea from the first flooding is now called into question. Fresh thinking suggests that the ocean waters rolled over the entire Adirondack region, which had been leveled by erosion and become a sort of continental shelf. Rivers from great northern highlands, of which the Canadian Shield now represents the root zone, spread their sediments widely across New York State, possibly as late as mid-Devonian time, while the Taconic ranges of New England were supplying the material that built the Catskill Delta. If the sedimentary rock layers, from earliest Cambrian time, had been deposited from the base of the Adirondacks onward, they would thin out as they near those mountains. On the contrary, those strata not only hold their thickness right up to the contact with the older Adirondack rocks, but are also found north of the Adirondacks at similar thickness. The only plausible explanation is that the Paleozoic sediments were laid across the whole region, and that the mountains as we now know them, including the Paleozoic layers, were afterward elevated. The sedimentary beds were arched up as the "roof" of the rising dome and have since been eroded away. At least 15 miles of rock, it is speculated, have been stripped from above these mountains while they were growing in stature.

Before meditating on the cause of the doming, it is important to note that the Adirondacks bear no relationship to the Appalachian mountain ranges farther east (principally the Green Mountains, the Berkshires, and the White Mountains). In fact, they are sharply set apart from the coast-long Appalachian chain by the down-dropped fault basins (graben) of Lake Champlain and Lake George. They are not folded mountains, as are the Appalachians. The Adirondacks are a topographical anomaly where they stand. They cannot be accounted for by the collision of crustal plates, which rumple up most of the world's major mountain chains (as the plate-tectonics concept so well demonstrates). In this respect, they are comparable to a number of independent uplifts in the interior plains of Africa which are now defined as "hot spots." Many of the African anomalies do not have volcanic caps and have never erupted. (In America, the Black Hills and the Ozarks are suggested as other possible "hot-spot" anomalies.)

In short, the Adirondack dome is now being proposed by some New York State geologists as a localized uplift over a "hot spot" where molten magma (or something called a "thermal plume") may be pressing upward from the depths. Such a deep-seated source of geothermal energy may or may not be a resurgence of the anorthositic material referred to earlier as being the primary ingredient of the High Peaks.

The enormous blob of molten anorthosite did not, of its own force, erect the dome. On the contrary, it was squeezed in more than a billion years ago while the stack of Grenville-age sediments was undergoing metamorphosis some 25 miles beneath the surface. The anorthosite melt burst into and through the buried rocks at depth. In that stygian turmoil, chunks of the metamorphic gneiss (of Grenville type) were broken loose and became embedded in the intruding magma. The doming of the Adirondacks is now theorized to have begun very much later—during the last 10 million years.

A recent gravity survey indicated that the principal mass of the metamorphosed anorthosite consists of a great slab two miles thick underlying the entire High Peaks region. One or more carrot-shaped "roots" are believed to project downward from this slab at least six miles, but detached from any deep source; perhaps these are remnants of the conduits up which the molten magma rose. The anorthositic rock, being ligher than the surrounding rocks, probably began rising plastically at a time of high pressure and temperature when the rock was viscous.

Whatever the mighty processes by which the Adirondack Mountains came into existence, they are, beyond question, New York State's most opulent natural spectacle.

*Perimeter highways make possible a complete circuit of the High
Peaks heart of the Adirondacks. Proceeding counterclockwise, one
drives the Adirondack Northway (I-87) north to Interchange 30;
thence on Route 73 to Lake Placid, Route 86 to Saranac Lake,
Route 3 to Tupper Lake, Route 30 to Indian Lake, and Route 28 to
Warrensburg. A recommended digression is Route 28-N east from
Long Lake to North Creek, affording a vista of several High Peaks
as viewed from the south side. The town of Newcomb maintains a
roadside lookout on this route, with a signboard identifying the
peaks.*

MOUNT McGREGOR
General Grant's Last View

In the 1880s Saratoga Springs was in its prime as a fashionable watering place. From there a narrow-gauge railroad ran north 10 miles to the top of Mount McGregor where there was a noted resort hotel, the Balmoral. One of its attractions was the Eastern Outlook, at the edge of a nearly vertical cliff 600 feet high. A marvelous panorama of the Hudson Valley rolled forth against a backdrop of Taconics, Green Mountains, and Berkshires.

Up the slope behind this vantage was a spacious cottage owned by one of the Drexels, who in the summer of 1885 lent it to General Ulysses S. Grant and his family. The retired president was dying from throat cancer, finishing his memoirs in a grim race with death. After scribbling the last word, Grant asked to be taken to the Eastern Outlook. His manservant trundled him down the stony pathway through the woods. Three days later Grant died. Ever since, the Outlook has been called Grant's Last View. Grant's Cottage, with the furnishings just as they were the day he died, is a State Historic Site.

Mount McGregor is a salient of the Palmertown Range, which stands out as a landmark between Saratoga and Glens Falls. This Adirondack spur extends on north to become the western rampart of Lake George as far as Northwest Bay. The range is the upthrust side of a great fault whose displacement (differential slippage) was over 1,500 feet. Southerly the escarpment lowers until it fades out entirely in the north part of Saratoga. Underground, a branch of the McGregor Fault is the crack up which Saratoga's famous carbonated mineral waters bubble to the surface.

**General Grant's last view: From the cliff's edge on Mount McGregor,
this spectacular view across the upper Hudson valley unrolls, with the
Green Mountains of Vermont as the horizon line.**

At the Eastern Outlook, downhill a bit from Grant's Cottage, a visitor scans not only a striking vista but a time gap of 650 million years—the difference in age between the rock of Mount McGregor and the horizontal beds of the valley floor below. The upthrust side of the fault line is ancient Precambrian rock from the crystalline basement of the Adirondacks. Spreading out from the foot of the range are shales representing waterlaid sediments of the far-later Paleozoic Sea, which originally covered the entire Adirondack region. This is the widest span of time between adjacent faulted rocks that is easily visible in New York State.

As seen from Mount McGregor, the Hudson River lowland is astonishingly wider than the valley at Troy and Albany. How this could be so has presented a geologic problem that is not yet satisfactorily solved. Obviously a gigantic job of erosion was done here by a preglacial stream of considerable size—but why did it not do a similar amount of work further south? One answer could be the buried river channel known to exist west of Albany across the towns of Colonie and Bethlehem. Moreover, the Champlain-Hudson lobe of the glacier had much to do with widening and deepening the valley. Borings in the glacial fill south of Lake Champlain have revealed a deep channel whose rock bottom is below sea level. Certainly the Mount McGregor escarpment was whittled back and scoured by ice action.

Apparently, two south-flowing rivers made a junction somewhere in the valley seen from Grant's Last View, forming the ancestral Hudson. The eastern stream would presumably have flowed from a divide in the neighborhood of Whitehall; the western one from the Northwest Bay of Lake George. The preglacial drainage picture of that region is still rather obscure.

As the ice front was in its final retreat, glacial Lake Albany extended far enough north to have lapped at the base of Mount McGregor.

N.Y. State Museum photo by Kenneth M. Hay

From the Adirondack Northway (I-87), take Exit 16 from Wilton. Where the Wilton road meets Route 9, follow the sign "Grant Cottage" five miles up a mountain highway. An alternative approach is Route 9 north out of Saratoga.

Looking down at the enormously popular south end of Lake George from the summit of Prospect Mountain. The "viewmobile" takes visitors the final lap from the parking lot to the top.

PROSPECT MOUNTAIN
Lake George Overlook

The State of New York supports highways to the tops of three
mountains: Prospect Mountain and Whiteface in the
Adirondacks, and Bear Mountain in the Hudson Highlands.

The newest of the ascending roads is the Prospect Mountain
Veterans' Memorial Highway, which was opened to public use in
1969. The motive for driving it is a long-famed view of Lake
George. The mountain rises directly west of the resort village of
Lake George, 1,714 feet above the lakeshore. The toll road,
spiraling like a carelessly tossed lariat, takes five-and-a-half miles
to reach its goal. The gradient is gentle enough not to boil a
healthy radiator. Three overlook stops are provided on the way
up.

As Adirondacks go, Prospect Mountain is in the minor league
with its elevation of 2,034 feet above sea level—less than half the
height of Whiteface. In the context of its environment, however,
it serves the purpose well enough to have a fire tower on top. All
the mountains enclosing Lake George, although ruggedly
picturesque, are modest in height. The tallest is Black Mountain
on the east side.

Prospect Mountain was mapped in early days as Rattlesnake
Hill, but that should not deter anyone from seeking its summit.
The rattlers long since decamped in favor of tourists. Anyone
desirous of reptile company may still find enough of them on
Tongue Mountain a few miles to the north. The Adirondacks as a
whole are free of venomous snakes.

In the late Victorian era, a fine resort hotel, the Prospect
Mountain House, defied thunderbolts on the pinnacle. Guests

arrived by cable car on an inclined railway up the steep flank of the mountain. The huge bullwheel of that facility, with some of its incidental machinery, remains as a curiosity in the park development on the top. The Prospect Mountain House burned after being struck by lightning.

Prospect Mountain belongs to the same fault escarpment as Mount McGregor, the Palmertown Range. The Precambrian granite-gneiss of the upthrust side of the fault line is on graphic display in the barren, domelike top.

The toll road ends in a parking area a short distance below the summit. From there, Viewmobiles—similar to those at Niagara Falls—transport visitors the rest of the way as a free service.

The chief spectacle is the south portion of Lake George up to the Narrows. Many of the charming islands are in this view. On an exceptionally clear day, one may pick up a distant horizon of Adirondack High Peaks. In the foreground valley leading to Glens Falls one may sense the work of the glacial tongue that pressed through the lake channel and left the moraine deposits damming the lake.

The toll road did not complete the state's plans for Prospect Mountain. Also anticipated is a Summit House with an observation tower that will enhance the view.

From the Adirondack Northway (I-87) take Exit 21 into Lake George village. The Prospect Mountain toll road turns west from Route 9 in the south edge of the village.

LAKE GEORGE
Queen of the Lakes

With a deep bow to Champlain, no other lake in America is so
steeped in history as Lake George, and few are as queenly. One
of the finest descriptive passages in historical literature is Francis
Parkman's picture of Abercrombie's army afloat in its advance
against the French at Ticonderoga. Parkman, who always visited
his scenes before writing, saw it like this:

*The spectacle was superb; the brightness of the summer day; the
romantic beauty of the scenery; the sheen and sparkle of those
crystal waters; the countless islands tufted with pine, birch and fir;
the bordering mountains, with their green summits and sunny crags;
the flash of oars and glitter of weapons; the banners, the varied
uniforms, and the notes of bugle, trumpet, bagpipe, and drum,
answered and prolonged by a hundred woodland echoes.*

Parkman pinpointed a key aspect of the lake's beauty—"those
crystal waters." The lake is mainly spring-fed and it receives little
surface drainage, so that the fine clay and organic content are
negligible. This, coupled with depths down to 190 feet, makes for
clear, cold water. Pollution is minimal, but is unhappily
becoming more of a problem in recent years. The frowning
mountains that hem in the lake produce a dramatic effect. And
then there are the islands, of which the official count is 225. The
state owns 154, lumping them together as the Lake George Islands
State Park. These were prized observation posts for scouts in all
the colonial wars. Now they are prized by canoe campers.
Lake George is 32 miles long, the longest lake in the
Adirondacks. Its written history dates from 1642, when the Jesuit

A spectacular view of Lake George islands sprinkled through the Narrows. Tongue Mountain rises at the left.

missionary, Isaac Jogues, gazed upon it and gave it the name Lac St. Sacrement, which clung until 1755. Sir William Johnson, after his victory over the French at the head of the lake, renamed it in honor of his sovereign, George II, who rewarded him with a baronetcy.

The genesis of the lake's basin is complex. Initially it was two valleys bearing streams, one flowing north, the other south, with a massive divide at the Narrows. Sometime in the process block-faulting occurred, deepening the valleys. This means that huge blocks slumped between faults on either side. The result might be compared to giant sunken bathtubs. In geologic parlance such an occurrence is known as a graben (a German word for "ditch"). In essence, the bed of Lake George is a series of graben, an outstanding instance of this feature. The mountain ramparts are the upthrust sides of the bordering faults, notably Tongue Mountain on the west and the Black Mountain–Pilot Knob massif on the east. An extension from the McGregor fault, leading north from Saratoga, accounts for Prospect Mountain and Northwest Bay where the south-flowing Lake George River headed up. The northerly Ticonderoga River of preglacial days flowed west of Rogers Rock in what is now the Trout Brook valley. Heavy glacial deposits across both river valleys choked off the exits, thereby damming up the lake.

A Lake George tongue of the ice sheet knocked out the old divide at the Narrows. The islands are mainly the tips of rock ridges that survived glaciation, but a few of those in the southern part of the lake are glacial deposits, of which the conspicuous Dome Island is the protrusion of an ideally shaped kame, heaped in deep water at the foot of the melting ice front.

The grandest concentration of islands is in the six-mile corridor of the Narrows, formerly called the Hundred-Island Archipelago. These had a dissimilar origin from the rest. The differential up-and-down movements along parallel fault lines did not occur at equal rates. The down-slipping rock divide between was caught in the jaws of a stone crusher, broken up into fragments, and jostled around. The islands of the Narrows are the end-products of that violent treatment. The pieces were so disarrayed that their composition cannot be matched with the shoreside rocks or even with each other.

The settling of the graben rocks into the main troughs left many sheer cliffs facing the water. These fault-line scarps frequently have a surprisingly fresh appearance, as if the slippage occurred only yesterday. It may, in fact, have resulted in some cases from postglacial readjustments in the crust as it "bounced back" from the weight of the ice. Other cliff faces were smoothed and grooved by ice movement. The best known of the fault-line scarps is Rogers Rock in the lower lake, west side, connected by legend with the Rogers Rangers. It seems that Major Robert Rogers was being pursued on snowshoes by hostile Indians. Coming to the top of this almost vertical pitch, he removed his pack and let it skid down the incline to the ice. Then he strapped his snowshoes on backward and stepped carefully in his previous tracks until he could leap into a thicket and attain the lake by an inconspicuous ravine. The Indians on his trail reached the rock, saw him crossing the ice in the distance, and believed he had taken the impossible slide. Deciding he must have supernatural aid to survive, they gave up the chase. About the only way Rogers Rock may be viewed to advantage is from a boat, although it can be seen across a mile of water from a cottagers' road along the east side of the lake out of Ticonderoga.

The abundant kame-moraine mounds at the south end provide rolling terrain for the Lake George Battlefield State Park, which was fought over by British, French, colonials, and Indians. Here Sir William Johnson built Fort William Henry after his defeat of Baron Dieskau. There are excellent statues of both Johnson and Father Isaac Jogues in this park, and a restoration of Fort William Henry is a commercial attraction in the village. The earthworks of Fort George, built by Lord Jeffrey Amherst a bit further east, are reasonably well preserved. It is noticeable that Amherst's troops made ample use of glacial cobblestones for outer facing of the fort. Erratic glacial boulders are sprinkled plentifully around the park.

A good way to take in the beauties of Lake George is a cruise on one of the sightseeing vessels of the Lake George Steamboat

Company (the name of which has been cherished since steam was introduced on the lake in 1817, though the boats are now diesel powered). The *Ticonderoga*, a made-over Naval Landing Craft (LCI) from World War II, covers the full length of the lake in a six-hour round trip. The smaller *Mohican* does a two-hour cruise, sampling the choicest part of the lake, turning around in Paradise Bay midway through the islands of the Narrows.

From the Adirondack Northway one leaves at either Exit 21 or Exit 22 for the village of Lake George. Beach Road leads to Lake George Battlefield State Park, passing the docks of the cruise boats and the celebrated bathing beach. Route 9-N is a scenic drive that skirts the west shore.

This eastward view from the summit of Mount Defiance plainly indicates the dilemma of Fort Ticonderoga when the British placed cannon on the mountain's crest. The restored fort is seen on the point below, with the narrows of Lake Champlain and the Vermont shore beyond.

MOUNT DEFIANCE
Overview on Ticonderoga

Except for Lake George, one will travel far to find a place where great scenery and great history are so closely interlinked as around the southerly narrows of Lake Champlain. The massive stone bastions, the barracks and vintage artillery of Fort Ticonderoga constitute one of the most faithfully restored and impressive colonial citadels in America. In New York State, only Fort Niagara and Fort Stanwix are in the same league. The summit of nearby Mount Defiance, 768 feet above the lake, offers one of the supreme panoramas of the state.

It was up the steep incline of Mount Defiance, on the opposite side from the fort, that British sappers hauled cannon during Burgoyne's invasion from Canada in 1777, to the dismay of the Ticonderoga garrison. General Arthur St. Clair evacuated the fortress under cover of night without the firing of a single shot, and Burgoyne took possession and marched on to his defeat at Saratoga. General William Phillips, the British artillery officer who executed that bold feat, promptly named the position Mount Defiance. To pioneer settlers of the locality it had been known as Sugar Loaf Hill, alias Rattlesnake Hill.

The present toll road to its top approximates the rugged route hacked out by Burgoyne's men, ironically enough on July 4. From the sight deck of the new summit house a viewer gets a sense of what the British fieldpieces could have done to the fort below. The strategic situation, in terms of geography, that made Ticonderoga such a vital point in all the French and Indian Wars as well as the Revolution is spread out far more graphically than any map or mock-up could depict it in a command headquarters. Lake Champlain slims down like a river past the muted gun muzzles, and Mount Independence stands opposite on the Vermont shore where the Yankees had an auxiliary fort. The two forts were connected by a floating bridge, across which the garrison retreated before the enemy could destroy it.

Apart from all the military history, the vista includes a distant reach of Lake Champlain to the north—the water highway that lured Samuel de Champlain from Quebec. In clear air some of the High Peaks can be seen. Off toward the sunrise a broad sweep of Vermont billows away toward a horizon of Green Mountains. The north end of the Taconic Range sinks from sight in the valley below. In the near foreground, between mountain and fort, appears the mouth of Ticonderoga Creek, which pours the outflow of Lake George over two waterfalls into Lake Champlain. The four-mile gorge has been cut since the glacier blocked off the prior southerly drainage at the present site of Lake George village.

The riverlike appearance of Lake Champlain past Ticonderoga, and particularly in South Bay, is no accident. The preglacial valley had been eroded by a river, presumably flowing north as the lake does now, from a rock divide near Fort Ann. The tight squeezes at Ticonderoga and Crown Point suggest a gorgelike condition at some time during the Ice Age, but geologists still puzzle over exactly how this happened. More than likely the gorge was the work of a southflowing outlet stream from a big glacial lake penned up against the retreating ice front across the Champlain valley.

Mount Defiance stands as an austere barrier between Lake George and the South Bay end of Lake Champlain. It is the terminal knob of an upreared fault block five miles long, forming the east wall of Lake George in that section. The gnarled old rock of its summit is a metamorphosed granite called charnockite, fairly plentiful in the Adirondacks.

After its brief moment of high drama in the Revolution, Mount Defiance returned to obscurity. All the while Fort Ticonderoga was being restored by the Pell family, its long-time owners, the mountain was neglected until in 1950 a group of Ticonderoga investors formed a corporation to build the road and develop the summit. The attraction was operated separately from the fort, despite its close relationship. In 1977, appropriately the bicentennial year of the Burgoyne incursion, the Ticonderoga Association purchased Mount Defiance, making it an integral part of the fortress tour.

From the Adirondack Northway take Interchange 28 and follow Route 73 east to Ticonderoga. An alternate approach is Route 9-N along the west side of Lake George. The toll road up Mount Defiance is easily located in Ticonderoga village, as is the way to the fort.

A visitor washing out stray garnets from rubble in the worked-out section of the Barton Mines at Gore Mountain.

GORE MOUNTAIN
Garnets in the Rough

The 1969 legislature decreed: "The garnet shall be the official gem of the State of New York."

The underlying reason for this statute is found high on the northwest flank of Gore Mountain in the Adirondacks. Garnets galore are on view and underfoot at the open-pit mines of the Barton Mines Corporation, which makes a point of being hospitable to visitors. The five-mile blacktop road up, maintained by the company, is a pleasant nature drive.

The Barton workings are the largest operating garnet mines in the world. Only one other garnet mine in the United States is currently worked and that is in Idaho. The bulk of the Barton product is marketed for abrasive uses, but the ore yields some crystals of gem quality that go for jewelry purposes. The garnet is also the January birthstone. Good rough gems may be purchased in a mineral shop on the property.

Gore Mountain, with an elevation of 3,595 feet, overlooks all its near neighbors. The summit may be attained by riding the ski lift, which is run for sightseers in the summer from the state-owned Ski Center on the east side of the mountain, aloof from the garnet mines. This is the only gondola (that is, enclosed) ski lift in the state. The peak is wooded, so that the scenic outlook requires the climbing of a fire tower.

The garnet mines have been worked since 1878 as a one-family industry. H. H. Barton, a Philadelphia dealer in woodworkers' supplies, desired a better grade of sandpaper than was then on the market. He recalled an incident of years before when he was apprenticed to a Boston jeweler. A stranger had come into the shop and spread on the counter a bagful of fine garnet gems, telling a vague story of having found them somewhere in the Adirondacks. Aware that pulverized garnets would lend a sharper bite to his sandpaper, Barton went prospecting in the Adirondacks and struck it rich. Unsure as to the extent of his strike, he bought up the whole of Gore Mountain to play safe. The deposit proved to be a lens-like mass three-fourths of a mile long and 300 feet wide. As the vein was thus limited, the Barton company some years ago donated the east side of the mountain to the state for a ski center.

The gaping open-pit mines are an impressive spectacle in themselves. A surprising waterfall leaps from the uppermost rim of the huge original quarry. The ore bodies are discerned in the walls of the working pit, embedded in a rock known as meta-gabbro, which was a molten intrusion in the older metamorphic beds. The garnet was crystallized deep in the earth from chemicals contained in the gabbro. The Barton Mines have turned up the largest individual crystals ever found. Crystals a foot in diameter are not uncommon, and a few have measured as much as three feet. The garnet is of a deep-red type, a hue that was highly fashionable in elaborate jewel settings of the Victorian era.

The guide service and mineral shop are managed under the company's supervision by a handpicked corps of college students for their own vacation profit.

Exit 23 from the Adirondack Northway leads into Route 9. Three miles beyond Warrensburg on this highway, take Route 28 branching northwest. Just before Route 28 enters the village of North River, there is a sharp reverse turnoff to the Barton Mines approach. The entrance to the Gore Mountain Ski Center is also off Route 28, but is in the larger village of North Creek.

INDIAN PASS
Wallface the Stupendous

Indian Pass, in the midst of the Adirondack High Peaks, is one of the most magnificent natural wonders in the state. Its west side, the Wallface Cliff, soars to 1,200 feet—the loftiest straight precipice east of the Rockies. It is a challenge to expert rock climbers. If Indian Pass were not aloof in the roadless wilds of the mountains, it would rank as a major tourist attraction in a class with Niagara and the Palisades.

Since there is no way to get into Indian Pass except by a long hike climaxing in some rough uphill going, the spectacle is not generally known outside of mountaineering circles. The forbidding notch may be glimpsed from a distance at a few spots along the Keene–Lake Placid highway (Route 73), incised between the McIntyre Range and Wallface Mountain. Because it cleaves the uppermost tier of the High Peaks, serious proposals were made in the past to push a highway, even a railroad, through the chasm. Luckily the Forest Preserve Act of 1885 protected it from so dire a fate.

Contrary to widespread belief, Indian Pass happens to be the authentic source of the Hudson River. The U.S. Geological Survey so maps the stream issuing from its southern portal. Partly because the name sounds so romantic, however, Lake Tear-of-the-Clouds up near the dome of Mount Marcy is generally believed by the public to be the Hudson's source. It is true enough that Lake Tear, a moss-bound pond, is the highest source water, but it is in reality the birthplace of the Opalescent River which joins the Hudson's main stem as a tributary several miles down the Tahawus valley.

Wallface Cliff, the west wall of Indian Pass, is the highest precipice east of the Rockies at 1,200 feet.

At the crest of the rise in the middle of the Pass, as someone once wrote, a wildcat might stand with its forepaws in the source trickle of the Hudson River, its hind feet in the headwater of the Ausable River, which belongs to the St. Lawrence watershed.

Besides the awesome Wallface cliff, the deep gulch of Indian Pass is remarkable for a jumble of enormous boulders strewn through much of its four-miles length. These rocks are angular, not rounded off as they wuld be if they had been transported by the glacier. They are of the same anorthosite composition as the cliffs high above. The trail threads its way among them and is often forced to climb over. Since little sunlight ever touches the bottom of the chasm, solid floors of ice lurk all summer in recesses beneath occasional boulders—a fact that has led some dreamers to speculate that the ice has remained there ever since the glacier.

The impact Indian Pass had upon early explorers of these mountains conveys some idea of its grandeur. In 1826, David Henderson, a young prospector for valuable metals, was approached in camp by an Indian who drew a lump of iron ore from beneath his blanket. When Henderson asked where he found it, the Indian guided him southward through the wild pass to the Tahawus iron and titanium ore deposit, which is mined today by NL Industries, Inc. Overwhelmed by the chasm he had seen, Henderson called it "the greatest curiosity in the country next to the falls of Niagara," and wrote: "If Niagara be the prince of waterfalls, the other exhibits the prince of precipices." Later on, Ebenezer Emmons, reporting to Governor William Seward on the first Natural History Survey of the Adirondacks in 1840, observed: "We look upon the Falls of Niagara with awe and a feeling of our insignificance; but much more are we impressed with the great and the sublime, in the view of the simple naked rock of Adirondack Pass" (as he identified it). A good prose description of the scene was given by Charles Fenno Hoffman, a New York author, editor, and poet who was presumably its first tourist-type visitor. In a book published in 1843, Hoffman wrote:

Loose boulders of solid rock, the size of tall city dwelling houses, hurled from a mountain summit into a chasm a thousand feet in depth, lying upon each other as if they had fallen but yesterday; each so detached from each that it is only their weight which seems to prevent them from rolling farther down the defile: their corners meeting in angles that defy the mathematician to describe, and forming caverns and labyrinthine passages beneath them that no draughtsman could delineate. . . . You would almost fear that your footsteps might topple over the gigantic masses, and renew the onward motion that was but now arrested. . . . The cliff opposite looks raw and recent, as if riven through but yesterday.

Without benefit of glacial knowledge, Hoffman, the amateur, sensed fairly well the reason for the extraordinary spill of boulders. Each recurrence of ice during the long glacial epoch filled the abyss, grinding it deeper and wider. At the final withdrawal, the ice tongue remained in the pass long after the main glacier had liberated the surrounding mountaintops. This plug of stagnant ice supported in place great blocks of stone that had been cracked loose by glacial pressure far above on the cliffsides. As the ice melted out at last, the boulders tumbled away helter-skelter, and their fall produced Wallface. If the boulders and glacial residue could be removed, Indian Pass would probably resemble a U-shaped glacial trough like the fjords of Norway.

The original fissure was already there preglacially, over a million years ago, in the form of a ravine, or at least a col between the flanking mountains, indenting a shoulder of the McIntyre Range. This cut is an outstanding example of the many fault lines slicing the Adirondacks on a northeast–southwest bias. Other instances within near compass are the two Ausable Lakes, the two Cascade Lakes, and Wilmington Notch alongside Whiteface Mountain. The displacement by slippage along a fault line creates a zone of broken rock that is relatively vulnerable to the wear of erosion. The creeping ice sheet from Quebec found the erosional fissure antedating Indian Pass a convenient avenue for its powerful southward movement.

Indian Pass may be attained, by the energetic visitor, from either north or south. The northern trail, seven miles long, sets out from Adirondack Loj on Heart Lake. The Loj is approached by turning due south from Route 73 at North Elba, near Lake Placid, and proceeding 4.8 miles. The trail in from the south side is shorter, about four miles, starting from the trail center at the location of the old Tahawus Club on NL Industries property. The approach to that focal point is via the company highway to its titanium mine. Turn north on this from Route 28-N, a distance of eight miles to the titanium workings. Near the entrance to the plant a bridge crosses the infant Hudson. Turn sharply left just before the bridge and follow a narrow dirt road four miles further along the bank of the river.

Blue Mountain Lake, with the Adirondack Museum in the foreground. In the distance are Eagle and Utowana lakes, which provide the outlet flow into Raquette Lake.

BLUE MOUNTAIN LAKE
Plus the Adirondack Museum

Of the Adirondacks' 2,000-odd lakes and ponds, Blue Mountain
Lake is one of the loveliest. It borrows its indigo hue from its
namesake, whose moods it reflects. The lake comes into view at a
major traffic junction southwest of the High Peaks. Roughly oval
in shape, a mile long at the extreme, it is not too large to be
visually grasped from a higher viewpoint such as the premises of
the Adirondack Museum. Its surface is broken by nearly a score
of wooded islets.

Blue Mountain Lake is the primary source of the Raquette
River, through which it sends its water by a devious, meandering
route over 100 miles into the St. Lawrence. Were it not for the
Hudson, the Raquette River (named for French snowshoes)
would be the longest in the state. From the Museum viewpoint
one picks up shining glimpses of Eagle Lake and Utowana Lake,
which are links in the outlet chain tying Blue Mountain into the
much larger Raquette Lake. By that defile, when Blue Mountain
Lake was in its heyday of big resort hotels, a steamboat line made
connections with the Raquette Lake Railroad to bring in
moneyed New Yorkers.

Blue Mountain itself towers over the scene, 3,759 feet tall,
popular among climbing vacationers. Its granitic bulk, seen from
afar, displays a chameleon quality of shifting colors ranging
through shades of blue, violet, and purple. Old-time guides gave
it the not surprising name; an early hotel proprietor transferred the
name to the lake.

In preglacial time, drainage of this area flowed eastward into
the ancient Hudson system. The stream headed at a ridge barrier

between Eagle and Utowana lakes, where the flow is now west through a short gorge. The valley was scooped and deepened, though not excessively, by ice erosion, which left behind remnants of rock for the islands. More pertinently, the glacier produced a quantity of drift material across the east end of the basin to impound the lake and reverse the flow. Probing for an escape to the west, the water hewed the short gorge through the barrier to Utowana Lake. It is true that a trench half a mile long and 20 feet deep would permit Blue Mountain Lake to drain off east into Hudson tributaries. Years ago a project was hatched to do this, but hasty passage of a state law halted it in the nick of time.

Around 1900, four wealthy New Yorkers banded together to buy up a parcel of land bordering the north shore of Eagle Lake, and built adjoining summer estates. Their private society was called the Eagle Nest Country Club. One of the four was Berthold Hochschild, a founder of the American Metal Company, Ltd. His son, Harold K. Hochschild, became so ardent an Adirondacks hobbyist and scholar that he built and endowed the Adirondack Museum, opened in 1957. The select spot he chose for it was an upland shelf, a spur of Blue Mountain jutting out to the verge of the lake, which had been the perch of a resort hotel, the Blue Mountain House. The museum has since grown into a complex of some 20 buildings.

The Adirondack Museum cannot be bypassed by anyone truly interested in the beauties and background of these mountains. A gallery in the central building contains a series of excellent dioramas illustrating phases of Adirondack history. At the far end of the gallery a visitor comes upon what looks like another well-crafted diorama, but turns out to be an artfully framed picture window focused on the lake below. By picking up an earphone, one then hears a recorded analysis of the scene.

The original curator of the museum, Dr. Bruce Inverarity, dreamed of getting the tip of a high Adirondack peak for an exhibit. Such sacrilege could not be committed upon any mountain within the Forest Preserve. His idea was finally realized, however, with the donation of a chunk from the summit of Gore Mountain by its owner, the Barton Mines Corporation. A visitor may become a vicarious mountaineer by stepping upon it.

The region of Blue Mountain Lake is bothered by recurrent micro-earthquakes, as many as 30 per month, and is occasionally shaken by a felt earthquake. For this reason it has received intensive study by seismologists of Columbia University, and is the site of the first successful attempt at earthquake prediction in North America.

The village center of Blue Mountain Lake is at the intersection of Routes 28 and 30. The entrance to the Adirondack Museum is a short distance up the grade going north on Route 30.

The river-like aspect of Long Lake is seen to advantage in this aerial view. The lake is thirteen and a half miles in length. The hamlet of Deerland lies in the foreground.

LONG LAKE
Javelin of the Mountains

Adirondack lakes come in many shapes, sizes, and varieties. The
repetition of Round Lakes, Mud Ponds, and Rock Lakes grows
monotonous and suggests a shortage of adjectives among the
wilderness pathfinders. Then one happens gratefully upon
Ampersand Lake and Antediluvian Pond. Curiosity alone might
impel somebody, someday, to go looking for Dishrag Pond, which
appears on topographic maps.

Linear lakes are plentiful in the mountains because of the
fault-line fissures that cross the dome. None of these is quite so
strikingly linear as Long Lake, which holds a solid claim to its
name. It is also one of the readiest to be seen. Indeed, it is
impossible to miss for motorists doing the western circuit of the
High Peaks area, as the major highway, Route 30, crosses it by
causeway. The vista straight down its length is one Adirondack
sight to remember.

Long Lake merits its name by stretching thirteen-and-a-half
miles diagonally athwart the midsection of the Adirondacks. In
its slimness it resembles a river, and it actually is a comparatively
recent enlargement of the Raquette River, which rushes in from
Buttermilk Falls at the west end and dawdles out in still-water
meanders at the other. Because of its uninterrupted length it is a
welcome segment of the celebrated Fulton Chain canoe route, by
which ambitious paddlers travel from Old Forge to Saranac Lake.

Because of the rocky, wild shores, it is impossible to drive the
length of Long Lake on either side. For only three miles, between
Deerland and the village of Long Lake, does Route 30 parallel the
south shore. A motorist's view of the lake is therefore practically

confined to his crossing of the causeway, where he may pull off
the road and have a good look. The village maintains a sandy
bathing beach beside the highway. Floatplane flights are
available at this beach for those who want an aerial perspective of
the lake.

Long Lake spears sharply northeast toward the Seward Range,
whose castellated purple profile may be seen distantly beyond the
lake's end from the causeway. The rugged Sewards, with their
four interconnected summits, are the westernmost bastion of the
High Peaks. Trailless and covered with blowdown timber, the
Seward Range is considered by Adirondack Mountain Club
members their toughest hurdle in pursuit of the mystical "46
peaks" over 4,000 feet (actually the number was reduced to 43 in a
more recent survey).

The axis of Long Lake probably originated as a crush zone
between two lines of fault slippage. The ancestor of the Raquette
River began the flow in that weakened zone, but somewhere
toward the present outlet of the lake it changed direction to
southeast as a headwater tributary of the preliminary Hudson.
The melting glacier left that escape route blockaded by ample
drift deposits, thereby imprisoning the lake.

Long Lake is distinguished as the birthplace of the Adirondack
guideboat, specimens of which are on view at the Adirondack
Museum. Mitchell Sabattis, a noted Indian guide who lived at
Long Lake, is credited with invention of the guideboat.

*Routes 30 and 28-N intersect in Long Lake village. Route 30 then
proceeds north across the causeway.*

LOWER AUSABLE LAKE
One of the Rarest Gems

The two slender Ausable Lakes, strung out in tandem, are marvelous examples of the many linear lakes in the mountains that owe their origin to diagonal faults (northeast–southwest) which determined stream channels long before the glacier's alterations. The Ausables gleam like shards of blue-glazed pottery caught between the bases of Mount Colvin and the Sawtooth Range. Both lakes are the property of the exclusive Ausable Club which, although restricting the recreational use of their waters to members, does not debar the public from enjoyment of their superb beauty.

The name Ausable, meaning "sandy," was bestowed by early Frenchmen in canoes, presumably in reference to the large delta of the Ausable River in Lake Champlain. The lakes are the source of the East Branch of the Ausable River. From the broad terrace fronting the Ausable Clubhouse, a bus maintains a shuttle over a three-mile woodland road to the lakefront boathouse from July 1 through Labor Day. Chance visitors who are not club members or sponsored guests may use the bus after purchasing tickets at the clubhouse, providing members and their guests have been accommodated. The boathouse at a corner of the lake is off limits to nonmembers, and no rowboats or canoes are available to the public. The dazzling scenery, however, is free and open to everyone. The Lower Ausable is certainly worth the slight inconvenience of finding it.

The lake is some two miles long, a quarter-mile wide, with a gentle bend part of the way up that prevents a full-length view from ground level. The sidewalls testify to the U-shape like that

Lower Ausable Lake, from the Fish Hawk Cliffs. A sliver of the Upper Ausable Lake peers from beyond.

of a fjord, eroded by a moving tongue of ice. Vegetation has trouble gaining a roothold on the near-vertical walls, and the sheer rock plunges beneath the serene water, forbidding lakeshore trails. A stunning overhead view, however, is the reward for panting up a half-mile trail on the east side to Indian Head. From there the Upper Ausable Lake shimmers in the offing, half as long as the Lower Ausable and at a level 32 feet higher. The two are separated by an alluvial natural dam built by Shanty Brook which drains flanks of six High Peaks.

Preglacially, the Ausable fault cleft was probably used by a south-flowing tributary of the ancestral Hudson system. It was later diligently scoured by a finger of the Keene Valley ice lobe. During final withdrawal the glacial front held in a large Keene Lake, which made its escape southwest through the Ausable defile. Ultimately Keene lake was emptied by a lower outlet into the Champlain valley. At both ends of the Ausable passage the glacier had left behind thick morainal deposits that served to dam up the single lake which was later divided by the work of Shanty Brook. The Ausable Club golf course makes use of glacial mounds. The lower lake has its deep vent through the moraine stuff against the north wall, behind the clubhouse.

After the mountains had been denuded by lumbering and were ravaged by forest fires, a group of New York sportsmen organized the Adirondack Mountain Reserve to heal them. As yet the state treasury was too poor to buy up much of the ruined land for the Forest Preserve. The Mountain Reserve acquired almost the entire Great Range along with the Ausable lakes, and began a large-scale program of reforesting, fire protection, and trail marking. The Mountain Reserve still exists as the property of the Ausable Club, into which the group evolved. During the 1920s the club sold 18,215 acres of restored land to the state, including the summit of Marcy. It retained both sides of the lakes up to the height-of-land, with the proviso that hikers be permitted to use the trails.

The matchless location of the Ausable Club used to feature a summer hotel known as St. Hubert's Inn, a mecca for vacationists in an Alp-like setting. St. Hubert is the patron saint of huntsmen, forests, and wild game. St. Hubert's is still the post-office address of the club. The tableland fronted by the clubhouse looks up at a spectacular circle of pinnacles that includes Giant of the Valley, Noonmark, Hedgehog, the two Wolf Jaws, and the serrated silhouette of the Sawteeth.

St. Hubert's is marked on highway maps between Keene Valley and the dramatic defile at the foot of Giant of the Valley. The entrance road to the Ausable Club turns left here.

HIGH FALLS GORGE
Mad Water in the Notch

The noted historian of the Adirondacks, Alfred L. Donaldson, referred to the West Branch of the Ausable as "a much-sounding river." Evidently he meant in particular the 10-mile gallop through Wilmington Notch where the agitated stream descends 624 feet in a gamut of rapids, chutes, and cascades.

Wilmington Notch is the pass followed by Route 86 between Lake Placid and Wilmington. The highway shares the cramped space with the river. At the height of lumbering the haul through the Notch on a narrow muddy road beside the torrent was the dread of all teamsters. The towering east flank of Whiteface is on one side, a sharp cliff of Sunrise Mountain on the other. Sunrise was a spur of Whiteface before a widened fault fissure separated them.

High Falls Gorge is a detail of a much larger scene. It is the tightest squeeze in a chasm that is itself a gorge of colossal dimensions. Within a stretch of a quarter-mile the West Branch drops 100 feet in a tormented channel that is nowhere more than a few feet wide. Under such constriction the river reaches a fortissimo of frenzy. The name "High Falls" is somewhat misleading. The falls proper is only 50 feet high, and then not a direct plunge but more of a sluice over fiendish obstacles. The water crashes headlong into a mishmash of cross-faults and slabs of basaltic dikes, injected in the crush zones of faulting. An intrusion of attractive pink granite, itself chopped up with the rest of the medley, throws in a snycopation of color.

Totally surrounded by the Forest Preserve, the High Falls segment is a surprising enclave of private ownership, managed as

The West Branch of the Ausable River hurtles its mad way through a narrow fracture zone of rocks in High Falls Gorge, at the base of Whiteface Mountain. Here it splits around a dike of granite.

a commercial attraction. The state is satisfied with this
arrangement, otherwise it might feel compelled to make a park
out of it and shoulder the expense and responsibility. It was a
difficult cleft to develop and safely maintain. Steel walkways are
solidly bolted into both cliffsides, with only angry water beneath.
Visitors pass down one side, cross over, and return on the other.
At key points railed outlook platforms are provided where
push-button taped remarks explain the scene with valid geology.

Before the glacier, the Notch probably had a col, or divide, still
tying Sunrise Mountain to Whiteface. Streams flowed from this
col in both directions. Under glaciation, a tongue of ice pared
down the rock divide and greatly widened the gorge. During the
retreat, two large glacial lakes were penned in the northern fringes
of the Adirondacks as forerunners of the East and West branches
of the Ausable. The eastern one, Keene Lake, filled Keene
Valley; the western, Lake Newman, was impounded in the
intervale between Lake Placid and Saranac Lake. Keene Lake
stood 2,000 feet higher than Lake Newman. The two lakes were
prevented from merging by the high barrier presented by the
Cascade–Porter Mountain complex. The east–west chasm of the
twin Cascade Lakes might have been a tie between them except
that it was plugged with ice.

Wilmington Notch now enters the plot in a dual role. The
retreating ice front freed an outlet toward Jay for the waters of the
Keene Valley lake, which then captured a lower escape to the
village of Wilmington. The sudden surge created Lake
Wilmington, which later burst southward through the Notch to
join up with Lake Newman. The combined lakes used an outlet
westward with the Saranac glacial waters.

Meanwhile the Champlain lobe of the glacier was shrinking so
that the Keene Valley arm of Lake Wilmington discovered
eastward escape vents into that valley. As Lake Wilmington
lowered its level accordingly, the flow through Wilmington Notch
was reversed. Water from Lake Newman now gushed
northward. All in all, the Notch got quite a housecleaning, and
anything that remained of the rock divide was scrubbed out.
With the final disappearance of the glacier, the East and West
branches of the Ausable River settled into their present channels.

Route 86 northeast out of Lake Placid threads the bottom of Wilmington Notch. The entrance to High Falls Gorge is three miles south of the village of Wilmington. From the Adirondack Northway the simplest approaches to the Notch are from either Exit 30 or Exit 34. From Exit 30, take Route 73 to Lake Placid and turn north on Route 86. From Exit 34, take Route 9-N southwest and turn right from Jay to Wilmington.

WHITEFACE
The People's High Peak

If any one of the Adirondack High Peaks was to be "sacrificed" for a public road to the summit, Whiteface was the logical choice. Its barren, windswept crown stands in aloof majesty across an intervale 10 miles north of the Great Range. Hence the highway could be built with minimal outrage to the "forever wild" doctrine of the Forest Preserve. This is the highest spot to which a motor vehicle may be driven in New York State. In a typical recent season, 40,000 cars made the eight-mile ascent. The tollgate is shut on many days when the peak is covered with clouds.

At 4,867 feet, Whiteface ranks fifth among the Adirondack pinnacles of which 43 exceed 4,000 feet (two are over a mile). Because of its outlying situation, it is a grandstand seat for a dozen or more of its fellow giants, including Mount Marcy, the champ. Its foreground vantage on ladder-shaped Lake Placid is classic. Northward the view gradually levels into the St. Lawrence Lowland, affording distant flashes of that river as far as Montreal.

During the 1920s conservation zealots fiercely battled a campaign spearheaded by the American Legion for a highway up Whiteface as a memorial to New York's war dead. Advocates argued that, among the many summits free to foot climbers, it was only fair that one be open to motorists. In a 1927 referendum, the state's voters approved an amendment making Whiteface an exception to the "forever wild" dictum. Governor Franklin D. Roosevelt pressed the road into construction in 1931 as a Depression make-work project. Keeping his promise, he returned as president in 1935 to ride up the completed toll road and give

Standing aloof from the main cluster of High Peaks, Whiteface Mountain ranks fifth in elevation.

the dedicatory address. The occasion became especially poignant when the polio-crippled president, standing stalwart in his steel braces, swept his glance over the horizon of the High Peaks and said: "Many persons, due to age or disability, cannot indulge in the luxury of camping or climbing. . . . For millions of people who have not got the facilities for walking up a mountain, we have now got the means for their coming up here on four wheels."

The topmost Adirondacks, as recounted before, are the remnants of a gigantic dome of rock pushed up within the past 10 million years. The primary material of the dome is metamorphosed anorthosite, a relatively rare rock in the world. The typical "Marcy-type" anorthosite is dark bluish-gray. As it radiates outward from the central core of peaks, this rock lightens in hue until Whiteface is almost milky white beneath the weathering. Avalanche scars are a trademark of the High Peaks. A tremendous landslip in 1816 inspired the naming of Whiteface. Three new scars were formed by slides in 1971.

And why is the Whiteface anorthosite lighter in hue than that of Marcy and Algonquin? One theory is that Whiteface was part of the outer crust of the huge blob of molten rock when it formed, cooling in contact with the enveloping strata into which it had been forced. At any rate, during metamorphism the dark blue-gray crystals were purged of their microscopic impurities.

Whiteface is hammered by the most savage winds of any Adirondack peak. This fact is attributed to the stratospheric jet stream that crosses the northern United States, oscillating frequently over this mountain as it does over Mount Washington in New Hampshire so that the two are kin in this respect, though the latter is over 1,000 feet higher. Although Mount Washington holds the United States wind record with a blow of 231 miles per hour, Whiteface sometimes gets winds up to 150. Alongside the stone summit house, with its circumambient window views, rises a 60-foot silo weather station operated by the Atmospheric Sciences Research Center of the State University of New York at Albany. In its lower level visitors are welcome for an exhibit of meteorological instruments.

Localized glaciers lingered in high mountain valleys for some

time after the parent ice sheets receded. Such tongues of ice
scooped out cirques, like amphitheaters, at the headings of their
valleys. Whiteface is the best example of an Adirondack peak
that was partially shaped by glacial cirques, one of which, having
a nearly vertical headwall, is used by the Whiteface Mountain Ski
Center on the eastern side of the mountain. Whiteface's almost
conical peak is the result of plucking by at least three mountain
glaciers whose headwalls were virtually back to back. These
cirques are separated by sharp ridges called arêtes. If the Ice Age
had lasted much longer, the arêtes on Whiteface would have
converged at the top to create a horn somewhat like the
Matterhorn in the Alps.

The principal ski lift of the Whiteface winter sports center is
operated in summer and autumn for the benefit of sightseers,
landing them at the top of Little Whiteface, a shoulder from
which they look up to the main summit.

The toll road terminates at a parking level 700 feet below the
pinnacle. The ascent is easily completed by elevator in a
perpendicular shaft, reached through a horizontal tunnel. The
more ambitious of visitors have the option of climbing the rest of
the way on foot along the spectacular trail following the hogback
arête that separates the north and west cirques.

*The Whiteface toll road starts its ascent from Wilmington, a village
reached by Route 86 from Lake Placid, or by Route 9-N going west
from Jay. The Whiteface Ski Center is a brief drive south from
Wilmington on Route 86.*

MOUNT MARCY
Monarch of the North

As the loftiest mountain in the state, Marcy—like its near neighbor, Indian Pass—demands a place in this book, even though its zenith may be won only by strenuous effort. Marcy stands 5,344 feet above sea level, 64 feet more than a mile. Although this is tame in comparison with the top Rockies and Sierras, it is only fair to say that climbing of a western peak starts from a much higher elevation at the base, so that the difference is not so great as might be supposed. Only six peaks in New Hampshire's Presidential Range, including Mount Washington, excel Marcy in the northeastern United States.

The profile of Marcy, once identified, cannot be mistaken. From a distance, its dome is seen as a uniformly contoured mound, rather elongated on the north–south axis, by contrast with the restless irregularity of the other High Peaks. The shape lends it an aura of proud dignity. The sculpturing was done mainly by ice. The glacier at maximum stood perhaps another mile over Marcy. Striations (glacial grooving and scraping) are visible on the summit, and erratic boulders from further north rest upon it where the ice unloaded them.

Because of its supremacy, if for no other reason, Marcy is the most frequently climbed of the Adirondack High Peaks, and it is one of the most interesting to be on. Its summit area for roaming about is larger than most and its scope of vision wider than any, encompassing a majority of the lesser peaks in the so-called Great Range. It reaches several hundred feet above timberline, its crown bald and footworn but fringed with sparse subarctic kinds of vegetation. Almost constantly swept by chill winds on the

Mount Marcy, monarch of the Adirondacks, as viewed from Haystack, with Panther Gorge between. On the right flank of the summit appears the snowfield that usually lingers into July, and just below it is a glacial cirque hollowed out by a lingering mountain glacier.

hottest days of summer, it is decidedly no place to be caught in a storm. A stone shelter that formerly huddled into the lee side of the peak for emergency use was once rebuilt with materials hoisted in by helicopter, but later had to be removed because of abuse and vandalism; sadly, the odious streak in human nature extends even to the clean mountaintops. At last accounts, a large bronze tablet celebrating the centennial of the first recorded climb was still firmly bolted into a vertical face of rock. A surveying benchmark attesting the highest spot in New York State is sunk in the pinnacle.

The substance of this mountain is chiefly that of all the High Peaks—anorthosite. The "Marcy type" of the unusual igneous rock is dark bluish-gray in color, in distinction from the whitish hue of Whiteface. The difference is accounted for by the fact that Mount Marcy is near the core of the gigantic mass of anorthosite that was intruded when it was molten, whereas Whiteface, part of the outer crust of this mass, was bleached because it was more severely metamorphosed.

Mount Marcy received its christening on the occasion of the original organized climb of 1837, in the course of the first Natural History Survey of the Adirondack region. The leader of the climb, Professor Ebenezer Emmons, reported to Governor William L. Marcy: "As this tour of exploration was made by gentlemen in the discharge of their duties to the State, and under the direction of the present Executive whose interest in the survey has been expressed both by public recommendation and private council and advice, it was thought that a more appropriate name could not be conferred on the highest summit of this group than Mount Marcy."

The fallacy that the Indians had an earlier name, Tahawus, is as indestructible as the dogma that Lake Tear-of-the-Clouds is the source of the Hudson River. Even as late as 1920 an eminent geologist, in writing a State Museum Bulletin, made this egregious error: "Marcy, we learn was called 'Tahawus' or the 'cloudsplitter' by the Indians and with all due respect to New York's great governor, one can not restrain a feeling of regret that the poetical and expressive name of the savages could not have remained attached to the peak."

In reality, Emmons was innocent of any such sacrilege. The vogue of "Tahawus" was planted unintentionally and with poetic license by Charles Fenno Hoffman, the same New York author and poet who described Indian Pass so well. Inspired by news reports of the Emmons expedition, Hoffman determined to climb Marcy for himself. This was a courageous resolution for him, as he walked on an artificial leg, the price of a boyhood accident. He set forth accompanied by a guide and a party of friends. Midway to the top, forced to confess defeat, he sat down on a log and wept. Nevertheless, Hoffman had seen enough of the great North Woods to write magazine pieces and verses about his wilderness adventures. Some Indian vocabularies just then coming into print fascinated him. He found the Seneca word "ta-ha-wus" defined as "he cleaves the sky." It was used by that western New York tribe as an expression of praise for gifted orators at their councils and powwows. It struck Hoffman as an appropriate descriptive term for the state's tallest mountain, and he wrote it into one of his poems. Readers picked it up and accepted it literally: Tahawus the "sky-cleaver" or "cloud-splitter."

An eccentric character indelibly connected with Marcy was "Old Mountain" Phelps, a bewhiskered and unkempt Keene Valley guide whose real given name was Orson. By his own count, he had scaled this peak more than 100 times. He adopted it as his own personal "mounting" and always spoke of it reverently as "Mount Mercy" (not that it was in the least merciful to amateurs). Every Adirondack Mountain Club member is familiar with "Old Mountain" Phelp's phrase for the sensation of standing on the peak of Marcy: "heaven-up-h'istedness."

There are three principal trails leading up Mount Marcy. The most popular and relatively easiest is the Van Hoevenberg Trail from Adirondack Loj on Heart Lake, a base hostelry of the Adirondack Mountain Club. (The name of this rustic camp is a relic of Melvil Dewey's crusade for simplified spelling.) The two other approaches are from Johns Brook Lodge, three miles in from Keene Valley on the east, and from the Tahawus (or Upper Works) trail center on the southwest.

A word of caution for inexperienced climbers: The ascent is no mere Sunday-afternoon hike. It should be well prepared for, especially in the matter of proper footgear, which should be comfortable and waterproof (Adirondack trails abound in boggy patches). Other essentials are a pack with flashlight, food, plenty of drinking water, and warm extra clothing. Drastic changes in weather sometimes keep climbing parties on the mountain overnight. And finally—never climb alone.

The nearest a car can get to Mount Marcy is the Adirondack Loj. From Route 73, a few miles east of Lake Placid, a marked secondary road turns due south. Five miles on this road brings one to Heart Lake and the Loj, where a parking area is provided for climbers. From the southern side, Route 28-N is the main highway approach. About halfway between North Creek and Long Lake, turn north on a well-kept company road, eight miles to the titanium mines of NL Industries, Inc. Near the plant entrance at a bridge, a narrow old road, sharp left, leads beside the Hudson four miles to the Tahawus trail center.

The river runs deep and strong through Ausable Chasm, down to its rendezvous with Lake Champlain. The Potsdam sandstone of its walls is the oldest sedimentary rock in New York State.

AUSABLE CHASM
Chuting the Rapids

N.Y. State Commerce Dept.

The Ausable is a dynamic, fast-flowing river that drains a number of the Great Range peaks of the Adirondacks. Since its outflow is into Lake Champlain, it is a relatively short stream for its volume, which helps to explain the unusual velocity of the current. From source brooks high in the creases of Mount Marcy, the McIntyres, Haystack, and the Gothics, it descends 4,000 feet in less than 50 miles. At flood periods the water of the West Branch travels from source to mouth in just a few hours.

It is hardly surprising that so energetic a river, rushing lakeward over boulders, has produced remarkable pieces of scenery besides itself. The climax of the performance comes in the Ausable Chasm, the deep cut by which the river lowers to the level of Lake Champlain. This impressive gorge, a mile-and-a-half long, has sheer walls rising 100 to 150 feet directly from the surging water. In places the cliffs are no more than 30 feet apart.

So swift a river, direct from the mountains, carries little silt. Instead it brings quantities of clean, washed quartz sand, which has built a large delta, Ausable Point, into the lake. This delta attracted the early notice of exploring Frenchmen out of Canada, perhaps of Champlain himself. They referred to it as *au sable*, literally "of the sand," or sandy.

The chasm has no waterfall, though two long rapids testify that the bottom is not yet leveled. The remainder of the cataract that did the work is Rainbow Falls, a half-mile upstream from the entrance pavilion. Long before the chasm was exploited for its scenery, these falls were harnessed for waterpower to run sawmills and gristmills. Before the mills, the Ausable River was famed for its annual salmon spawning. The great fish were ruthlessly speared during their run, and not a salmon has been seen in the Ausable since 1830.

That the chasm might be more lucrative than the mills was realized in 1874, when it was opened as a commercial tourist attraction. It is now owned and smartly managed by the Ausable Chasm Company.

From the pavilion, visitors proceed downstream in the chasm on railed walks that are ledges in the cliffsides. Tricks of erosion in combination with joint planes and faults have left offsets, cornices, and recesses and have created curious forms that bear fanciful names such as Pulpit Rock, the Elephant's Head, and Jacob's Ladder. Occasional informative signs along the route uphold a good standard of scientific accuracy.

The walkways are placed at a level high enough to be safe in the event of a heavy downpour in the mountains, which can raise the water in the chasm dangerously fast. Movable facilities such as bridge spans and a ticket booth for the boat trips are hauled up the cliffside every fall to preserve them from the spring runoff, in which the chasm is at least half filled.

The second half of the chasm tour offers an exciting boat ride which is optional but highly recommended. The vessel, about the size of a whaleboat, rides the strong current under control of an expert steersman who also gives a running spiel during the trip. It shoots two sets of rapids, pirouettes in a whirlpool, and while doing the rapids splashes some passengers in spite of canvas shields raised along the gunwales. The adventure ends in still water at a dock where the people are loaded into buses for return to the pavilion. The boat is hauled back by a powered cable along the sidewall of the gorge.

Ausable Chasm has been hewed entirely in a single rock formation, the Potsdam sandstone, some of the oldest sedimentary rock in New York State—the bottom layer of the Paleozoic pile which reaches its top (in this state) with the Olean conglomerate of the rock cities in southwestern New York. The Potsdam beds were laid in an early influx of Paleozoic seawater beginning around 515 million years ago. More than 1,000 feet thick, the Potsdam sandstone is of Cambrian age.

The Potsdam seashore was somewhere northwest of the present Adirondacks. Only recently has it been recognized that the water submerged the whole Adirondack area, meeting land at the margin of the Canadian Shield. That the waters of the Potsdam Sea were generally shallow is indicated by pronounced ripple marks in slabs of the rock, which are on display near the entrance to the chasm walk. The pebbles and coarse sand grains cemented into the Potsdam sandstone show a surprising freshness—that is, they are not very much waterworn—indicating that they were not carried far by streams or shuffled on a beach. This fact suggests that the Canadian Shield of that time consisted of high mountains that descended abruptly to the sea.

The rock takes its name from the village of Potsdam in St. Lawrence County, on the far side of the Adirondacks, in whose locality it is typically seen.

The preglacial Champlain valley was almost certainly occupied by a river flowing north into Canada, and the Ausable River of that period must have joined it as a tributary. The Champlain lobe of the sheets erased any sign of such a stream, but it was surely off to one or the other side of the present chasm. After the glacier the reviving Ausable River, finding its former route buried by glacial fill, was deflected. When it was able to stake out a new course across the barren Potsdam sandstone shelf, the river set to work chiseling out the Ausable Chasm.

The entrance to Ausable Chasm is 12 miles south of Plattsburgh, two miles northeast of Keeseville. Leave the Adirondack Northway at Exit 34 to Keeseville if driving north or at Exit 35 if driving south, and follow Route 9 a short distance to the Ausable Chasm entrance. There is a large pavilion for shelter, refreshments, and souvenirs.

The historic Cohoes Falls at full flow in the spring floodtime. This is the drop by which the Mohawk lowers to join the Hudson. Much of the year the cataract is reduced almost to trickles by diversion of the water for power and canal locks.

COHOES FALLS
Final Plunge of the Mohawk

The Mohawk River's logical junction with the Hudson would be somewhere south of Albany, as it was in the ancient past. The fact that it now occurs 11 miles to the north, instead, signifies one of the profound changes wrought by the great ice invasion. Cohoes Falls and the lower gorge of the Mohawk are results of a drastic deflection of the river at Schenectady. That swerve ordained the founding of Albany where it is; the waterpower of the cataract brought about the city of Cohoes.

Long before Niagara came to notice, Cohoes Falls gained international renown as an American scenic spectacle and was sought out by European travelers. An Irish poet, Thomas Moore, saluted it in verse. This premature fame was a result of the early settlement of Fort Orange and Rensselaerswyck by the Dutch. A contributing factor was that the falls, in colonial days, roared with an unflagging supply of water out of the western wilderness. Its repute was eventually eclipsed by Niagara and given a body blow by the wholesale diversion of its volume for textile mills and the Erie Canal locks during the nineteenth century.

In recent years Cohoes has taken steps to revive the esteem of its waterfall as an item under its Community Development Agency. The city has established Overlook Park on the best viewpoint of the clifftop, commanding a full sweep of the falls. This lookout has been improved with concrete- and brick-paved platforms, benches, and a protective chain-link fence around the rim. The fact remains that the cataract performs seasonally, putting on a good show only in short periods of spring flooding (April) and autumnal rains (October–November); at those times, however, it really booms. During summer drought the flow dwindles to a filigree of white rivulets over waterworn black rock.

This cataract has a descent of 65 feet and measures 600 feet along the crest. Nowhere is it a vertical drop. Rather, when at flood, it is a furious display of foaming leaps and plunges down an irregularly bulging facade. A large buttress or rock, locally dubbed "the Nose," juts out in one place, producing a forward plume of water when the volume is full. The river churns over a series of rapids above the falls.

The northward digression of the Mohawk from Schenectady was caused by a vast, sandy delta distributed over the floor of glacial Lake Albany by the Iro-Mohawk River when it was carrying the copious outflow from Lake Iroquois at Little Falls. Lake Albany was essentially the Hudson River backed up by an obstruction downstream and fed by meltwater. With this lake's subsidence, the postglacial Mohawk came up against that deltaic mass, which made the Pine Bush region between Schenectady and Albany. Digging into this barrier with a loop at Schenectady, the river was compelled to make a long northeasterly detour to rejoin the Hudson. Remaining souvenirs of that excursion are Ballston Lake, Round Lake, and the sand plains of Malta.

Ultimately the Mohawk settled upon a shorter spillway across rock beds from Rexford down to Cohoes, cutting two sequential gorges en route. The last descent to the level of the Hudson created the Cohoes Falls, which have receded 2,000 feet. The entrance to the upper gorge may be seen from the Rexford bridge of Route 146 (Balltown Road).

The rock formation over which the river pours is interesting in its own right. Geologically known as the Snake Hill shale, this almost black formation is intricately crumpled and contains vari-sized blocks of graywacke (an impure sandstone), a condition that helps to relate the formation with the westward thrust of the Taconic klippe. (See chapter on the Taconic Range). The klippe was a rock slide that avalanched off the steep flanks of the great New England highlands at the time of the Taconian Revolution. The awesome landslip reached into the margins of the Paleozoic Sea, which was then lapping at the base of the eastern mountain ranges. The makings of the Snake Hill shale were at that stage a thick accumulation of soft clay layers on the sea bottom near shore. The clay was ruffled up by the advance margin of the

Taconic klippe and became consolidated in later aeons. The layers can be distinguished in the gorge walls, slanting upward toward the falls.

The first dominie of the Dutch Reformed Church at Rensselaerswyck, sent out from Holland by Patroon Kiliaen van Rensselaer in 1642, wrote an enthusiastic description of Cohoes Falls after a visit. The settlers heard Indian tales about the name, which was variously rendered as Ga-ha-oose, Kah-hoe, Ca-hoos, and Co-hoe. The word was in some way connected with the wrecking of canoes. One Mohawk legend held that Hiawatha, after organizing the Iroquois Confederacy, deliberately went over the falls in a white canoe and vanished into the mist.

To avoid the dangerous cataract, the Mohawks adopted an overland route direct from Schenectady to Fort Orange for their fur trading with the Dutch. For the same reason the Erie Canal called for a series of locks around the falls to lift barges up to the Mohawk. Canvass White, an engineer on construction of the canal, was impressed with the waterpower potential of the falls and organized the Cohoes Company in 1826 to exploit it, thereby becoming the "father" of Cohoes. In their heyday some 40 knitting mills hummed at Cohoes, drawing many French workers from Canada. Although some of the mill structures have been adapted to other uses, the remainder stand idle.

Toward the end of the nineteenth century a big resort hotel, the Cataract House, did a thriving business on the clifftop above the falls. Its guests had a thrill in 1899 when a noted daredevil, Bobby Leach, who had shot the Niagara Whirlpool in a barrel, rode the same barrel over the Cohoes Falls—not once but twice.

More and more water was withdrawn upstream as a hydroelectric plant was installed near the foot of the falls, and a new and larger series of locks were built on the Waterford side for the State Barge Canal, superseding the Erie Canal in 1917. The city of Cohoes now diverts anywhere from six million to 11 million gallons a day for its water supply.

A collateral claim to fame is the Cohoes mastodon. In 1866, workmen excavating high on the south wall of the gorge for foundations of the Harmony Mills uncovered bones and teeth of an Ice Age mastodon (an extinct member of the elephant family). These remains were buried under 50 feet of muck and peat in two

large potholes that had been bored in the rock, presumably by
water surging through crevasses while the glacier still stood over
the site. It appears that the mastodon died during the ice
withdrawal on a lingering swampy floodplain and was washed
into the river and downstream, becoming dismembered; and that
its bones were caught in the two adjacent potholes.

The fossil remains were taken in custody by the State Museum
and reassembled into an almost complete skeleton. Using this
skeleton for a model, museum experts in 1922 made a life-size
restoration of the animal as it probably looked in the flesh,
complete with tusks and shaggy hempen hair. Still the only such
replica of its kind in the world, it was an extremely popular
exhibit in the old State Museum for more than half a century, but
was rejected for use in the new museum now in the Cultural
Education Center of the Empire State Plaza.

In 1977 the celebrated Cohoes mastodon was "taken home" to
Cohoes, on loan from the State Museum, and set up as a free
exhibit in the city's Human Resource Center. The skeleton was
left behind in the abandoned old State Museum. The Human
Resource Center occupies what was formerly the edifice of St.
John's Episcopal Church at 169 Mohawk Street. The mastodon is
at home in a mezzanine compartment built into the altar end of
the defunct church, kept company by winged angels in
stained-glass windows.

*A handy way to reach Cohoes is from Exit 7 of the Adirondack
Northway. After a brief jog on Route 9, take Route 9-R east.
Entering Cohoes, Route 9-R merges into Columbia Street, which
leads downhill, crossing Remsen Street, direct to Mohawk Street.
Turn left on Mohawk Street and follow it through to North
Mohawk, back uphill past numerous mill buildings. Just before the
last of the mill structures, turn right into a narrow one-way street,
then left into Cascade Street. Overlook Park is near the intersection
with School Street. Returning downhill, Mohawk Street veers right
at a grassy open triangle. The graystone church, with a sign
"Mastodon Exhibit," will be found on the left after several blocks.*

THE INDIAN LADDER
Thacher State Park

The Helderberg Escarpment, one of the most striking geographic features of eastern New York, stretches out as an irregular frowning bluff some 15 miles west and south of Albany. It is the horizon line that catches the eye of Thruway travelers while they are making the swing between the Hudson and Mohawk valleys. Relatively few of them turn aside for a closer look because most tourists are unaware of the merits of the park along the clifftop, or of the stupendous panorama.

John Boyd Thacher State Park is the most popular recreation tract within easy range of the capital district. It is the sort of showplace to which residents drive their out-of-town guests. Apart from the view, this park has such facilities as picnic grounds, campsites, and an Olympic-sized swimming pool.

Thacher Park is locally known as the Indian Ladder, in reference to a hallowed tradition. Only the upper face of the escarpment is limestone; below that is a long talus slope. The Indians had a trail up the slope, and a primitive ladder leaned against the cliff to complete the ascent. The ladder was a tall tree trunk from which the branches had been lopped, leaving stubs for footrests. It was dispensed with in 1820 when white settlers graded an Indian Ladder Road slanting up the talus, and blasted a cut through the limestone at the top. For the sake of sentiment, Thacher Park used to have a rustic ladder as part of its Indian Ladder Trail, but it was since replaced by a fieldstone stairway.

A benchmark at Thacher Park bears the figure 1,226 feet above mean tide level in the Hudson River at Albany. The view from that height takes in a vast spread of the Mohawk-Hudson

Two massive beds of limestone are the reason for the Helderberg
Escarpment, and the Indian Ladder Trail runs along their base at
Thacher Park. The upper is the Coeyman's limestone, the lower is the
Manlius. The photo clearly shows the narrow dividing line of shale, which
represents an interval of perhaps a thousand years.

lowland, its cities and farms. The Cliff Edge Overlook is a strip with a stone parapet at which cars may draw up facing the scene. An outline of Adirondack foothills appears dimly in the north. The intervening terrain is the distance over which the Helderberg cliff has been eroded through millions of years by predecessors of the Mohawk and Hudson Rivers.

The escarpment is the beetling front not only of the Helderberg Mountains but of the Allegheny Plateau. The Helderbergs are not foothills of the Catskills, as many believe. They are an intermediate step up to the Catskills, reaching an elevation of 2,000 feet, whereas the Catskills loom beyond at the 4,000-foot level. The Helderberg Plateau represents an erosion remnant of an incipient peneplain that became involved in an uplift. The limestone of the cliff face shows grayish-white. The Albany Dutch pioneers called it the Hellerberg, meaning bright or clear mountain.

The preservation of the Helderberg Escarpment was partly inspired by the crusade to save the Palisades of the lower Hudson from quarrymen. In 1902 cement companies were making offers to farmers whose cows grazed to the edge of the cliff. John Boyd Thacher, an Albany industrialist and former mayor, had a summer home on the verge of the Helderbergs. Outraged at the possibility of the Indian Ladder being blasted away, he began to systematically purchase lands bordering the cliff with the intention of piecing them together as a public preserve. Thacher died in 1909 before his plan was completed. Five years later his widow presented 350 acres, including three miles of cliff frontage, to the American Scenic and Historic Preservation Society as a memorial to her husband. The society later transferred title to the State Conservation Department, which made the site into a state park.

The upper front of the cliff is formed by two massive beds of limestone with an interval between them that could represent the passage of as much as a thousand years. The capstone is the Coeymans limestone, 55 feet thick. Below it is the Manlius limestone, 45 feet thick, an earlier deposit of the immense Devonian series. Voluminous beds of shale and sandstone underlie that. As at Niagara Falls, the weathering out of weak shales removes support of the limestone, causing blocks to break off.

The Helderberg cliffs have a venerable scientific background. Because of their fossil content, they became a mecca for both American and European geologists as early as the 1840s. Sir Charles Lyell, the foremost British geologist of his day, did field work on the escarpment in two visits during that decade. He wrote that the Helderbergs were "a key to the geology of North America . . . a place which every geologist must know if he is to understand his science." Anchored in a facade of limestone near the crest at Thacher Park is a bronze tablet that says: "In memory of those pioneer geologists whose researches in the Helderbergs from 1819 to 1850 made this classic ground." Seventeen names are listed on the plaque, among them Sir Charles Lyell, Louis Agassiz, and Dr. James Hall, a pioneering geologist and the first state paleontologist of New York. Hall's collecting of fossils while still a student at R.P.I. called the world's attention to the Helderbergs. Scientists from foreign nations continue to seek out the Indian Ladder, and busloads of university classes are brought to study the strata. The collecting of fossils within the park is prohibited even to scientists, but there are ample hunting grounds near at hand.

The escarpment has two large reentrants, the Indian Ladder Gulf and the Cave Gulf. In former times, perhaps interglacially, streams pouring over the cliff eroded these notches with high waterfalls. The Helderberg drainage is now nearly all southward because the rock strata dip in that direction, and also because much of the drainage is underground. Only one cataract of any size comes over the cliff today. This is the Indian Ladder Falls, 116 feet high. The Indian Ladder Trail ducks behind it. This trail runs for a half-mile at the base of the Manlius limestone. The limestone beds are honeycombed with caves and solution channels. The mouth of Hailes Cavern is on the trail. Spelunkers have explored this bat-inhabited cave 2,800 feet back in the cliff, crawling nearly half of it in a dangerous passage averaging two feet high.

Thacher Park may be reached from the Thruway by leaving at Exit 24, the west approach to Albany. After passing the tollbooths, keep straight ahead on the arterial, turning off at the Slingerlands exit. From Slingerlands, pursue Route 85 through New Salem and up the hill. From Schenectady, Route 146 leads through Altamont, and the park is then approached from the west side.

A passageway in Howe Caverns. The flowstone formation at left is designated as the Pipe Organ.

HOWE CAVERNS
Subterranean Beauties

The same limestone beds that show up so boldly in the Helderberg Escarpment also underlie a large part of Schoharie County. Their solubility in water is manifest in several caves around Cobleskill, especially Howe Caverns, the largest and best developed in the Northeast. A mile away is Secret Caverns, far less pretentious and more akin to a "wild" cave.

From a pleasant lodge styled after an English manor house, commanding a splendid view of the broad Schoharie valley, the Howe Caverns are entered by riding down 156 feet in an elevator. The passageway of the cave is three-fourths of a mile long and reaches its climax with a boat trip on the low-ceilinged Lake of Venus, part of the stream dammed up. Groups are taken on a guided tour of the many novel formations, such as the Pipe Organ and the Great Beehive. The walks, concrete and brick, are kept surprisingly dry with controlled dripping.

An effective feature, introduced near the end of the return trip, is the Winding Way, a side passage 550 feet long. This is an extremely tortuous corridor, a continuing series of "S" curves with sudden twists every few steps. Some of the bends are a tight squeeze even for normal waistlines. At the inner end the group convenes in a small rotunda called Pluto's Niche, where a pardonable bit of theatricality is indulged. The guide calls for absolute silence and switches off the lights for a long moment. The effect is eerie. The Winding Way is no place for anyone with claustrophobia.

The main portion of the cave is wholly in the Manlius limestone. Exploration in adjacent passages has shown that the visited section is only a fraction of an elaborate network of tunnels and crevices. Attempts have been made to reckon the age of Howe Caverns by the rate of deposit of the calcareous minerals in the stalactites, stalagmites, and flowstones. Someone found that the drippings from the ceiling contain one teaspoon of dissolved mineral matter per one gallon of water. From this he calculated that it takes 85 to 100 years to accumulate one cubic inch of a stalactite's growth (stalactites hang from the ceiling, stalagmites grow from the floor).

Howe Caverns have an interesting history. During the Revolution a peddler named Jonathan Schmul, plying his trade among the Palatine German settlers in the valley, discovered the cave "when the Indians were after me" and adopted it as his residence. He imparted the secret to a Lutheran clergyman, who helped to conceal some parishioners there when danger threatened. Strangely, the cave faded from memory after the Revolution. It was rediscovered in 1872 by a local farmer named Lester Howe.

Howe noticed that his cows, in hot weather, gathered around a thicket of small trees and bushes on the hillside. Investigating, he felt a strong, cool breeze issuing from the vegetation. Pressing through, he discovered the entrance to a dark hole in a rock ledge. Returning later with a lantern and a long roll of tape, he tied the tape to a tree in order to find his way back and began exploring the cave. He spread the news, and his discovery was widely publicized as Howe's Cave. Howe made rudimentary improvements and opened the cave to the public, charging a 50-cent fee. Each visitor carried his own oil torch. The ceiling still shows black smudges from the torches held overhead. Howe built a hotel and air-conditioned it with a conduit from the cave. His enterprise was not a financial success, and the cave was closed for at least 50 years.

During the 1920s a corporation was organized to rejuvenate the caverns. An elevator shaft was bored straight down to the inner end of the passage, and the reclaimed Howe Caverns opened in May, 1929. Following the precedent set by Lester Howe, the entrance lodge obtains its air-conditioning today from deep within the cave.

The nearby Secret Caverns are also channeled in the Manlius limestone, and a stream gurgles through. This cave lacks the sophisticated and costly improvements of Howe's, and the entrance fee is correspondingly less. It even has a few bats clinging to the ceiling, which Howe's does not. The secret of the Secret Caverns may be the underground waterfall featured in its signboard advertising. The 100-foot fall is at the inner end of a rather damp passage, and it performs only on demand. As the patrons draw near, the guide pokes a button and the sound of falling water is heard from the darkness ahead. The supply comes from a pond in a field aboveground, dammed up for the purpose. As a result, small frogs and salamanders are unexpected inhabitants of the cave.

Access to Howe Caverns is expedited by the new Interstate Route 88 between Schenectady and Binghamton. Leave the expressway at the Howe's Caverns exit. Across the valley, where this exit road joins the old Route 7, turn east a short distance on Route 7 to the well-marked cavern entrance pavilion. For Secret Caverns, keep on ahead past the private drive of Howe Caverns and follow the signs.

A bucolic look at the Taconic Range in the vicinity of Petersburg. In effect, this mountain barrier serves as the geographic boundary between New York and New England.

THE TACONIC RANGE
A Landslip from the East

Along some 100 miles of its length, the frontier between New York and New England is coincident with a straight and narrow rank of mountains known as the Taconics. Their altitude rarely exceeds 2,000 feet, the tallest being Berlin Mountain (2,798 feet), four miles due east of Berlin village near the Massachusetts border. Their marked steepness, however, makes up somewhat for their modest heights. They are uniformly wooded.

The Taconics supplied a natural dividing line between Indian tribes and their hunting territories, and later served a similar function for the colonies. Breaks in the range are almost nonexistent; a major exception is the pass at State Line through which the Berkshire spur of the New York Thruway ties in with the Massachusetts Turnpike. A very few other roads, notably Route 20 and Route 2, climb over the ridge through high gaps, affording nice views from their crests.

The Taconics are often confused with the fabled Berkshire Hills of western Massachusetts. In fact, they are a separate and distinct range, set apart by wide intervening valleys, yet the two are related from far back in time. The Berkshires are eroded stumps of a once tremendous mountain range of Himalayan dimensions. The Taconic Range, along with its forefront, broke loose from the steep west side of those lofty peaks and skidded to its present position in colossal landslips. The awesome event happened around 445 million years ago, in mid-Ordovician time. Such a rock avalanche is termed a klippe (pronounced clip-pa), a German word for similar phenomena in today's Alps. Hence the Taconic klippe, as geologists know it.

In a general way, the range marks New York's boundaries with Connecticut, Massachusetts, and southwestern Vermont. The range extends from the Hudson Highlands nearly to Hubbardton, Vermont, gradually becoming lower toward the north until it vanishes near Ticonderoga.

Between the Taconic Range and the Hudson River lies a strip roughly 20 miles wide that is a strikingly unique segment of New York State. This is a hodgepodge of fractured, folded, and weirdly contorted rock beds scattered in the form of low hills and ridges, making for an intriguing, storm-tossed kind of landscape. What this zone represents is a frontal apron—a mélange of rubble that swept on ahead of the Taconic klippe as it slumped into place. The Paleozoic Sea was at that time washing the base of the New England "Alps," and this advance mélange plunged underwater. (A fine illustration of how the gigantic slide swept ahead of it the soft layers of mud and silt on the seabed may be seen in rumpled, uptilted, dark-hued stratification of the walls of the Mohawk River gorge below Cohoes Falls.)

The Taconic phenomenon as a whole is the state's classic example of a direct consequence from a long-ago clash between the African and the North American continental plates. This interpretation is a by-product of the dramatic new concept of plate tectonics and continental drift which, only since 1965, has taken the scientific world by storm. The theory suddenly makes sense of geographic manifestations all around the globe that have hitherto defied explanation.

The continents are now seen as "passengers" riding on granitic crustal plates perhaps up to 60 miles thick that are in constant slow motion, floating on a plastic or semimolten material underneath. The oceans are similarly carried on plates, but theirs are of basalt, an igneous rock denser and heavier than granite, hence floating lower. Periodically, plates "collide," remain welded together for lengthy periods, then pull asunder to create new oceans. The amazing "fit" of the Atlantic coastlines of Africa and the two Americas, like that of pieces of a jigsaw puzzle, has been remarked since accurate maps were drawn. Plate tectonics verifies that these continents were indeed formerly jammed together as a continuous land mass. The last time they began to separate along the weld line was around 165 million years ago, and they are currently drifting apart at the approximate rate of two inches per year. While the Atlantic widens, the Pacific is narrowing.

During episodes of collision, it is typical for one plate to underthrust another, plunging its bent margin deep into the crust, thereby creating an oceanic trench near the point of contact into which seawater floods. One result is that the diving edge taps hot-rock zones at depth, while at the same time intensifying the heat by its own friction. This action, which permits molten rock to rise, produces volcanoes and other geothermal effects such as hot springs and geysers. Another outcome is that sediments long accumulated on the continental shelf and turned to rock are bulldozed up in great slabs and slices on the surface of the opposing plate. Continuing horizontal pressure rumples this transferred material, along with the prior surface features, like folds in a carpet. This accounts for the uprearing of the immense mountain ranges that so often parallel coastlines (for example the Appalachians, the Andes, and the Cascade Range of the Pacific coast). Offshore chains of volcanic islands—such as Japan and the Aleutians—are results of the heat reactions that are generated at great depths by an underthrust plate margin.

For some 200 million years, sediments had been piling up on the continental shelf of an ancient "Proto-Atlantic Ocean" off the east coast of North America. Around 450 million years ago that ocean began to close, with the eastern edge of the American plate sliding beneath the approaching African plate. The heat of the underthrust produced a chain of volcanic islands some distance offshore. The intervening water—comparable to the Sea of Japan today—collected thick, black sediments on its floor from the erosion of the volcanic islands. The progressive downthrust of the American plate beneath the island arc scraped up huge slabs of the newer Ordovician sedimentary rocks, stacking them on top of the previously laid sandstones and limestones of the continental shelf. The steadily encroaching African plate eventually smashed into the offshore chain of islands and shoved them, along with the already bulldozed slices of dark Ordovician rocks from the sea bottom, against and upon the coastal margins of northeast America. The northwest bulge of what is now Africa fitted into the pattern of the New England coast and the Canadian maritimes (see the appendix section on Stark's Knob).

This, the Taconic Orogeny, was the opening episode of the long-continued Appalachian upheaval. The scooped-up material from the island arc and the intervening sea bottom was compressed and buckled skyward into the earliest Taconic mountain range. The Taconic klippe skidded off the precipitous west side of this range at a relatively early stage (445 million years ago). Those high Taconics were only a segment of the vast Appalachian mountain chain, which was simultaneously being folded to lofty altitudes from Newfoundland to Alabama.

After that violent encounter the continents drifted apart, and there followed a quiescent period of some 100 million years, with enormous wearing down of the mountains and heaping of sediments in the adjacent seas. Then the African and American plates collided afresh in the Acadian Orogeny, even more radical than the Taconic had been, and this event rejuvenated the Appalachian Range into what must have been an overwhelming spectacle, 4,000 miles long and higher than Mount Everest. Aeons of subsequent erosion have left the Berkshires and Taconics what they are today.

The name Taconic is derived from an Indian word, Tagh-ka-nick, of uncertain or at least multiple translation. It may have been a local name applied to a spring on the mountainside above Copake, meaning "water enough." It was broadened to cover the entire range ("a great woody mountain"). The same root word occurs in other locations and forms, notably at Taughannock Falls, which was in Iroquois territory.

The handsomely groomed, much-traveled Taconic State Parkway runs up the middle of the forward apron of the Taconic klippe after emerging from the Hudson Highlands. Almost every road cut in that section of its route exhibits the wondrously distorted rocks. Off to the east, a matter of 10 miles, looms the skyline of the Taconic Range itself. When the Taconic State

Parkway (not to be confused with the Taconic State Park) was developed in the late 1920s, it was widely publicized as a "ribbon park" and became a model for other such parkways around the country on which engineers collaborated with landscape architects to harmonize roads with the scenic terrain through which they pass.

Olana, the Persian-styled mansion of the artist, Frederick Church, preserved as a State Historic Site south of Hudson, stands on a hill which is a huge block that tumbled off the Taconic klippe, in contrast to the bulk of the mélange which was "snowplowed."

The well-known Route 22 (sometimes dubbed "Park Avenue North") follows the base of the Taconic Range through most of its length. Route 22 can be reached by a number of crossover roads from Hudson River bridges or the Taconic State Parkway. A convenient point of access is Exit B-3 of the Berkshire Spur of the Thruway (Route I-90). Viewpoints from the crest of the Taconic Range are available where Route 20 crosses it to Pittsfield, and where Route 2 crosses to Williamstown, Massachusetts. The best of these outlooks is from Petersburg Pass, after a picturesque, winding drive up Route 2 from Petersburg on the New York side.

Splitting around a giant boulder, Bash Bish Falls is just across the Massachusetts border, at the foot of the Taconic Range, but is reached through an extension of the Taconic State Park.

BASH BISH FALLS
Taconic State Park

The Taconic Range is too steep and narrow to generate streams of much consequence. It sheds rainwater like a barn roof. There is, however, one notable exception. Bashbish Brook collects runoff from a number of tributaries in a wider, plateaulike area of ponds and marshes near the summit of the range, to do some whitewater rampaging down a deep, wild ravine that is almost a gorge, culminating in a 70-foot cascade.

Bash Bish Falls is the only waterfall worth attention in the Taconics, and it offers quite a novelty. Just before its final plunge, the stream splits angrily around a giant pyramidal rock, creating a twin cataract. The boulder, wedged firmly in the V-shaped notch, plummeted from a crag somewhere high above. Bashbish Mountain rises steeply from the falls on the south side to a height of 1,600 feet, opposite the 1,000-foot Cedar Mountain. The boiling plunge basin, framed by tall vertical cliffs, makes a striking picture.

The odd name, Bash Bish, is reputed to be of Indian origin, and is obviously a case of onomatopoeia (i.e., imitating the sound of the subject). With a little imagination, one side of the falls is saying "bash," the other "bish." It used to have another name, Copake Falls, which survives in the small village of Copake Falls near the entrance to the glen.

The waterfall happens to be on the Massachusetts side of the boundary, but is most conveniently reached from the New York side. For this reason the Massachusetts Conservation Department, in an unusual interstate working agreement, shares in the maintenance expense of the only practical approach to the falls—a gorge trail, one-and-a-half miles long, part of New York's Taconic State Park.

Bash Bish Falls was one of the scenes that attracted artists of the Hudson River School during the Victorian era. Two resort hotels were maintained in the adjacent hamlet of Copake Falls. Incidentally, a Copake Iron Works was also operated there, taking waterpower from the lower creek. A level area spreading from the gorge entrance was developed into a pretentious summer estate by a wealthy New York attorney, Alfred Douglas. His cluster of buildings were in the Swiss chalet style, and included greenhouses and horse stables. Douglas was the first to beautify the glen up to the foot of the falls.

The Gilded Age passed into history, the automotive era ensued, and Bash Bish Falls lapsed into neglect. In 1922, Mrs. Francis P. Masters purchased 400 acres of mountainside surrounding the falls for their protection. She later sold the property, at cost, to the Commonwealth of Massachusetts, and this spurred the Massachusetts legislature to create the Bash Bish State Forest.

Meanwhile, a group of New York conservationists were agitating for a state park in the Taconic Range. Governor Alfred E. Smith took up the idea, and the New York legislature established the Taconic State Park adjoining the Bash Bish State Forest at the border. This park was afterward enlarged until it extended 15 miles along the Taconic Range, with recreation facilities at the base of the mountains. Governor Smith appointed a Taconic State Park Commission, with Franklin D. Roosevelt of Dutchess County as its chairman. Today this commission has eight additional parks east of the Hudson under its jurisdiction.

Both the Taconic State Parkway and Route 22 are approaches to Bash Bish Falls. From the Parkway, exit for Route 23 east to Hillsdale, thence south on Route 22 to Copake Falls. From the west and the north, take the Berkshire Spur to Exit B-3, thence south on Route 22.

THE CATSKILLS
"Land in the Sky"

Washington Irving was America's first full-fledged man of letters, as well as the pioneer publicist of the Catskill Mountains. Although the silhouette of those romantic highlands had stirred river travelers since Henry Hudson, they were still remote from the mainstream of civilization. Europeans knew but vaguely of their existence until Irving's *Sketch Book* appeared in 1820. At that time the young author had never set foot in the Catskills, admiring them only from boat decks. With a single story he won them world renown. The tale was *Rip van Winkle,* and it began:

Whoever has made a voyage up the Hudson must remember the Kaatskill mountains. They are a dismembered branch of the great Appalachian family, and are seen away to the west of the river, swelling up to a noble height, and lording it over the surrounding country. Every change of season, every change of weather, indeed every hour of the day, produces some change in the magical hues and shapes of these mountains, and they are regarded by all the good wives, far and near, as perfect barometers. When the weather is fair and settled, they are clothed in blue and purple, and print their bold outlines on the clear evening sky, but sometimes, when the rest of the landscape is cloudless, they will gather a hood of gray vapors about their summits, which, in the last rays of the setting sun, will glow and light up like a crown of glory.

Irving can hardly be censured for mistaking the Catskills for a branch of the Appalachians, since they had not been geologically studied in his day. At any rate, his graceful prose would exonerate him. In reality, these erosional mountains pertain to

A somewhat bumpy horizon is written against the sky in this camera study of Catskill high peaks terrain.

the Appalachian Plateau, as distinct from the crumpled
Appalachians. During the Appalachian Revolution, 350 to 300
million years ago, while the big range was being reared on a scale
as magnificent as the Andes, a level plateau behind it was being
jacked up slowly, its stratified rock beds unbroken. The Catskills
were a part of this Appalachian Plateau.

The Catskills present a high and formidable front to the
Hudson River for a distance of 30 miles. They have no
pronounced western wall but merge gradually into the lower hill
country of the Allegheny Plateau crossing the state. The majestic
horizon as viewed from the east is one of New York's
unforgettable spectacles. Bluish-purple or purplish-blue, this
backdrop often looks insubstantial, a curtain of gauze. During
colonial times and well into the nineteenth century, the Catskills
were known as the Blue Mountains. The River Indians had an
earlier name for them—Onteora, "land in the sky."

As noted before, the Catskills were considered New York's
loftiest mountains until the Natural History Survey of the
Adirondacks in 1837. Their interior summits average 3,500 feet
high, but two peaks exceed 4,000 feet—Slide Mountain at 4,180
feet and Hunter Mountain at 4,040. The Adirondack Forty-Sixers
(climbers who have scaled all Adirondacks over 4,000 feet) can
become Forty-Eighters by adding Slide and Hunter to their
conquests. The central fortress is divided loosely into northern
Catskills, over which Hunter Mountain presides, and southern
Catskills, with Slide Mountain as their chief pinnacle. The valley
of Esopus Creek separates them. Approximately 1,600 square
miles of highland are, properly speaking, Catskills. Together with
the Adirondacks, they are protected as State Forest Preserve.

The mountains were formerly covered by vast hemlock forests
that gave rise to tanning industries—hence the village of
Tannersville. The giant trees were peeled of their bark and then
left to rot. The industry died with the trees, and the forests grew
back to hardwoods. The advent of steamboats and railroads,
coupled with the nearness of New York City, made the Catskills
the first great summer resort of the United States. Hotels sprang
up and were thronged by the elite of the metropolis as well as

European travelers. The matchless scenery drew artists, and the Catskills became the cradle of the Hudson River School of painting. The resort industry still flourishes, though the center of gravity of the great hotels has shifted to the southern Catskills. New York City gets the major share of its water supply out of the Catskills, and the Ashokan Reservoir is a genuine scenic asset.

Geologists view these mountains as the Catskill Delta. The huge heap of Devonian sediments was accumulated beginning around 370 million years ago as a complex delta of rivers flowing down from the lofty mountain ranges in New England. More correctly, it was a series of coalescing deltas that fanned out in the Devonian Sea. The Catskill Delta grew all the way across the state until its last gushes left their record in the conglomerate rock cities (except for the Olean). At its full extent, it was perhaps comparable to the present Mississippi delta. The most common rocks in the Catskills pile are green, slabby, crossbedded sandstones and reddish shales known as the "old red beds." The rock strata of the Catskills are flat-lying and horizontal, in sharp contrast to the Taconics and Hudson Highlands.

The origin of the name Catskill is debatable. No amount of scholastic delving will erase the legend that early Dutchmen so christened the mountains because of the wildcats screaming in their dark cloves (as ravines are known in the Catskills). But "kill" was the Dutch word for a creek. This suggests that the mountains were named for the Catskill Creek, the major tributary debouching at the village of Catskill, which is not even in the mountains but in the valley just north of them. The mouth of this creek afforded good overnight anchorage for river craft. Logic favors the guess that some early skipper may have named the creek in tribute to Jacob Cats, an admired Dutch figure of the seventeenth century. Cats was the best-known poet of the Netherlands as well as an eminent statesman. He was the Grand Pensionary of Holland and also the Dutch Ambassador to London. Moreover, the Old Dutch word for a cat was spelled "kat." If the Dutch settlers had wished to name the highlands for bobcats, they would have said Katzbergs—meaning cats' mountains.

Thruway exits for access to the Catskills are 19, 20, and 21. The major scenic highways through the mountains are Route 23-A up the Kaaterskill Clove to Tannersville, Haines Falls, and Hunter; and Route 28 from Kingston to Phoenicia and Shandaken.

The panoramic outlook over the Hudson valley from the clifftop of the
Catskill mural front was famous in the heyday of the Catskill Mountain
House. The view is still there, though the great resort hotel is long gone.
In the foreground are century-old initials and dates of hotel guests carved
in the rock ledge.

WALL OF MANITOU
The Catskill Mural Front

When the "floating palaces" were in their full glory on the
Hudson, the Night Line boats would beam their searchlights on
the Catskill Mountain House in passing. The great resort hotel
made an elegant picture on its rock platform 2,100 feet above the
river. Greek revival in architectural style, it faced the east with a
stately portico of 13 gleaming white Corinthian columns. It
reigned as an American classic of its kind for well over a century.
Newcomers on its register practiced the ritual of getting up
before dawn to greet the sunrise from the brink of the cliff known
as the Wall of Manitou.

Gone is the Mountain House from its height and vanished are
the palatial side-wheelers from the river, but the breathtaking
outlook remains undiminished in its latter-day obscurity. The
precipice was a landmark for woodsmen long before the hotel was
built. Apparently James Fenimore Cooper was there at some
time in his roving youth, storing up details of his beloved York
State scenery for the novels he would write. In *The Pioneers*, the
first of his Leather-Stocking Tales, he quoted Natty Bumppo, his
intrepid hero of the wilderness, describing the spot to a wide-eyed
boy. A man might stand there, said Natty, and see "all creation,
lad," spread forth at his feet.

The panorama brackets 50 miles of the Hudson River from
near Albany almost to the Hudson Highlands, with its far-flung
valley rolling away in the knobby avalanche of klippe hills to the
opposite barrier of the Taconic Range. The intervening trough
gives some appreciation of the enormous quantity of rocks that
have been worn away by the Hudson and its ancestral drainage
systems. The greater share of that eroded thickness was the

landward beginning of the Catskill Delta. The cutback of the delta from its New England origins has left the Catskills fronting the valley with a precipitous rampart which, for a distance of 30 miles, is virtually a straight line. To geologists this is the Catskill mural front, otherwise the Wall of Manitou.

Manitou was the Great Spirit of the Algonkians, to which peoples the River Indians belonged. Their legend was that Manitou chose the fastnesses of the inner Catskills (Onteora) for his private sanctum. He uttered the word creating the Wall of Manitou as a defensive bastion to ward off evil spirits. But it was the fine view from Manitou's protective wall that triggered the influx of vacationers, summer hotels, and tourist hordes that ironically drove Manitou out.

The mural front has stood as solidly as it has because of its caprock, the Kaaterskill sandstone, almost as resistant as limestone. The strikingly linear aspect of the Wall of Manitou is the result of glaciation. Grooves and scratches of striation from moving ice are found on the top of the Mountain House ledge. The Hudson valley was a main thoroughfare for the glacier. Geologists have estimated that the Catskill front may have protruded at least two miles further into the valley before the Hudson Lobe sheared it back.

The rear of the sandstone shelf on which the hotel stood slants off markedly to the west. In a depression at the foot of this slope are nestled two small lakes—North Lake and South Lake. These were part of the extensive Mountain House preserve, now state property. A camping and trailer site centers around North Lake, which also offers a bathing beach. South Lake has been left in the custody of nature. The lakes are of glacial origin. The Hudson Lobe overlapped on the clifftop and scooped the rock basins in which the lakes are cupped. The two are separated by only a low arch of rock, and their combined outlet leaps the Kaaterskill Falls.

The Catskill Mountain House was opened in 1824 with a dozen rooms, and expanded rapidly as patronage grew. Thomas Cole, founder of the Hudson River School of painting, quickly discovered it, and other artists followed his lead. No other part of

the Catskills is represented on the walls of so many art galleries.
A favorite vantage of the painters was Artists' Rock, which may
be reached with a short hike up a cliffside trail.

The legend that Rip van Winkle slumbered his 20 years' sleep
in the vicinity of nearby Kaaterskill Clove somehow took root,
and the early management of the Mountain House is not above
suspicion. Washington Irving publicly denied that he had
intended to pinpoint any specific setting for his story. In 1832 he
checked in at the Mountain House, confessing that this was his
first venture into the Catskills. Irving remarked that "the wild
scenery of these mountains outdoes all my conception of it." In
reality, the basic plot idea of *Rip van Winkle* was old in German
folklore. Irving transferred it to an American locale, and so
greatly improved upon it as to make it his own.

At first the hotel's guests were trundled by stagecoach up a
rough road from the Catskill steamboat landing. After the Civil
War a circuitous railroad was built from Kingston, by way of
Stony Clove, to Tannersville, whence a spur ran to the Mountain
House station on South Lake. In 1892 the hotel put an inclined
cable railway up the front of the escarpment, thereby reducing
travel time from New York to three-and-a-half hours.

With World War II the famous old hotel lapsed into a sad
decline, brooding among its memories. The State Conservation
Department acquired its lands, which included three miles of cliff
frontage, and also took over the abandoned hotel. The building
was growing decrepit, and gale winds toppled the decaying
Corinthian pillars. Although the place was dangerous for
intruders, a high chain-link fence failed to keep them out. Before
dawn of a January morning in 1963, a match was struck and the
Mountain House burst into towering flames. The idea had been,
in choosing the early hour, that no one in the valley would witness
the fire, but this hope was vain. Someone spread the word, and
neighbor called neighbor. Afterward a bulldozer shoved the
charred remains over the cliff.

The last visible reminders are initials and names of onetime
guests chiseled in the hard sandstone out near the rim. Dates run
as far back as the 1840s.

From Exit 21 of the Thruway, one follows Route 23-A out of Catskill and up the Kaaterskill Clove to Haines Falls. In that village, turn sharp right for the Mountain House Road, which loops back to the state campsite at North Lake. From the bathing-beach parking lot, a trail leads upgrade to the clifftop.

KAATERSKILL FALLS
The Forgotten Jewel

Thomas Cole's painting of the Kaaterskill Falls in 1825 marked their debut as a favorite subject of nineteenth-century landscape art in America. Cole himself pronounced the falls "the most famous beauty of the Catskills." Others spoke of them as "the jewel of the upper Catskills." Virtually every artist of the Hudson River School painted them at one time or another. A Currier and Ives print of them enjoyed wide circulation. William Cullen Bryant put them in a poem. Travelers by thousands came to look at them.

If allowance is made for two plunges in the descent, then the Kaaterskill is the highest waterfall in New York. A break on the way down disqualifies it for the title, which is held by Taughannock Falls. Nevertheless, the Kaaterskill, when seen in full stature, is graceful enough to have merited the earlier superlatives. Curiously, the Kaaterskill has faded out of favor and is today little known. Since the decline of the resort hotels around it, the main reason for its neglect is the difficulty of finding a public viewpoint that will fully show it. The only real way is the upward look from the foot of the falls, and this demands a rough climb on a rocky trail over a half-mile long.

The forgotten waterfall, 260 feet in total height, pours over a chute of the same Kaaterskill sandstone that has made the Wall of Manitou so durable. Its unbroken first drop is 180 feet, exceeding Niagara by 13 feet. The plunge pool for this drop is in a wide projecting ledge, across which the creek takes a brief respite before falling an additional 80 feet down a cascade. From there on, the stream frets its way down a steep ravine that is tributary to the Kaaterskill Clove.

When its two separate plunges are added together, the Kaaterskill Falls
may be considered the highest waterfall in New York State, at 260 feet. It
was a favorite subject of the Hudson River School of painters.

In passing, it is worthwhile to know that in the Catskills anything resembling a gorge or deep ravine is called a clove. This usage is derived from the Dutch word "kloof," for a cleft.

Spray from the intermediate plunge basin has weathered a large concavity in the soft shale behind the upper fall. A popular thrill for Victorian visitors was a somewhat daring detour behind the falls on a narrow path hugging the wall of the semicavern. The detour can still be taken, but getting to the ledge, from either above or below, is now strenuous although it used to be easy. The Laurel House, erected near the top of the falls as a competitor of the Catskill Mountain House, maintained a sturdy wooden stairway alongside the falls all the way down. The stairs disappeared long ago, and more recently the state tore down what remained of the Laurel House.

The crest of the falls is now readily attained on a pathway from the lingering Laurel House Road, but the view, with only a narrow creek dropping out of sight, is rather disappointing. A dog was once carried over the falls, and his mourning owner built a monument for him on the ledge below.

The Kaaterskill Clove, a dramatic scene merely from a drive on the twisting Rip van Winkle Trail, is the front door to the Catskills. It is a postglacial gorge carved into the mural front by the Katterskill Creek. Its remarkable depth in contrast to its length of only four miles may be party attributable to a tremendous volume of water from a glacial lake that remained for some time in the back country before the ice was entirely melted from the northern Catskills.

The Clove abounds in waterfalls, some in the channel, others dropping over the sides. Only a few can now be glimpsed from the highway. Another lost pleasure of the past was walking the bed of the gorge, which, with stairways gone, is no longer safe. Haines Falls, at the head of the Clove, used to be a real spectacle, plunging 240 feet in two drops. It is now only partially seen from a bridge abutment.

The trail to the base of Kaaterskill Falls starts at the crook of a hairpin curve in Route 23-A, just three miles up the Clove from Palenville. There is a small parking area at the nearby Bastion Falls outlook. The crest of Kaaterskill Falls is reached by taking a right turn on Laurel House Road off the Mountain House Road.

SCENIC CHAIR LIFTS
Belleayre and Hunter

Winter sports have passed on a summer dividend for the tourist trade. Ski lifts to high viewpoints are of special value in the Catskills, where no toll road climbs a mountain and narrow valleys do not permit expansive vistas. Two cable rides fairly well cover Manitou's inner fortress, north and south. These are the Belleayre Mountain Chair Lift and the Hunter Mountain Sky Ride. Both are reopened for weekends during the fall foliage season.

With the help of such mechanical aids, the Catskills are seen in midsummer as a green and friendly kind of mountains, with little of the barren-rock drama of the Adirondacks. Easily distinguishable as separate peaks and ranges, they do not appear so much like a plateau as might be expected of the Catskill Delta. A practiced eye will note that they were much less worked over by glaciation than the Adirondacks. For example, there are very few natural lakes. The principal ranges and valleys trend east–west, so that they served as a brake on the movement of the glacier across them. Spilling over a ridge, the ice would drop into a valley beyond, fill it, and stagnate there while upper levels of ice slid over it. The grooving of striations is abundant on the higher mountains, and some valley moraine deposits testify to the action of localized glaciers after the main front withdrew.

The Belleayre Mountain Ski Center is state-owned. The summer lift operates to an elevation of 3,325 feet and offers the best prospect of the central Catskills attainable without legwork. Belleayre Mountain stretches out for six miles, with the main summit and three subsummits spaced along the spine. The ski-lift landing is between two of the subsummits, and a welcome

**Ski-lift cables near the top landing of the Belleayre Mountain chairlift in
summer use.**

surprise awaits the visitor there. The ridge top, entirely
unwooded, has been graded into a nearly flat plateau, topsoiled,
seeded, and kept groomed like a lawn. Picnic tables lend the final
touch of a mountaintop park.

This landscaped crest presents two views for the price of one. A
short stroll to the opposite slope of the ridge shifts the scene. The
comprehensive eastern vista is down the Esopus Creek valley
toward Kingston, framed between two major peaks. Toward the
west the Catskills diminish in height, and the hollows give rise to
Delaware headwaters. Out there is John Burroughs country. The
famed naturalist and author grew up in nearby Roxbury and
roamed these mountains as a youth.

The Hunter Mountain Ski Bowl, a commercial enterprise, is
among the best-known winter meccas of the East. The upper
landing of the Sky Ride is on a curiously shaped spur known as
the Colonel's Chair, 825 feet lower than the summit of the
mountain. The summit, with a fire tower sticking up, is within
plain sight across a long mile of thickly wooded gulches. A
Hunter Mountain trail to the top starts from the lift landing. The
widest panorama is from the porch of a small hut nearby, taking
in a sweep of the northern Catskills and of the Tannersville valley
looking east through the notch of Kaaterskill Clove. The
mountain horizon includes Windham High Peak and the range of
three peaks called the Blackheads. In the foreground is a huge,
hollow amphitheater slashed by ski runs. This is a glacial
cirque where one of the lingering mountain glaciers headed up.

The surface of the Colonel's Chair is rocky, with ledges of the
slabby, crossbedded gray sandstone that is the commonest rock in
the Catskills. Sometimes the surface shows ice polishing.

*For Belleayre Mountain, take Thruway Exit 19, then Route 28 west
from Kingston 37 miles; turn at Highmount for the Ski Center. For
Hunter Mountain from the Thruway, there are two choices: quit the
Thruway at Exit 20, drive north on Route 32, then west on Route
23-A past Tannersville to Hunter; if southbound, leave the Thruway
at Exit 21 to Catskill, then take Route 23-A up the Kaaterskill
Clove to Hunter.*

The rambling Mohonk Mountain House, with its deep-sunk Lake Mohonk.

MOHONK AND MINNEWASKA
Lakes of the Shawangunks

A conspicuous stone edifice thrusts upward, like a castle turret, from a crag six miles west of the Thruway stretch between Kingston and Newburgh, attracting the curious glances of motorists. This is the Sky Top lookout tower, landmark of the Mohonk Mountain House and of the Shawangunk Range, on which it sits. Two of the state's most fascinating lakes, owned by the celebrated resort hotels overscanning them, are within close radius of the tower. Wholly spring-fed, sunken in solid rock basins, they are perhaps the least polluted lakes of New York State.

Lake Mohonk is the property of the Mohonk Mountain House. Lake Minnewaska's longer size accommodates two hotels under the same ownership—Wildmere House and Cliff House, separated by an expanse of water as blue-green as if it were dyed. Although use of the lakes for boating and bathing is restricted to guests of the hotels, roaming about the alluring grounds is permitted to the general public upon paying a modest entrance fee at the gates.

The Shawangunk (pronounced shon-gum) Range is not a row of mountains, but an elongated, table-topped ridge broken now and then by a widened fault fissure or a gap permitting a highway to pass through. A peculiar erosional remnant, it extends further southwest more than 100 miles. In New Jersey it becomes the Kittatinny Range, across which the Delaware River has cut the Delaware Water Gap; from there it reaches a short distance into Pennsylvania.

The Mohonk-Minnewaska segment is the north end of the Shawangunks, where they attain the highest elevation and are most diversified on the crest, which varies from one to three miles in width. Here they stretch out benchlike about halfway between the Catskills and the Hudson Highlands, with no geologic kinship to either. The double-faced escarpment looms above the Wallkill River valley on the east and the Rondout Creek valley on the west. The capstone of the entire range is the highly resistant Shawangunk conglomerate of wave-washed pebbles and sand. The fallen talus blocks of this rock were formerly used by surrounding settlers for grindstones and millstones.

Fortunately this unique section of the Shawangunks was purchased over a century ago by two nature-loving brothers, and the third generation of the Smiley family still holds control. In 1869, Alfred H. Smiley, a Quaker schoolmaster newly arrived in Poughkeepsie, heard of a strangely beautiful lake hidden away on a mountain west of New Paltz. The Indians knew it as Lake Mogonck. Renting a horse and buggy, he endured a day's rough trip to find it. Captivated by the lake, he wrote his twin brother, Albert, headmaster of the Friends' School in Providence, Rhode Island, to come and share his discovery. Albert agreed that it would be an ideal spot for a summer home for both their families and purchased the Lake Mohonk property from a farmer who was running a small, sleazy tavern beside the lake. They soon learned that the costs of development, including a road up the mountain, were beyond their resources. Enlarging the tavern, they started taking in boarders to raise money, and gradually found themselves in the hotel business. The onetime tavern grew into the Mohonk Mountain House with successive additions, and had a long waiting list for guests. With the profits, adjacent properties were bought up.

Ten years after the original purchase, Alfred Smiley acquired Lake Minnewaska, three miles south, and erected his two hotels there. A deep gully separates the two lakes, making it impossible to get from one to the other except by bridle path or hiking trail. A car must go all the way down to the valley and back up a different highway. Cars are not permitted on the networks of carriage roads.

The Sky Top lookout tower of Mohonk stands on a point of

rock 1,200 feet above the Wallkill valley, a half-mile walk from
the hotel by an uphill trail. It is a memorial to the founder, Albert
Smiley. When the state set out to put a fire tower on that point in
1923, the Smileys objected to such an unsightly, skeletal structure.
Instead, they offered to build at their own expense a handsome
stone tower of the native conglomerate, with a corner turret for
the fire-watcher. As it turned out, friends and perennial guests of
the Smileys made up a subscription fund for the tower. The State
Department of Environmental Conservation now uses the turret
for its fire watch without cost. Massive stone stairs lead to an
observation deck that surveys a vista deep into New England, and
in the other direction a comprehensive look at the southern
Catskills, including the only full profile to be had of Slide
Mountain.

The deposition of 1,000 feet of the Shawangunk quartz-pebble
conglomerate took place during the Silurian period 425 million
years ago. The coarse debris was washed down from the great
Taconian mountains in New England to the shore of the
Paleozoic Sea. Under the spur of northwestern winds, the gravel
was shuffled along the beaches, worn finer, and then carried out to
sea. This deposit in turn was buried deeply under beds of mud
and clay, and became solidified. Finally, some 50 million years
ago, the conglomerate was laid bare in the Schooley peneplain,
uplifted, and subjected to the differential erosion that has left the
present-day narrow remnant.

Lakes Mohonk, Minnewaska, and a third one named Awosting
are ascribed to glacial action. Yet they were not gouged or
bulldozed by ice. The rock-walled basins are angular, as if
quarried. The bottom ice of the moving glacier seems to have
frozen to blocks of the stone already loosened along fault fissure
lines, and carried them away. Lake Mohonk is 60 feet deep, Lake
Minnewaska 80.

Lake Awosting is the focal point of Minnewaska State Park, for
which 7,000 acres of the Minnewaska estate's total 10,000 acres
were acquired for the purpose by the Nature's Conservancy.
Meanwhile 6,000 acres of the Lake Mohonk estate have been
transferred to the Mohonk Trust, set up by the Smiley family to

guarantee its future preservation.

Four miles of the vertical eastern cliff below Lake Mohonk are in active use by rock climbers, who consider it the best practice cliff in the East. Such climbing, with rope and pitons, is carefully regulated under permits issued by the Mohonk Mountain House.

The New Paltz exit, 18, from the Thruway is the key to the lakes of the Shawangunks and their hotels. Pass through New Paltz and drive west on Route 299. For Lake Mohonk, bear north on Route 299 and watch for signs. For Minnewaska, remain on Route 299 until its junction with Route 44 near the base of the cliff; take Route 44 to the top of the hill. On the west side of the range, turnoffs from Route 209 point to the same destinations.

SAM'S POINT
Ice Cave and a Great View

According to folklore, Samuel Gonzales, a noted hunter and
Indian fighter during the last French and Indian War, was
pursued by a gang of warriors on top of the Shawangunk Range.
Seeing that he was about to be cornered on a projection of a cliff,
Sam backed off and took a running jump, landing unhurt in the
yielding boughs of a hemlock wood. The Indians, well fortified
with rum, peered over the cliff, decided that he must have been
killed, and continued on their way. Ever after, the jutting ledge
has been Sam's Point.

The legend is oddly akin to that linked with Rogers Rock on
Lake George. Perhaps one yarn is as true as the other.

The Mohonk-Minnewaska section of the Shawangunk Range is
nearly amputated from the remainder by a deep gap through
which Route 52 climbs over from Walden to Ellenville. Sam's
Point, at an elevation of 2,255 feet, is the southern tip of that
section. As a lookout, it is well developed with masonry of the
native conglomerate, including platforms, stairways, and parapets
interestingly shaped to fit the uneven margins of the ledge. The
visual sweep takes in portions of five states. With strong
binoculars on a rare smogless day, the highest skyscrapers of
Manhattan may be glimpsed. A wide-angle view of the northern
front of the Hudson Highlands is also obtained.

The terrain back of Sam's Point is a weird, windswept plateau
with a sparse and stunted vegetation. It is owned by the village of
Ellenville for the water supply it derives from Lake Maratanza,
which the access road encircles en route to the Point. A squatter
colony of berry pickers used to harvest lush crops of blueberries in

One of the great scenic viewpoints of the state is Sam's Point, an eroded
bastion of the Shawangunk Range. The Ellenville Ice Caves are operated
in conjunction with it as a tourist attraction.

the neighborhood, and a few shacks of their shantytown can be seen on the way up.

A private company, Ice Caves Mountain, leases the frontal cliff area from the village and operates both Sam's Point and the Ellenville Ice Caves near at hand. The so-called ice caves are fissures between huge blocks of the conglomerate gradually breaking loose from the escarpment. A guide leads tourist groups on a nature trail along the base of the bluff, ducking in and out of the alleyways. The Ice Cave is the climax of the trip. It is a passage where two massive blocks have tilted together at the top, creating the effect of a peaked room. A door shields the entrance to keep the interior air refrigerated. Walking through on a wooden flooring, visitors peer over railings into fissures filled with solid ice left from the previous winter. The guide declares that the ice never completely melts.

From Thruway Exit 17, one picks up Route 52 in the outskirts of Newburgh and drives west toward Ellenville. Midway through the Shawangunk gap, just before the highway begins its descent to Ellenville, a steep, twisting road turns off north to Sam's Point and the Ice Caves, three miles to the entrance gate.

A cable car ascends the incline railway to the crest of Mount Beacon.
The city of Beacon spreads beyond the base to the east bank of the
Hudson River.

MOUNT BEACON
Last of the Incline Railways

The Hudson Highlands, a belt of crumpled old mountains 15 miles wide through which the Hudson River flows in a steep canyon, were an extremely important barrier in the Revolution. Thanks to their presence, the patriots were able to contain the British occupation forces in New York City and Westchester County, save for a temporary breakthrough by three warships in 1777. On that occasion, a huge signal fire blazed on one of the summits of the north-facing Fishkill Heights. A series of warning beacons had been piled for lighting, each within sight of the next, the length of the Hudson from the Palisades to Albany.

On the east bank of the river, nestled at the foot of the Highlands on the upstream side, lay the town of Fishkill, where the Americans kept a store of munitions safe from a surprise enemy raid. In aftertime both the riverside village and the signal mountain were renamed Beacon in historic pride. The Daughters of the American Revolution dedicated an obelisk monument on top of Mount Beacon in 1900. A year later the Otis Elevator Company ran an incline railway up the steep mountainside, and a resort hotel and casino were erected at the upper landing.

The funicular lift was the third such railway built in New York State, preceded by those at the Catskill Mountain House and Prospect Mountain on Lake George. (In a funicular lift, cable-linked cars move up and down simultaneously, passing at midpoint.) The Mount Beacon Incline claims to be the last one operating in the United States, as well as the world's steepest. In 2,384 feet of length, it has an average gradient of 64 degrees. The actual rise in elevation is 1,540 feet.

At the summit landing, passengers find a steel lookout tower of modest height. Nearby are the foundations of the vanished hotel.

The old casino building has been revived as a refreshment haven. A footpath leads through light woods to the Daughters of the American Revolution monument.

There is no comparable location from which to scan along many miles of the north rampart of the Hudson Highlands in both directions. The panoramic overview takes in the cities of Beacon and Newburgh, with the Hudson River bridge connecting them; a grand sweep of the river past the Mid-Hudson Bridge at Poughkeepsie; and, in the further distance, the Shawangunk Range and the southern Catskills.

The Hudson Highlands lie on a southwest bias athwart the river, which long ago broke through its deep gorge. Vexing geologic problems remain as to how the river could have carved such a gorge crosswise of a mountain range standing as a barrier in its path, and also as to what the narrow belt of the Highlands was doing there in the first place. (The question of the gorge is discussed in the following chapter on Storm King Mountain.)

These Highlands are largely composed of an exceedingly ancient type of metamorphic rock, old as the metamorphosed sedimentary rocks of the Adirondacks and originally laid as sediments in the same shallow sea that extended from Labrador to Mexico. Radioactive dating has set their age in the bracket of 1,150 million years. Surprisingly, the country rocks on either side of the range are less than half that age. The strata immediately to the north in Dutchess County are sedimentary rocks of early Paleozoic vintage. The rocks outcropping southward through Westchester County look different in that they are crystalline, but for the most part they also were sedimentary beds of Paleozoic age before they were metamorphosed. A positive age correlation has been established between the two sides. Thus the range of the Highlands has the appearance of being an intruder; that is, "rootless" where it stands. It is classified as a portion of the Reading Prong extending southwest, like a thrust spear, from New England (so called because its tip reaches to the environs of Reading, Pennsylvania). Scientists now believe that the Reading spear-point is without "roots" at its location. Until quite recently, geologists had speculated that the Reading Prong—and perhaps its neighbor on the southeast, the Manhattan Prong—had been thrust

southwestward during a "collision" between North America and
Africa. Geologic thinking on this score has since undergone a
radical shift.

The original sedimentary rocks of Grenville age were forced
deep underground, like those of the Adirondacks, to be
metamorphosed by extreme pressure and heat, while also being
infused here and there with molten granite. Over the aeons, these
metamorphics were gradually lifted nearer the surface, in time to
become involved in a great new mountain-building spasm, the
Acadian Orogeny. This upheaval occurred around 380 to 350
million years ago when the bulge of Africa and the North
American coastline came together and were welded for an
eternity of time. The entire rock package of southeastern New
York was squeezed like an accordion into crazy folds and crinkles,
which now show up abundantly in Manhattan, the Bronx, and
Westchester County.

According to this fresh interpretation, the Hudson Highlands,
as a block, were shoved northwestward and, at the same time,
sideward along a fault line into their present position. As Dr.
Yngvar W. Isachsen of the New York State Geological Survey
avers in a Museum leaflet on this subject: "Earthquakes must
have been frequent and severe during this tumultuous time as the
crust was ruptured and offset along fracture zones."

Of course this displacement of the Hudson Highlands block
was occurring underground, and the landscape as we now see it
has been laid bare by an enormous amount of erosion since that
time. The Acadian Mountains that were reared skyward in that
orogeny would have made an awesome spectacle, if any eyes had
been around to see them. They are estimated to have reached
altitudes as high as Mount Everest of today. All that range was
ultimately pared down and carried off to become new sediments
on the floors of later seas.

*To reach the city of Beacon from the State Thruway, leave at Exit
17 and cross the Newburgh–Beacon bridge. At the east end of the
bridge, turn abruptly south on Route 9-D. In the southern outskirts
of Beacon, the incline railway up Mount Beacon is readily located.*

The notch was blasted in the granite flank of Storm King Mountain for construction of the scenic Storm King Highway. Together with Breakneck Ridge on the opposite side of the river, it forms the north portal of the Hudson Highlands gorge.

STORM KING MOUNTAIN
North Gate of the Highlands

.

During the era of "floating palaces" on the Hudson River, the passage through the Highlands was the most scenically dramatic part of the cruise between New York and Albany. On the down trip, the portal to the gorge loomed ahead like a grand gateway with Storm King Mountain and Breakneck Ridge as the sideposts.

Owing to its location and the handsome pinkish granite of its composition, Storm King is the most striking eminence of the Hudson Highlands. It is well seen today from Amtrak trains. The name itself conjures up the capricious gusts and gales that were once the bane of sailing vessels. Passing over this mountain in his 1910 flight from Albany to New York, Glenn Curtiss was almost pitched out of his flimsy little biplane by boisterous air currents.

After the widewater of Newburgh Bay, the river is abruptly pinched into the narrowing jaws of the gorge. It then pursues an angular course between precipitous mountainsides past Constitution Island, West Point, and the Bear Mountain Bridge, before broadening out afresh into the Tappan Zee. The gorge, subject to strong tides, displays the characteristics of both a fjord and an estuary. The water is partly salt as far north as Newburgh. It was undoubtedly this false promise of a strait leading through to the Pacific that lured Henry Hudson to sail on. Indeed, Hudson's chief mate Robert Juet, who kept the log of the voyage, wrote that the *Half Moon* "came to a straight between two points"; that the "high land hath many points, and a narrow channell, and hath many eddie winds."

The Storm King Highway, constructed in 1922, brought the mountain into the limelight. The roadbed was dynamited into the

granitic gneiss as a shelf girdling the waist of Storm King 400 feet
above the water. Convenient turnouts along the highway provide
excellent overlooks on the gap across to Breakneck on the east
side of the river. The rounded contours of both mountains tell of
the enormous pressure of ice that was funneled into the gorge
during the glacial age.

To say that the Highlands gorge was overdeepened by
glaciation would be an understatement. The maximum sounding
for navigation off Storm King Mountain is 81 feet, but this is only
the depth to the level of the loose glacial fill. Nobody had
dreamed of the great thickness of that fill until 1909, when test
borings were being made for a siphon beneath the Hudson River
in construction of the Catskill Aqueduct for New York City's
water supply. The Storm King—Breakneck line was chosen for
the crossing because the siphon could be tunneled in
impermeable Storm King granite. The engineers were astounded
when slanted diamond-drill borings from both shores proved that
the granite bottom of the gorge at that location was somewhere
between 768 and 950 feet. There could be only one explanation
for such abnormal depth: the rock must have been gouged by a
tongue of ice being forced by immense pressure into the funnel of
the two guardian mountains.

The attractive and durable Storm King granite was an
intrusion, in molten form, into the more ancient metamorphic
rock of the Highlands. It accounts for not only Storm King
Mountain but a cluster of summits around the Highlands gorge,
among them Breakneck, Mount Beacon, Mount Taurus, the
Torne, Crown Ridge, Bear Mountain, and Dunderberg.

The problem of how the river could have hewed a gorge
through a tough mountain barrier lying across its path continues
to inspire geologic debate. One theory is that the ancestral
Hudson flowed to the sea in thick sedimentary beds overlying the
Highlands. While the land surface was wearing down, according
to this thinking, the Highlands were being gradually uplifted.
Thus the river might have superimposed its prior channel upon
the harder metamorphics, stencilwise.

A flaw in this reasoning is the three sharp angles encountered through the Highlands chasm—namely, at West Point, Anthony's Nose, and Dunderberg. A long-held course in overlying sedimentary rocks would be highly unlikely to contain such angular bends. Another school of thought suggests that the gorge developed along three zigzag zones of weakness, or cleavage, in the Highlands rock. A short stream draining the coastal slope of the Highlands worked its headwaters northward in a vulnerable zone. Meanwhile, the upstate forerunner of the Hudson came up against the mountain barrier and was deflected southwest along its base. Eventually—so runs the theory—the stream flowing south on the coastal side eroded backward until it captured the northern river into the present course.

Storm King Mountain was formerly known as Butter Hill. In 1777, General George Clinton sent a message posthaste to Kingston warning: "I am this moment informed by a light horseman from my guard at New Windsor, that twenty sail of the enemy's shipping . . . are in the river below Butter Hill."

The Storm King Highway is Route 218 north from the West Point Military Academy. After rounding the nose of Storm King Mountain, the road descends into Cornwall, there connecting with Route 9-W. By turning south on Route 9-W, a driver may complete a circle back to Bear Mountain Park. From a lookout point along 9-W, a fine view of West Point and Constitution Island can then be obtained.

Captured artillery pieces from historic battles frame a spectacular view of the Hudson Highlands gorge from West Point's Trophy Point. Storm King Mountain on the left, Breakneck Ridge on the right.

WEST POINT
Pride of the Army

The U.S. Military Academy, with its stately ranks of stone buildings rising like battlements behind the parade ground known to cadets as the Plain, is reason enough for a detour to West Point. Aside from the college itself, the setting deep within the river gorge of the Hudson Highlands is one of New York's prime spectacles. In addition, the locale is a trove of Revolutionary history.

The name West Point originally referred to the promontory—a flat shelf of rock 160 feet above the tidewater of the Hudson estuary—that juts midway across the steep-walled mountain chasm. The Point forces the river into a sharp eastward bend against Constitution Island, shaping an elbow as the stream veers abruptly south again. The island was once part of the same rock ledge. The channel now slicing it off is the narrowest passage of the river between New York and Albany, and was recognized as the "choke point" of the navigable Hudson long before the Revolutionary War brought the situation into military focus.

Glaciation prepared the ground for fortifications against enemy ships attempting to sail up the Hudson and chop New England off from the other colonies. Although the tongue of ice that so drastically overdeepened the gorge in the funnel at Storm King Mountain did not ream it to so extreme a depth all the way through, it changed the course of the river in such a way as to make West Point the ideal spot for a citadel in the Highlands. Thus did geologic processes help write a dramatic chapter in American history.

The preglacial route of the Hudson River was wholly on the

east side of the rock ledge, including the portion that was to become Constitution Island. The older course is indicated today by a strip of marshland lying between the island and the precipitous east bank. The main thrust of the glacier moving through the gorge bypassed that angular jog, preferring a straighter route. During the slow retreat of the ice tongue lingering in the gorge, while its own front and heaped debris still blocked off the prior course, the gushing meltwater began hacking the new channel, which amputated Constitution Island from West Point. The liberated postglacial river simply retained the newer route and hewed it deeper.

Millenia passed. As hostilities with the mother country loomed, colonial leaders were keenly aware that the Hudson defile could be the key to victory or defeat. By May, 1775, the Continental Congress at Philadelphia prodded New York's Provincial Convention to look into its defenses. The Convention sent two members upriver to study the pass. They strongly recommended forts on "the west point" and Martelaer's Rock (as Constitution Island was then known); also a boom of heavy logs strung across the river between. This report was forwarded to the Continental Congress—and left dangling.

The Battle of Bunker Hill, fought and lost on June 17, diverted attention from the Hudson Highlands. After taking command of the Continental Army and mounting the siege of Boston, General George Washington warned New Yorkers that British warships might stage a surprise raid on their city and the river at any time. This startled the New York Convention into creating a five-man Commission to get started fast on a Highlands fortification. Bernard Romans, a former Dutch botanist who had helped Benedict Arnold repair Fort Ticonderoga after its capture, was assigned as engineer and drew plans for a Grand Bastion on Martelaer's Rock; he envisioned only a blockhouse opposite on the "west point," ignoring the fact that the point stood higher than the island.

The Commission voted to name this citadel Fort Constitution, in honor of the *British* Constitution. The colonists thus far considered themselves Englishmen standing up for their rights.

The Declaration of Independence was still in the future. In this way Constitution Island acquired its name.

Delay followed delay until it was plain that Romans would not have any fort finished by the first snow. Sensing that affairs along the Hudson were "in a mess," the Congress at Philadelphia sent a committee of its own to investigate. This group observed the fatal flaw that the "west point" overlooked the island; it also took serious note of a height of land at the mouth of the Popolopen Kill, near the foot of Bear Mountain, some three miles south of West Point. The latter site commanded the south gateway into the Highlands gorge. In January, 1776, the Congress resolved that no further works be erected on the island, and that the height on the Popolopen Kill be fortified without delay. Adjudged "incompetent," Romans was fired—but the "west point" was once again scorned.

That winter the colonial assault on Canada was bloodily repulsed at Quebec, where Brigadier General Richard Montgomery was killed and Colonel Benedict Arnold sustained a bad leg wound. This defeat raised the specter of invasion from Canada, making the Hudson defenses doubly urgent. The Congress ordered that work on the Popolopen fort be expedited and that it be called Fort Montgomery for "the brave General Montgomery" who fell at Quebec.

After driving the British out of Boston, Washington correctly guessed that General Sir William Howe would sail for New York, and swiftly marched his army there to meet the threat. Washington was dismayed to learn the true state of the Highlands defenses, and sent three trusted officers upstream to look into the matter. They found conditions at Fort Montgomery "deplorable," and noted that the opposite (south) cliff of the Popolopen gorge stood higher than the fort being built. At their insistence, a second fort was erected on that rise, named Fort Clinton after General James Clinton, whom Washington was soon to appoint as commander of the Highlands forts.

Clinton reasserted his earlier proposal for a log boom across the river, with the added improvement of a strong iron chain floated on the logs. The huge links of the chain were forged from iron mined nearby in the Highlands. The location of this first chain crossed the south entrance to the gorge, between Fort Montgomery and Anthony's Nose, loosely on the line of the present-day Bear Mountain bridge. Only a small garrison was left on Constitution Island while labor was rushed on Forts Montgomery and Clinton, whose guns were trained on the river below. Washington appointed George Clinton, younger brother of James, to command the militia being called up for defense of the Highlands.

Early in the summer of 1777 the feared invasion from Canada came to pass, with General John Burgoyne leading his redcoats, Hessian mercenaries, and Indians south on Lake Champlain, taking Fort Ticonderoga without firing a shot. The enemy strategy was for Lord Howe to sail in force up the Hudson and join Burgoyne at Albany, but Howe chose to take Philadelphia instead, leaving the New York command to Sir Henry Clinton (a distant cousin of the American Clintons).

Meanwhile that same summer, New York was constituted a state and General George Clinton was elected its first governor, establishing his capital at Kingston while worrying about the defense of the Highlands.

In the haste and confusion of trying to close off the Highlands gorge, the twin forts of the Popolopen were but weakly protected at the rear, where the terrain was wild and rugged. A squadron of British war vessels sailed upriver at the start of October as Burgoyne became entangled in the two Battles of Saratoga. The British under Henry Clinton sprang a surprise by landing a force at Stony Point in a dense fog, marching around behind Dunderberg and Bear Mountain in the night, and assaulting the forts at the rear. Both forts were captured within a half-hour on October 6. The victors made short work of the chain and sailed on up the Hudson, spreading havoc along its banks and putting the torch to Kingston. When he learned that Burgoyne had been halted at Saratoga and surrendered his army, Sir Henry Clinton contented himself with demolishing the Popolopen forts and retired discreetly to New York.

After the breach of the Highlands, Governor George Clinton

urged immediate fortification of the "west point," also a new and
better chain to block the river at this location. The legislature
backed him. Colonel Rufus Putnam, because of his experience in
erecting the works on Dorchester Heights for Washington's siege
of Boston, was detailed with his regiment to begin a fort at the
river margin of the West Point "plain." The need for a
professional engineer was clear, however, and one was found in
Colonel Tadeusz Kosciuszko, a young Polish nobleman who had
cast his lot with the American freedom fighters. Formerly a
captain in the Polish army, Kosciuszko had studied military
engineering in Paris and built the earthwork bastions on Bemis
Heights for the Battle of Saratoga.

Looking up the sharp incline behind West Point, Kosciuszko
saw a jutting, round-topped spur of the mountain, known as
Crown Hill, several hundred feet above. In enemy hands, this
salient could nullify any fort at West Point and command the
river. Colonel Rufus Putnam led his men up the steep flank of
Crown Hill to plant there a secondary fort, Fort Putnam, which a
French engineer later pronounced "the key to all the others." In
the meantime the new chain and log boom were in place by the
end of April, 1778, and a battery was hurriedly installed on
Constitution Island to help protect them.

West Point was activated as a fortress—now quite
formidable—later in 1778, and is today the oldest military post in
the United States that has been in continuous occupancy by
American troops since its completion. The main fort was first
designated as Fort Arnold in tribute to General Benedict Arnold,
who was at that time acclaimed as the real hero of Saratoga. In
1780, Washington acceded to Arnold's urgent request for the
command of West Point. After Arnold's attempted betrayal of
the fort, it was renamed Fort Clinton for General James Clinton,
who had been in command of its construction.

Neither West Point as a fortification nor the chain across the
river was ever challenged in warfare. After the Revolution, only a
small garrison remained on duty and the structures were allowed
to deteriorate. Actually, the government did not even own the
land, which had been leased from a private owner, Stephen

Moore. In 1790 Congress appropriated $11,085 for its purchase. As president, George Washington strongly advocated a military academy, and West Point was the only federal post available for the purpose; but he was unable to get the proposal through Congress, which feared a standing army. By 1794, however, some volunteer cadets were being informally trained in barracks on the Plain. West Point, so to speak, became an academy by default. At the same time some reconstruction work was done on Forts Clinton and Putnam to give them higher and stronger walls.

It remained for President Thomas Jefferson to get his proposal for a "military school at West Point" past the Congress, and to appoint Major Jonathan Williams as its first commandant. On March 16, 1802, Congress passed an act creating the U.S. Military Academy.

The peculiar, high-standing shelf of rock that provides the main campus and parade ground is an erosional surface to which the river had leveled the solid floor of its gorge before the Ice Age. It coincides in elevation with another remnant, which affords the level recreation area of Bear Mountain State Park adjacent to the Bear Mountain Inn.

The principal visitors' attraction on the West Point grounds is Trophy Point at the north margin of the Plain, noted for its historic monuments, captured artillery pieces, and Flirtation Walk. Nearby are several of the two-foot iron links of the Revolutionary chain, arranged on posts in circular pattern. Trophy Point also offers an excellent outlook on the Hudson upstream, capturing the fjordlike appearance of the gorge framed by its northern gateway between Storm King Mountain and Breakneck Ridge. A more recent viewpoint, a trifle further east, was added as a gift from the Academy's Class of 1938 on the occasion of its fortieth reunion. This takes the form of a long stone platform with a parapet along which are ranged a series of brass plates that knit together the story of West Point as a fortress.

A popular spectacle is the close-order drill of uniformed cadets on the Plain. The parade drills are performed on Saturdays in spring and fall seasons (from April to June in the spring). Ferryboat tours from the South Dock to Constitution Island are available at stated times, for which reservations are required. The West Point Museum in Thayer Hall with its fine military relics draws many visitors. A Visitors' Information Center is maintained near the south gate to the campus, and directions may also be obtained from the military police on guard duty.

No visit to West Point is complete without a climb up the hill to Fort Putnam. Long neglected and vandalized in private ownership, this important old fortification was gradually salvaged during this century. Its restoration was finally completed in 1977 as part of the Revolutionary Bicentennial activities. Visitors game for the 15-minute ascent on a foot trail may leave their cars in Parking Lot G of Michie Stadium, the Army's football field on the hillside. They are rewarded by superb downviews of the Academy grounds and the Highlands gorge from the elevated ramparts.

From the Thruway, one may leave at Exit 16, taking Route 6 east through Harriman Park to Bear Mountain Park; thence north on Route 9-W a short way to Route 218, which runs through the West Point campus. Alternatively, leave at Exit 17 for Newburgh, thence south on Route 9-W to the Route 218 intersection. A recommended scenic approach from the north is Route 218, off Route 9-W in Cornwall, which rounds the nose of Storm King Mountain.

The Bear Mountain Bridge as viewed from Bear Mountain. The mountain across the way is Anthony's Nose.

BEAR MOUNTAIN
South Gate to the Highlands

Where the Hudson emerges from its gorge, Bear Mountain rears its ursine head in a position comparable to that of Storm King at the northern gateway; and it is made, in fact, of the same kind of pinkish granitic gneiss. Here the analogy ends, as Bear Mountain is a heavily visited attraction with a blacktop highway circling to the top and a good trail up for hikers. Bear Mountain State Park is headquarters of the Palisades Interstate Park Commission.

In Revolutionary time this mountain showed on military maps as Bear Hill, because a large bear population was lured by its lush crops of blueberries and bearberries. The last bear on the mountain was shot by a thoughtless man named Sickles in 1845, but at least he shared its meat with his neighbors.

The eastern gatepost is Anthony's Nose, comprising a different rock, the Canada Hill granite. Once there was a landmark projection on the river side of that mountain resembling a huge, bulbous nose. The name, we are told, was bestowed by early Huguenot missionaries, in probable reference to a nose swollen by St. Anthony's fire (erysipelas), the disease miraculously cured by St. Anthony. The proboscis was blasted away in 1846 by an engineer who intended to build a bridge but never got around to it.

When the eventual Bear Mountain Bridge was finished in 1924, it was the southernmost bridge across the Hudson, a greatly admired suspension span. Its exits provide access to Bear Mountain Park, to the ruins of Forts Montgomery and Clinton, and to West Point. Nearly on a line with the bridge, the patriot army under General James Clinton strung the first chain across the Hudson as related earlier.

The level portion of Bear Mountain State Park, on which stands the well-known Bear Mountain Inn, fans outward from the foot of the mountain on a rock plateau 160 feet above the river, at the same level as West Point.

Near the Bear Mountain Inn, Hessian Lake—one of the prettiest small lakes in the state—curves around the base of the mountain. Nearly 100 feet deep in places, spring-fed and cold, Hessian Lake is off limits for swimming, but is popular for rowboating and for strolling along its perimeter walk. The lake traces a line of contact between the Storm King granite of the mountain and the surrounding metamorphic rocks, which are slightly less resistant to weathering than the granite. The glacier felt out a fissure along that contact and hewed it larger into the deep basin of the lake.

Hessian mercenaries were with the British troops who sneaked around back of Bear Mountain to capture the two nearby forts. After the brief battle, according to durable legend, bodies of friend and foe alike were carried and tossed into the little lake in lieu of decent burial. For that reason the lake was long known as Bloody Pond; later it came to be known as Highland Lake. At the time Bear Mountain became a state park, it was renamed Hessian Lake after the mercenary German soldiers (a rather peculiar tribute, it would seem).

Save for a timely deed of philanthropy, a penitentiary would have been built on the site of the Bear Mountain Inn. Sing Sing State Prison at Ossining, a few miles downriver on the east side, was in deteriorated condition in 1908 when the legislature authorized a new Sing Sing at Bear Mountain. A work gang of prisoners, quartered in a stockade built for the purpose, leveled off most of the site by hand labor before a public protest boiled up at this desecration of so scenic and historic a location. Mrs. Mary Harriman played the role of Lady Bountiful to halt the outrage.

The Palisades Interstate Park was just then in the developmental stage. Mrs. Harriman was the widow of E. H. Harriman, the railroad magnate and financier, who had long been gathering up forest acreage in the Hudson Highlands with an idea

of donating it to the state for preservation and public recreation.
Before his plan matured, Harriman died. Spurred by the prison
project, Mrs. Harriman wrote Governor Charles Evans Hughes
that she was prepared to convey 10,000 acres to the state plus a
gift of $1 million for further land acquisition, with the stipulation
that work be stopped on the new prison and that Bear Mountain
be added to the Harriman parklands. In the face of such generous
terms the state complied, and the existing Sing Sing penitentiary
was rehabilitated instead.

Upon the site already graded for the prison, the colossal Bear
Mountain Inn was erected with a rustic architectural theme.
Before the proliferation of superhighways, the vast majority of
users of the Bear Mountain–Harriman State Park complex were
from the New York metropolitan area, many traveling by
riverboats that ran scheduled excursions to the Bear Mountain
landing. The present Hudson River Day Line still operates one
boat daily from the city, during season.

The Perkins Memorial Drive spirals to the summit of Bear
Mountain, at an elevation of 1,305 feet. The top is largely bare
rock—the Storm King granitic gneiss of which the Perkins
Memorial Tower is built. The glass-enclosed observation deck of
the tower permits a sweeping view of the Highlands, including the
wild and rugged Harriman section of the park, and a direct view
up the lower gorge toward West Point. Both the road and the
tower commemorate George W. Perkins, an ardent promoter of a
park system along the west side of the Hudson and president of
the first New York Commission for the Palisades Interstate Park.

The ruins of Fort Clinton and Fort Montgomery, which were
only briefly held by the British victors, had been neglected all
through the years. They stood on either side of the Popolopen
Creek's gorge where it empties into the Hudson, and became a
part of Bear Mountain Park when it was established. Fort
Clinton, on the south flank of the gorge, was the better preserved
of the two, and remains of its ramparts and a star bastion are on
view today beneath the west approaches of the Bear Mountain
Bridge. These are adjuncts of the Trailside Museum, in which
battle relics have a place along with nature specimens. Across the

Popolopen, archeologists in recent years have uncovered large sections of the masonry and barracks of Fort Montgomery, but these are not as yet open to the public.

From the south, leave the Thruway at Exit 13, taking the Palisades Interstate Parkway north to Bear Mountain State Park. From the north, quit the Thruway at Exit 16 and drive east on Route 6 through the Harriman Park to Bear Mountain. Route 9-W, paralleling the river on the west, passes Bear Mountain Inn. From Peekskill on the east side, get onto U.S. Route 6 heading west and cross the Bear Mountain Bridge into the park.

THE PALISADES
East Face of New Jersey

The celebrated Palisades of the Hudson confront the river for a
distance of more than 30 miles, from the vicinity of Nyack, New
York to Hoboken, New Jersey, before vanishing underground in
Bayonne. This magnificent cliff—400 feet high opposite uptown
Manhattan and rising higher to the north—was the first significant
landmark which persuaded Henry Hudson that this tidewater
estuary might be a through passage to the Pacific.

The main stretch of the Palisades is located in New Jersey,
although they reach several miles into New York and are under
jurisdiction of the Palisades Interstate Park Commission.
Aesthetically, the better part of their scenic value accrues to New
York City, Yonkers, and a slice of Westchester County. This was
the negative argument used by some New Jersey legislators when
that state's cooperation was first solicited in purchasing waterfront
properties to halt quarrying operations that were chewing away at
the cliff.

The State Line Lookout of the Palisades Interstate Parkway
attains a height of 550 feet above mean tide level. Through most
of its length not more than the upper half of the rock wall is
visible, the lower part being concealed behind the talus slope of
fallen blocks and weathered fragments. Most of the talus
accumulation is wooded, and the striking contrast of the green
apron with the stark precipice is part of the latter's beauty.
During colonial days, rocks from the talus were used as ballast for
sailing ships. The talus slope is beneficial in another way. The
sheer igneous wall does not descend to water level. Concealed
behind the rubble heap are the vulnerable shale and sandstone

A southward view along the Palisades from the State Line Outlook on the New Jersey side. The George Washington Bridge and Manhattan skyline are dim in the distance.

beds of the Newark Group, upon which the sill of Palisades diabase rests.

When examined at close range, the precipice is seen to consist of distinct columns fitted snugly together. Basically, but not always, the columns are hexagonal. They vary in size up to several feet in diameter. In their polygonal, turretlike shape, they are comparable to the Giant's Causeway in Ireland and Fingal's Cave in Scotland. Presumably the Palisades received their name from early fur traders or ships' crews because of their vague resemblance to the stockades with which upstate Indians protected their villages, a practice quickly adopted by white settlers. The columnar structure was caused by tensional cooling of the molten magma intrusion underground. (Magma becomes lava when it erupts at the surface.)

The Palisades rock, grayish to dark in color, is diabase—more commonly known as traprock (from a Swedish word, *trapp*, for stairs). Radiometric measurement has set the date of its origin at 195 million years ago in the Mesozoic Era (the age of dinosaurs). The Palisades are an indirect consequence of the last collision between Africa and North America, which produced the Acadian mountain-building epoch and sky-high ranges across New England. After a long period of being welded together, the two continental plates began pulling apart 200 million years ago, leaving a raw "wound" at the cleavage accompanied by widespread faulting, earthquakes, and volcanic spouting. One localized result was the down-dropping of a large block to create the Newark Basin in northeastern New Jersey. This basin, holding water, was gradually filled with a great thickness of sediments from the stream erosion of the nearby Acadian highlands. The evolving dinosaurs roamed the marshy surface of these sediments.

Continued faulting of the Newark Basin ultimately tapped a deep-down reservoir of magma. The molten rock welled up until it was able to squeeze laterally between two layers of the Newark sediments, prying them apart, where it slowly cooled and solidified. The tabular sheet of diabase, up to 1,000 feet thick, was pressed eastward underground like toothpaste from a tube, never reaching the surface. Subsequent erosion stripped away the topping of sedimentary strata and cut back the Palisades sill to its present position. Since the sill dips to the westward, outcrops of the resistant diabase in that direction have made possible an accurate computation of its total thickness. What is seen today in the cliff front is approximately only the lower 300 feet of the original sill.

Fossil bones and footprints of lizardlike saurians have been found in the rock beds of the Newark Group behind the Palisades escarpment. A specimen with rudimentary wings—a reptile evolving into a bird—was found in New Jersey not long ago. The first discovery of actual dinosaur footprints in New York State was made in 1972 by a couple of students near Nyack. The three-toed prints in a slab of rock were trackways crossing one another, made by at least two specimens of an upstanding, meat-eating, four-foot-long creature whose scientific name is *Coelophysis*. Some of the tracks, along with a lifelike reproduction of the small dinosaur, are on exhibit at the State Museum in Albany.

Toward the north end, near Haverstraw, the Palisades cliff curves inland for five miles in the shape of a sickle. The blade terminates in two camel's humps named High Tor and Little Tor (the word *tor* is Old English for a hill). High Tor at 827 feet, is the peak elevation of the Palisades, and was used for beacon fires during the Revolution. Both Tors may be climbed via a popular hiking trail.

High Tor has a broad, flat summit which the playwright Maxwell Anderson made famous in the 1930s as the setting for his play *High Tor*. Anderson had a house behind the Tors, and his play carried a "message." Its villains were officials of an Igneous Traprock Company; its hero a young idealist and poet who said: "They want to chew the back right off this mountain . . . leave the old Palisades sticking up here like billboards." An Indian supporter of the hero's crusade muses: "Nothing is made by men but makes in the end good ruins."

The successful play did serve its political purpose by spurring public sentiment for further control of traprock quarrying in that

area. Some quarry operations however, still continue to the rear
of High Tor, but outside park property.

The peculiar inland hook is thought to have originated as a
low-angle, semicircular dike. In other words, the sheet of molten
rock that was being injected between layers of sedimentary rocks
broke out of bounds in this direction, cross-cutting through beds
of the Newark Group. The result may be likened to the uptilted
rim of a saucer.

The density and hardness of the Palisades diabase invited the
interest of quarrymen. For a period right after the Civil War,
great chunks of the rock were carted off to become "Belgian"
paving blocks in New York and other cities, though most of these
were taken with comparative ease from the talus slope at the foot
of the cliff. The market died out and the Palisades were left alone
for a couple of decades. Around 1890 a more disastrous threat
appeared. New York City began to macadamize its streets on a
large scale. The asphalt was laid on broken stone, and the
picturesque rock just across the river was ideal for this purpose, as
it was for railroad ballast. A frontal attack on the precipice was
launched in earnest by quarrymen. Before long, four quarries
were operating from Fort Lee, New Jersey, northward, just
opposite Washington Heights in Manhattan. One firm alone was
taking 12,000 cubic yards of traprock a day. Stonecrushers went
to work at the riverfront, and scows lined up to ferry the broken
stone across the river.

Quarries worked around the clock during the 1890s and
frequent blasting was done at night, disrupting the slumbers of
upper Manhattan residents and rattling dishes on their shelves. A
newspaper editor, awakened in the small hours by the explosions,
roared "They're blowing up the Palisades!" and launched his
paper on a campaign to stop the quarrying. Soon the whole New
York press was in full cry.

The incipient crusade to "save the Palisades" soon came to a
standstill. The blasting continued and ugly scars multiplied in the
face of the cliff. Some opposition to state intervention was heard
in the statehouse at Trenton. The objections were summed up by
one legislator who pointed out that the aesthetic value of the

Palisades "inured entirely to the State of New York." To a large
extent that statement was true. The cliff is best viewed from the
east side of the river.

A mile north of Fort Lee a craggy projection of the cliff was a
favorite landmark of river travelers. This showed two differing
profiles, one known as Washington's Head, the other as Indian
Head. In September, 1897, what little remained of Washington's
Head was "blown into a million fragments," to quote one news
report. Three weeks later, a part of Indian Head tumbled.
Newspapers gave vent to frustrated rage.

The climax came on March 4, 1898. The quarry operators
made no secret of their preparations to demolish Indian Head in
its entirety. A five-foot tunnel was bored 100 feet into the
landmark and 7,000 pounds of dynamite was planted within. A
strange kind of beauty contest was conducted among young ladies
of the area for the honor of touching off the explosive. The
winner was an Irish colleen named Alice Haggerty, of Coytesville,
New Jersey. A large crowd of spectators assembled to see the
sport, along with the quarry workmen. Prettily gowned for the
occasion, Miss Haggerty giggled as she pushed the plunger, then
turned and fled to a safer distance. Down came Indian Head into
a heap of 350,000 tons of Palisades diabase. Loudly the audience
cheered, but a tidal wave of public wrath arose with the dust.
And still the dynamite vandalism went on.

When conservation-minded Theodore Roosevelt took office as
Governor of New York in 1899, one of his first acts was to appoint
a fresh Commission on the Palisades. New Jersey followed suit in
1900, although it was mutually admitted that New York held "a
vastly greater interest in preservation of the natural scenery of the
Palisades." The international campaign to preserve Niagara
Falls, not many years earlier, had established a cogent precedent.
Before the year was out, the governors of New York and New
Jersey signed bills creating a joint Interstate Palisades Park
Commission, with New York sharing the costs of land
acquisition. Between them, the two states appropriated $500,000
as a start toward purchasing cliff frontages. J. Pierpont Morgan,
the noted banker and financier, donated $122,500 for purchase of

the most active quarry of all, at Fort Lee, New Jersey, and putting it out of business. By 1905 a total frontage of 14 consecutive miles was in government control, and the commission opened that stretch up for camping, picnicking, and other recreations. The shabby homes of fisherfolk along the waterfront disappeared and a road was developed along the base of the cliff. The Palisades Interstate Park was dedicated in 1909 as part of the Hudson-Fulton Celebration while battleships of many nations lay at anchor below the precipice as far north as Spuyten Duyvil.

Today six individual state parks are strung along the line of the Palisades, while the area as a whole is one grand interstate park. Four miles south of Nyack, adjacent to the Tallman Mountain State Park, is an impressive gorge called Sparkill Gap. Route 9-W climbs its south wall to the village of Sparkill. The wide upper wind gap represents an ancient course of the Hudson River where it flowed across New Jersey to reach the ocean. A narrow notch in the floor of the wind gap has been cut by the present Sparkill Creek, much too small a stream to have made the broad trench above. The mouth of the gap is the point at which the ancient river was captured out of its Jersey route by the lustier new Hudson in the present direct channel.

From the outset, the Interstate Park Commission had hoped for a scenic road along the crest of the Palisades. That dream finally materialized after World War II through a gift of bordering lands by John D. Rockefeller, Jr. and his son Laurance. Rockefeller had previously benefited the city of New York by his donations of Fort Tryon Park and the Cloisters on Washington Heights, across from the Palisades. The Palisades Interstate Parkway, completed in 1957, was the crowning touch for a sequence of related parks that, in their totality, have been termed the "greatest park in the world." Simultaneously the Henry Hudson Drive was developed along the base of the cliff, enabling drivers to look upward at the Palisades.

By means of the Palisades Parkway, New Jersey is afforded the best of cross-river views of the Manhattan skyline. Three lookout points are provided along its route. Northward from the New Jersey exit of the George Washington Bridge, these are:

1. *The Rockefeller Lookout.* Installed as a memorial to John D. Rockefeller, Jr., this is the one from which to see the midtown Manhattan skyline, partially framed by the George Washington Bridge. It faces across at the Henry Hudson Bridge, the gorge of Spuyten Duyvil, Inwood Hill Park, the Cloisters, and Fort Tryon Park.

2. *The Alpine Lookout.* This is two-and-a-half miles further. On the opposite shore spreads the city of Yonkers. A shining strip of Long Island Sound is discernible over the intervening Westchester landscape.

3. *The State Line Lookout.* A little south of the New York boundary, this is the choicest of the viewpoints and also the highest (550 feet). The rock platform juts forward, with sidewise bastions from which the columnar structure of the cliff may be examined and photographed at near range. The platform gives a sweeping view upriver past the Tappan Zee Bridge of the Thruway. Hastings-on-Hudson is directly across, and a sliver of Long Island Sound peeps up.

The finest views of the Palisades are from the New York side. The best outlook places there are Fort Tryon Park, the Cloisters, and Inwood Hill Park; also along Riverside Drive, Riverside Park, and Riverdale Park. The exit of the George Washington Bridge into New Jersey ties directly into the Palisades Interstate Parkway. The Henry Hudson Drive is reached by descending at either the Englewood Cliffs or the Alpine interchange. Route 9-W is the link connecting the parks in New York State related to the Palisades. In the outskirts of Haverstraw, Route 202 veers off west, following the curve of the ridge past High Tor and Little Tor.

WARD POUND RIDGE
High Spot of Westchester

In the extreme southeast corner of the state, against the Connecticut border, lies a landscape feature whose rock structure long presented geologists with some puzzling problems that have yet to be entirely untangled. The Ward Pound Ridge Reservation, besides being a much-favored recreational center for a metropolitan and commutertype populace, offers scenic attributes that are rather out of the ordinary. The largest unit of Westchester County's park system, with 4,100 acres of semiwild terrain, it sponsors such sophisticated events as art shows, and has a small but well-ordered nature museum. It is laced with 35 miles of trails for both hiking and horseback riding.

The original name of this unusual piece of raised countryside was Pound Ridge. The area became Ward Pound Ridge because William L. Ward of Portchester spearheaded a campaign in 1925 to have it preserved as a public park. Mr. Ward persuaded the owners of 32 farms to sell them to Westchester County instead of to real estate developers who were busily making lucrative offers.

The park is not, strictly speaking, a ridge. It stands above the largely residential surrounding region as a sort of elliptical dome rougly three miles in diameter. Ranging from 700 to 800 feet high, it is the highest land in Westchester County with the exception of Anthony's Nose, overlooking the Bear Mountain Bridge on the Hudson. At the eastern extreme, it faces into Connecticut as a somewhat gloomy escarpment, a portion of which is called Raven Rocks. Westward from this escarpment, the irregular landscape is chopped up by hillocks, ridges, ravines, hollows, marshes, and a few lakelets.

Wooded terrain of Ward Pound Ridge, broken by one of its many ponds, as seen from the Lookout.

The key goal for transient sightseers is Fire Tower Hill, which tops the Raven Rocks. Many visitors climb the mile-long upgrade trail from park headquarters to enjoy the outlook from an observation tower. The panorama in all directions picks up Manhattan skyscrapers, the Palisades, Bear Mountain, Slide Mountain in the Catskills, the Hudson Highlands range, a broad sweep of the Connecticut highlands, and Long Island Sound.

Geologically, Fire Tower Hill is the apex of a bow-shaped mass of pink-hued Poundridge granite (or granitic gneiss), a unique kind of rock not yet found elsewhere in the world. This mound of attractive rock, smoothly polished by ice and showing glacial striations, is the platform on which the lookout tower rests. The outer tips of the granite crescent, pointing west, partially embrace a profusion of Fordham gneiss, the very ancient basic rock of the New York City formations, which commonly surfaces all over the Bronx. The rocks of the Manhattan group are traced northeastward across Westchester and deep into Connecticut. They show up in the Pound Ridge Reservation as concentric ridges on both sides of the exposure of Poundridge granite.

The structural complexity of the Pound Ridge rocks has tantalized earth scientists for many years. The currently accepted solution is that the stratified beds of the Manhattan-Westchester set of metamorphosed rocks had been folded once in a corrugated east–west pattern. After many millions of years, they were caught in a diagonal squeeze during the next collision between the bulge of Africa and the North American continent. This time the pressure came from the southeast, and the jaws of the vise were the Connecticut highlands and the solid buttress of the Hudson Highlands on the north. Thus the older folds were folded afresh from a different direction, wrenching them into a hodgepodge of twisted and tilted arcs. At some time during this ordeal, the Poundridge granite was intruded from below and forced into a similar arc shape, between the layers.

The name Pound Ridge was derived from an ingenious method the Indians used to capture wild game, saving themselves considerable energy in hunting. At the base of the escarpment on the southeast side was an indentation in its steep front, across which the Indians built a high stockade with outward-swinging gates. By beating the woods in a communal effort they rounded up deer, herded them into the pen, and slammed the gates shut. This trick reminded the white settlers of the word "pound," for a trap or enclosure.

The entrance road to Ward Pound Ridge is near the junction of Routes 35 and 121. The best approach from New York City is the Sawmill River Parkway to Katonah, thence east on the Cross River Road (Route 35). With careful map reading, a route may be traced eastward from the Bear Mountain Bridge tying into the Cross River Road. An alternate approach from the State Thruway is to leave at Exit 17, cross the Newburgh–Beacon Bridge over the Hudson and follow arterial Route 84, then Route 22 to Katonah.

CENTRAL PARK
New York's Village Green

"To appreciate Central Park, consider the City of New York without it." These words from a map leaflet handed to visitors distill the essence of this best-known of urban parks in America. They conjure the nightmare of solid blocks of tall buildings filling the space instead. The man who was its designer, Frederick Law Olmsted, explained his chief objective as "simply to produce a certain influence in the minds of people and through this to make life in the city healthier and happier."

A person cannot be truly acquainted with the metropolis without a stroll or a drive in Central Park. This is the big city's breathing space. Because it preserves an extensive, if considerably altered, section of Manhattan Island's original rock floor, it merits a niche among the scenic gems of the state. Its rockiness, once frowned upon as a disadvantage, proved, as we shall see, to be its greatest asset. Owing to its association with the Revolution, the park is enrolled as a National Historic Landmark.

The name meant what it said. Central Park is situated at the approximate geographic center of Manhattan Island. It is a rectangle, two-and-a-half miles long and a trifle over a half-mile wide, and usurps 843 acres of some of the most valuable real estate in the world. In the pre–Civil War era every quaint New England town boasted its shady and grassy village green, but few people looked for natural beauty or graciousness in a large, rapidly growing American city. Central Park set a precedent for dozens of municipal parks, with Brooklyn for a starter.

A movement for a park to meet New York's future needs was launched in 1849. At that time the population was around 500,000 and the strictly urban part of Manhattan was confined

The contrast between a hillock of the Manhattan schist formation and a skyscraper background is typical of Central Park scenery.

below Fourteenth Street. The thought was to lay out a park
somewhere up in the boondocks and let the city grow around it.
The central area was chosen largely because it was so rough,
rocky, and inhospitable to building as to be regarded as worthless
for anything else. In 1776 George Washington's drooping army,
after the humiliating Battle of Long Island, retreated across the
future Central Park terrain to Washington Heights for its next
stand. The area had since become a pesthole, grown to briars and
poison ivy, although it had a census of some 5,000 squatters
domiciled in hovels and shanties. Mongrel dogs roved in packs
and the air hung putrid with the aroma of stables, pigsties, and
bone factories. Converting the spot into a park might be a fine
way to clean up the eyesore, but nay-sayers objected to the rock
formation as "bald and unpicturesque." Perhaps what really
tipped the scales was the cogent argument that a park would
greatly increase the value of surrounding properties.

In 1853 the state legislature passed a bill enabling the city to
take over that no-man's-land for purposes of a park. Washington
Irving was chairman of a City Park Commission to consider
plans. A young man from Hartford, Connecticut, Frederick Law
Olmsted, applied for the job of park superintendent. In travels
abroad after his graduation from Yale, Olmsted found that he
disliked the formal gardens that passed for parks in France, but
was pleased by the natural, parklike landscapes of the English
manors.

While the squatters, goats, and pigs were being evicted, the
Park Commission opened a design competition. Olmsted joined
with Calvert Vaux, a fledgling architect, in submitting a plan
entitled "Greensward" which won the contest in 1858. Olmsted
was appointed architect-in-chief, with Vaux as his assistant. In
the performance of this task, Olmsted became America's pioneer
and leading landscape architect. His primary object was to adapt
the park to its scenic environment. Five streams flowing across
the area into the East River were utilized to create ponds,
waterfalls, and lakes, with appropriate walks, bridges, and
ornamental plantings. Carriage drives were made curvilinear to
conform to the landscape, and Olmsted invented the term

"parkway" for these roads. He was the city's original traffic
planner, introducing transverse east–west parkways on the
principle of grade separation from north–south drives and walks.
A sophisticated person of strong artistic tastes, he granted Vaux
liberal scope for architectural flourishes in gateways, plazas,
fountains, and sculptures. The northerly reaches of the park, at
the Harlem end, are the more ruggedly picturesque, with rock
mounds rising as much as 100 feet. This section was deliberately
given minimal treatment to counterbalance the more "cultural"
development of the southern end.

In the final analysis, it was the area's rockiness that gave
Central Park its most distinctive characteristic. All the bedrock
obstacles, ledges, and hummocks in the park belong to the
Manhattan Formation, which comprises the primary surface of
the entire island save for a wedge of Inwood marble in the
Broadway valley at the extreme north. Fortunately this is an
attractive and interesting rock, crystallized, folded, and rumpled
by intense metamorphism; its typical ingredient being mica schist,
which is often iridescent and glistens in the sunshine. Bands of
granite frequently intersect the mica schist. The granite was
probably intruded as molten rock deep underground, although
the more recent geological thinking accepts the possibility that
granite is sometimes produced "in place" by partial melting of
preexisting rocks of the right composition.

The boroughs of the Bronx and Manhattan occupy the southern
extension of the Manhattan Prong, so called as a southeasterly
relative of the Reading Prong (the Hudson Highlands, etc.). It
was long speculated that Manhattan Island had been moved in
from a location further east. In the light of the new concept of
plate tectonics, it is believed that the Manhattan Prong was
shoved into its present location during the Acadian Orogeny,
while the African continental plate was jammed against that of
North America. The Manhattan Prong might be considered as a
second wave of that gigantic squeeze, coming along behind the
Hudson Highlands.

The island can be compared to a crumpled layer cake, with the
far more ancient Fordham gneiss at the bottom, the Inwood

marble as the middle layer, and the Manhattan schist on top. The
Fordham gneiss crops out in the Bronx and Westchester. At all
events, this rock pile is durable and stable. No other city in
America has so reliable a footing for such lofty buildings. The
fact that the skyscrapers appear in two main clusters, midtown
and downtown, is attributable to a pronounced depression in the
rock floor between those two areas, the sag having been filled by
glacial material.

Glaciation had greatly helped to prepare the ground for
Olmsted and Vaux in Central Park, by polishing and rounding off
the bedrock and grooving it with striations. The ice also dropped
large, erratic boulders liberally around Central Park, most of
them carried from the Hudson Highlands and the Palisades.

Central Park was essentially completed before the first guns of
the Civil War. Since that time it has undergone many changes,
usually occasioned by the bequests of wealthy people. Some
examples are the Heckscher Playground, the Wollman Skating
Rink, and the Delacorte Shakespeare Theater. The chances are
that Olmsted would have bemoaned such tampering with his
original "Greensward" design in order to take advantage of
generous gifts. Some critics have branded such additions as
"aggressive philanthropy."

An unpleasant fact cannot be evaded in any discussion of
Central Park. "Crime in the park" is no figment of the
imagination. Muggings, holdups, rapes, and murders do take
place in Central Park and visitors must be careful. Large portions
of the park are no longer safe for pedestrians to explore, even in
broad daylight. The best means of gaining an overall impression
of the park is by automobile with the aid of maps that may be had
at the main entrances. The more romantic horse-drawn carriages,
especially popular among young couples and children, may be
engaged near the southeast entrance gate and the Plaza Hotel.

The sections that are generally safe for walking are the southern
part, nearest to Central Park South; and the traverse starting from
the Eighty-first Street gateway on Central Park West, opposite the
American Museum of Natural History. These walks are nearly
always well frequented.

The two main entrances at the south end are the one at
Fifty-ninth Street and Fifth Avenue (the Scholars' Gate) and the
one near Columbus Circle. Between these entrances may be
found the Zoo, the Pond, the Promontory and Bird Sanctuary,
and the Mall, which leads to the Terrace with its ornamental
Bethesda Fountain and view of Rowboat Lake and the Ramble.
The promenade from the Eighty-first Street gate passes the
Shakespeare Garden and the Delacorte Theater, where
Shakespeare plays are performed. Near at hand is the charming
Belvedere Lake, with the old Belvedere Tower perched on the far
side. The tower is now used for the municipal weather station.
This route ultimately leads to the famed Egyptian obelisk,
Cleopatra's Needle—which Olmsted and Vaux did not place there
and Cleopatra never saw. The Needle has long been cited to
schoolchildren as an example of what Manhattan air does to stone
when it is exiled from its desert home.

*Central Park is bounded on the east by Fifth Avenue, on the south
by Central Park South (Fifty-ninth Street), on the west by Central
Park West, on the north by 110th Street. The main fact for drivers
to know is that one-way traffic is south on Fifth Avenue. Transverse
drives are at Sixty-sixth Street, Seventy-ninth Street, Eighty-sixth
Street, and Ninety-seventh Street.*

FORT TRYON PARK
Comrade of the Cloisters

Transients come and go by the thousands in New York
City—seeing theater, nightclubs, museums, and lofty
buildings—but generally unaware that, far uptown on Washington
Heights, the metropolis boasts one of the truly superior
scenic-historic heirlooms of the state. This treasure is Fort Tryon
Park, situated on a rocky knob on which General George
Washington planted an outpost of the hurriedly prepared fortress
where his bedraggled army made its last stand before being
driven into New Jersey.

A circular viewing platform, with a stone parapet around and a
flagstaff in the middle, affords a peerless sweep of the North River
(alias Hudson) north and south, and of the Palisades in ideal
perspective across the water. Just far enough seaward to blend
softly into the picture is the gracefully suspended arc of the
George Washington Bridge. When air pollution permits, the
Statue of Liberty may be glimpsed. The viewpoint also looks east
over the lowland valley of upper Broadway to the Fort George
ridge, which was Laurel Hill to the retreating colonials who
paused to set up a small fort there. The triumphant British
enlarged that fort to protect their occupation of the city and
called it Fort George in tribute to their distant sovereign. The
depression between the two ridges is due to the water-soluble
Inwood marble of its floor.

The elongated spine of the Manhattan Ridge, upland of the
borough, includes not only Washington Heights but Morningside
and St. Nicholas Heights. Reaching over five miles, it drops off
steeply on both sides. Fort Washington Park, Riverside Park,

Fort Tryon Park, on Washington Heights, offers a superb overview of the Hudson River and the Palisades on the Jersey side. Across this water, George Washington withdrew the remnants of his battered army.

Riverside Drive, and the Henry Hudson Parkway skirt its base on
the west; Morningside Park, St. Nicholas Park, and High Bridge
Park on the east. The campuses of Columbia University and City
University of New York are on its more southerly crest.
Washington Heights constitutes the northerly mile-and-a-half.
All in all, the Manhattan Ridge serves the city well.

Fort Tryon Park was for many years marked as the highest spot
on Manhattan Island, but this was not quite accurate. A resurvey
has awarded that title, by a hair's breadth, to Bennett Park, a
fenced-in green rectangle above the entrance ramps to the George
Washington Bridge, where the benchmark says 270 feet. Bennett
Park is the former site of the mansion built by James Gordon
Bennett, Sr., publisher of the *New York Herald.*

Fort Washington lay between Bennett Park and Fort Tryon
Park. A little beyond its upper end was the knob then known as
Forest Hill which Washington chose for the outwork. When Sir
William Howe staged his assault on November 16, 1776, it was
spearheaded by 4,600 Hessian mercenaries who labored up the
forbidding rock incline of Forest Hill under heavy fire from 600
Maryland and Virginia troops at the top. The Germans were
pinned down for three hours and suffered many losses.

General Washington was in the main fort at the time, having
come over from Fort Lee, New Jersey for an inspection. He was
reluctantly persuaded to row back immediately, escaping capture
by a scant half-hour, which could have meant his trial for treason.
Legend says that Washington then stood on the Palisades and
wept openly at seeing his men being bayoneted across the river.

The victors made Forest Hill into a strong bastion and named it
Fort Tryon, in honor of William Tryon, a prominent Loyalist who
was the last colonial governor of New York. While the battle
raged, Tryon was safe aboard an enemy warship in the harbor.
After the fall of Fort Washington, he was brought ashore and
instated as nominal governor under the British occupation. As
soon as the Revolution ended, the Americans wiped Fort Tryon
from the map. In view of that fact, it seems ironic that Fort Tryon
Park is today one of New York's best.

History aside, not the least of the park's attributes are its

upright exposures of the Manhattan Formation, already
encountered in Central Park. The characteristic mica schist of this
interesting rock is displayed to advantage, its flakes gleaming
blackish, pearly, often with nuances of iridescence. The
crystalline schist was metamorphosed from shale, and the shale
was hardened from mud and silt on a sea bottom.

Much of the northern extremity of Washington Heights was
acquired piecemeal by John D. Rockefeller, Jr. for donation to
the city. The Fort Tryon hill was occupied by a lavish estate
owned and developed by C. K. G. Billings, a capitalist of the early
twentieth century. The 40-room mansion, Tryon Hall, in Louis
XIV style, was noted as one of the most palatial homes in the
nation. Rockefeller purchased the property in 1917 for a reputed
$5 million and presented it, along with two adjacent estates,
during the 1920s on condition that the city preserve it as a park.
The mansion was badly damaged by fire in 1926.

Looking north along the ridge from Tryon Park, one's gaze is
riveted by a great, castlelike structure in the chaste and gentle
architectural mood of medieval monasteries, crowning the next
rise in the landscape. This spectacle is the Cloisters, widely
renowned for its collections of Gothic and Romanesque sculpture
and other art forms in a setting well adapted to their spirit. A
branch of the Metropolitan Museum of Art, the Cloisters is
linked, for maintenance purposes, with Fort Tryon Park, and a
visit to either should by all means include the other. The pleasant
walk between, through a sag in the terrain, is only a quarter-mile.

The Cloisters was developed over a period of 20 years by an
eminent sculptor, George Grey Barnard, to contain his hoard of
rare statuary and architectural relics. It evolved around elements
from the cloisters of five French monasteries dating from the
twelfth to the fifteenth century. There are interior garden courts,
chapels transported bodily from Europe, and dimly lighted halls
that produce a semi-ecclesiastical effect. The Western Terrace
gives impressive vistas of the Hudson and the Palisades from a
slightly different angle.

Barnard had a special fondness for France. Many of the
choicest items of his collection were salvaged from stone walls,

barns, attics, even pigsties. Lacking the means to do business with
dealers, and knowing the peasants' habit of using stone objects
from decayed buildings, he sought out the ruins of medieval
abbeys and systematically searched farms in their vicinity.

Rockefeller gave $600,000 to the Metropolitan Museum in 1925
for purchase of the Cloisters from Barnard and its expansion to
house the museum's existing store of art from the Middle Ages.
From his private collections, Rockefeller then added 30 sculptures
and other art objects, including the marvelous series of six
tapestries, "The Hunt for the Unicorn," one of the main
attractions. Rockefeller had acquired the tapestries for his own
home in 1923 at a cost of $1,100,000. They are believed to have
been woven in or around 1499 as a gift from Louis XII to his
bride, Anne of Brittany.

*To reach Fort Tryon Park by car from the Henry Hudson Parkway
(West Side Highway), one takes the first exit north of the George
Washington Bridge, then Fort Washington Avenue. By subway,
which is generally preferable, take the Independent "A" train to the
190th Street stop, from which an elevator unloads passengers almost
at the entrance walk to the park. The Number 4 uptown bus makes
its turnabout in the Cloisters parking lot.*

The northern heights of Manhattan Island are dominated by parks. The wooded area at top center of the picture is Inwood Hill Park. The castlelike structure just south is the Cloisters; Fort Tryon Park is lost in the nearer trees. The major traffic artery at the left is the Henry Hudson Parkway.

INWOOD HILL PARK
A Forest in the City

The rock-ribbed island of Manhattan stretches for 13.4 miles, all the way from the Battery to Spuyten Duyvil. Surprising even to many residents is the fact that the northern finger of their overcrowded borough is mantled by woodland thick enough to be the haunt of birdwatchers, dog-walkers, and people who simply want to stroll a real forest path as a relief from sidewalks. Only the muted hum of traffic on the Henry Hudson Parkway down below, well out of sight, intrudes on the stillness.

This unexpected haven, Inwood Hill Park, is situated on the bluff jutting 220 feet above Spuyten Duyvil Creek which, as a ship canal, links the Harlem River with the Hudson. A grassy open space at the crest, with railing on the west, provides yet another splendid view across the mile-wide Hudson to the Palisades. The woods are almost as wild, in some parts, as if they had been lifted out of the Catskills. And yet the eastern border is within a few hundred yards of solid ranks of apartment houses, and subway trains stop within easy walking distance.

Once hailed as "the last bit of virgin territory on Manhattan," the beautiful headland remained virtually untouched since the days of Indian occupation. The reason it escaped urbanization was its relative inaccessibility, with its sides too steep for roads and, in particular, a large ravine that cleaves its northeast section. In spite of these handicaps, realty interests were starting to move in during the forepart of this century. A citizens' crusade formed to save its wilderness charm, and the city acquired the nucleus of Inwood Park in 1922, later enlarging it to 196 acres and a length of nearly a mile.

N.Y. City Dept. of Parks and Recreation

The hill is properly an extension of Washington Heights, although it is totally detached from that ridge, just beyond the Cloisters, by the deep, precipitous Dyckman Street valley, an eroded cross-fault that meets the Hudson at Tubby Hook. During his brief and harried sojourn on Manhattan, George Washington installed another outpost, the Cock Hill Redoubt, on what later became Inwood Hill. The general locality around upper Broadway and Dyckman Street has long been referred to as Inwood.

Although Inwood Hill is capped by the same mica schist rock as all of Washington Heights, it is best known geologically for the Inwood marble, which outcrops near the base of the bluff and along the banks of the Spuyten Duyvil.

Manhattan was not always an island. The origins of the waterways surrounding it are complex and not yet fully understood. The place at which the island was finally amputated altogether from the mainland of the Bronx was the nose of Inwood Hill, by the cutting through of the Spuyten Duyvil channel. It is theorized that a Spuyten Duyvil Creek was flowing south out of Westchester, in the vicinity of Van Cortlandt Park, veering west to the Hudson along a weak fault zone between Inwood Hill and the Bronx. At the same time, the Harlem River flowed southeast as a tributary to the East River. The Harlem River eroded its way headward in the soluble Inwood marble until only a thin divide, perhaps, separated it from the Spuyten Duyvil. Glacial action probably knocked out this final divide and then left the land surface of the coastal area depressed so that the former stream channels became tidal estuaries.

Inwood Hill is rich in historic associations. The Harlem River shore of its northeast margin was the site of a well-known Indian village, whose inhabitants cultivated the river's flats. Excavations have indicated a group of cave dwellers in the flanks of the Inwood ravine, bringing to light weapons and utensils centuries older than those in use when the first whites arrived. An ice-cold spring literally spouted from the north base of the cliff, giving the Indians a splendid water supply. The spring inspired the Dutch name Spuyten Duyvil, meaning "spitting devil." The spring still spouts, but nowadays from a pipe. Inwood was the Indians' last foothold on Manhattan Island. These Indians paddled out to meet Henry Hudson's *Half Moon*, on his return from upriver. They had become hostile since Hudson's prior visit, and blood was shed. The Inwood natives took no part in the subsequent "sale" of Manhattan to Pieter Minuit, but held onto their isolated land until 1715 when freeholders of New Haarlem were assessed a special tax for its purchase.

Mounds of oyster shells around the Spuyten Duyvil site have testified to its lengthy inhabitation by Indians. Huge, fallen wedges of rock from the Inwood heights form a disorderly cluster locally known as the Indian Caves. Many artifacts retrieved in the vicinity are exhibited at the Museum of the American Indian in New York.

The West Side Express Highway becomes the Henry Hudson Parkway north of the George Washington Bridge. One leaves the northbound lane of the Parkway by the Dyckman exit, which leads to the Inwood Park approaches. No public parking area is available—only street parking. Visitors will be better advised to travel the West Side subway, "A" train, to the 207th Street station, near which a walkway leads up the Inwood slope.

A scene in the out-of-place Bronx River gorge, which cuts across a corner
of the Botanical Gardens in Bronx Park.

BRONX PARK
The Zoo and Botanical Garden

The Bronx is the northern borough of New York City, bordering
on Westchester County, and the only borough situated on the
mainland. The name is a slight corruption from that of Jonas
Bronck, a Dutchman who acquired the grant of the land in 1638.
The Bronx chiefly comprises people—close to a million-and-a-half
of them—who pride themselves on being a tribe apart. Outlanders
know it best as the location of the Bronx Zoo and the Bronx
Botanical Garden, both of which are in the Bronx Park. The park
is at the approximate middle of the borough and was in existence
some years before the Botanical and the Zoological societies came
into the act.

The park in itself would be a distinctive recreational preserve
even without the flora and fauna introduced by the two
nature-oriented societies, which have brought it to national
acclaim. It is distinguished by its abundant exposures of
Fordham gneiss—a strikingly ornamental kind of rock because of
its black-and-white banding, crinkled into varied patterns by the
ordeals of metamorphism deep underground in ages past. The
Bronx River gorge is an offbeat feature of the Botanical Garden.

The Fordham gneiss is so called for its type locality on the
Fordham University Heights and the campus adjacent to the
Bronx Botanical Garden on the west. Appearing in ridges, ledges,
spines, and humps, the Fordham gneiss provides one vast rock
garden for the floral and horticultural displays. The decorative
aspects of the gneiss are diversified by the smoothing and
grooving of horizontal outcrops by the passage of glacial ice.
Since the exposures are generally more massive and assorted in
the zoological section south of Fordham Road, they lend

themselves admirably to imaginative uses in naturalistic
environments for certain privileged animals such as lions, bears,
antelopes, and mountain goats, and to the spread of landscape
designated as the "African veldt."

Glacial erratic boulders are abundant throughout the Bronx
Park. For the most part these are identifiable as rounded chunks
of rock transported from the northern Palisades and the Hudson
Highlands. One such boulder, called the Rocking Stone, draws
special attention on the zoo grounds. Standing seven feet tall,
perched where the ice dropped it on a pedestal of Fordham
gneiss, this oddity may be set rocking by a push of the hands.

As already noted, the Fordham gneiss is far and away the oldest
formation of the New York City triad. The other two—the
Manhattan Formation and the Inwood marble—have in late years
come to be recognized as of Paleozoic sedimentary origin, after
being long mistaken as of Precambrian age.

The confusion was aggravated by the vast difference in age
between the Fordham gneiss and the two upper members of the
New York City structures. Beneath the streets of Manhattan there
exists an immense time gap (unconformity) of at least 500 million
years between the Inwood marble and the Fordham gneiss, with
practically no intervening rock formation to provide a clue as to
what happened in the great interval. This puzzling unconformity
has at last been explained through the concept of plate tectonics.
Whatever vanished rock layers may have been deposited on the
Fordham gneiss in the eternity between were eroded away.
During the Acadian mountain-building epoch beginning some
350 million years ago, the American and African continents were
welded together. Before they again parted company as the
Atlantic Ocean was reborn, the previous sedimentary rocks caught
in the vise had been thrust underground, metamorphosed at
depth, uplifted, then shoved northwestward. Incidentally, the old
Fordham gneiss had undergone a fresh metamorphism in the
process.

The aforementioned Bronx River gorge is no great scenic
spectacle as gorges go, but it is a pleasant novelty. Located in the
southeast corner of the Botanical Garden, it is less than half a
mile long, and is something of an enigma in its own right. A river

more by courtesy than size, the stream flows south past Bronxville and Mount Vernon in a straight valley eroded in the water-soluble Inwood marble, paralleled by the Bronx River Parkway. It then veers aside eastward into the Bronx Park, drops over a modest waterfall, and babbles through a narrow gorge with steep, jagged walls 60 to 70 feet high.

The odd thing about this behavior is that the gorge is hewed through a spur of the quite resistant Manhattan schist, which contrasts sharply with the more vulnerable marble of the valley just left behind. Obviously the preglacial river must have gone on straight ahead to join the Harlem River. In early attempts to explain this aberration it was suggested that the gorge detour was begun as the diverted outlet of a glacially impounded lake. That theory had to be discarded when no symptom could be found of a glacial barrier deposit that might have dammed up such a lake. An alternative guess was that the river was prevented by a huge block of ice lingering across the valley from resuming its normal course; but in that case, the brevity of time while the ice block was melting would hardly account for a gorge 70 feet deep in so tough a rock. To complicate matters, three sizable potholes found in the gorge are of relatively recent origin and indicate a rapid and larger stream heavily charged with gravel and grit.

A more mature hypothesis is that the errant gorge was begun during an interglacial period, in a weak fault zone through the spur of Manhattan schist, then grew with recurrent flooding episodes until it gained control over the river's direction. The diversion was probably abetted by the fact that the new route to the East River is shorter by some two miles than the prior one.

Incidentally, the Bronx River played a minor but amusing role in the Revolutionary War. General Sir William Howe, persuaded that he had Washington's battered army securely trapped on Harlem heights, moved north with a strong detachment in a scheme to outflank it in Westchester County and thereby force its surrender. The British War Office, studying maps in London, sent orders for the naval squadron on patrol in Long Island Sound to set sail up the Bronx River and capture or sink all rebel ships lurking there. The trouble with this tactical maneuver was that no vessel larger than a rowboat had ever navigated the Bronx River.

Thus deprived of naval support, Howe's troops had to ford the stream as best they could en route to White Plains. A British officer reported to London, with tongue in cheek: "We have crossed the Bronx [River] without the loss of a single man!"

Since early colonial days, the waterpower supplied by a 50-foot drop in level in the Bronx gorge was utilized to turn mill wheels. In 1800 a French émigré named Pierre Lorillard built a stone snuff mill on the rock floor of the gorge near its mouth. From that mill evolved the hugely successful Lorillard tobacco industry. The gorge was enveloped by a wonderful stand of virgin hemlocks, which Lorillard had the good judgment to preserve. A remnant of that forest, now called the Hemlock Grove, is today an admired part of the Botanical Garden. Lorillard erected his family mansion nearby and cultivated roses on a lavish scale, using their petals to perfume his snuff. His once famous "Acre of Roses" is now the park's alluring Rose Garden.

In order to be near the large tobacco growers, Lorillard ultimately removed his industry to the South. Attracted by the hemlock forest and the rose garden, the New York Botanical Society acquired the Lorillard estate in 1891 for its Garden Project. The New York Zoological Society followed the precedent in 1899 by establishing the Bronx Zoo in the southern half of the Bronx Park.

Pierre Lorillard's original snuff mill still stands in the lower Bronx gorge and is operated as a restaurant for visitors. A natural stone walkway beside the stream leads up to the falls.

The Cross Bronx Expressway (U.S. Route 95) carries traffic eastward from the George Washington Bridge. Passing just to the south of the Bronx Park, it affords an exit direct to the Bronx Zoo as well as an interchange with the Bronx River Parkway, which leads north along the eastern boundary of the Botanical Garden. Both the Lexington and the Seventh Avenue subway lines serve a Bronx Park station (elevated) near the zoo's main entrance. Closer to the Botanical Garden, the Woodlawn train on the Lexington subway line has a Fordham Road station.

FORT WADSWORTH
Sentinel of the Narrows

The mile-wide gap between Brooklyn and Staten Island is known
as the Narrows. Through it pass all ocean vessels in and out of
New York Harbor. The bluffs rising sharply on either hand are
the sawed-off stumps of a glacial terminal moraine where it has
been cut through by the Hudson River. These severed ends have
been reconnected since 1964 by the Verrazano-Narrows Bridge,
whose center section of 4,260 feet is the world's longest suspension
span and one of the most aesthetically pleasing.

Shadowed beneath the landward extensions of the bridge are
forts that guarded the passage in bygone wars: Fort Wadsworth at
the west, or Staten Island end, and Fort Hamilton at the east, or
Brooklyn end. Fort Wadsworth has a legitimate claim to being
the oldest continuously manned military post in the United
States; the earliest Dutch settlers of New Amsterdam placed a
blockhouse on that point of Staten Island, which was later
enlarged into a fortification by the British. The Fort Wadsworth
Military Reservation is accessible to visitors and affords a
convenient scenic viewpoint on the "front door of America."

The magnificent bridge has belatedly given his just dues to
Giovanni de Verrazano, a Florentine navigator in the French
service who was the first recorded European explorer to probe the
mouth of the Hudson River. In the year 1524 he dropped anchor
outside the Narrows and, with exemplary caution, had himself
rowed in the ship's boat into Upper New York Bay. Afterward he
reported to his royal employer, Francis I: "At the end of a
hundred leagues we found a very agreeable situation located
within two small prominent hills, in the midst of which flowed to

The Staten Island end of the Verrazano-Narrows Bridge shadows Fort Wadsworth. The grounds of the historic fort are laid out on a stump end of the Harbor Hill moraine where it was cut through by the Hudson.

the sea a very great river, which was deep within the mouth. . . .
On account of being anchored off the coast in good shelter, we did
not wish to adventure in without knowledge of the entrances. We
were with the small boat, entering the said river to the land, which
we found much populated. . . . We entered said river, within the
land about half a league, where we saw it made a very beautiful
lake with a circuit of about three leagues."

A sudden onshore wind threatening to drive his ship aground,
Verrazano hastily weighed anchor and withdrew to open sea. He
never did get a second chance at the Hudson River because he
was eaten by cannibals on a Caribbean island where, exercising
less prudence than at the Narrows, he unwisely stepped ashore.

The Narrows was formerly closed off by the Harbor Hill
moraine, which dammed up a vast lake behind it. This ridge was
continuous with the moraine belt that extends the entire length of
Long Island and, westward, comprises the bulk of Staten Island.
Some idea of its dimensions at the gap can be gotten from the
existing heights of land on both sides of the Narrows. Todt Hill
on Staten Island has an elevation of 410 feet and is the highest
point on the Atlantic coast from Maine to Florida. The high spot
in Brooklyn's Prospect Park is 188 feet above mean tide level. A
drive on the Todt Hill Road affords views across New York Bay to
downtown Manhattan, and south to the Atlantic Highlands of
New Jersey.

The upland surface features of Long Island are almost wholly
the product of two separate advances of the Wisconsin Ice
Sheet—that is, the end moraines that were built up at the frontal
margins during prolonged stands of the ice at its extremes. The
older Ronkonkoma moraine terminates in Montauk Point, the
so-called south fluke of the island. The Harbor Hill moraine,
which overlaps and buries the Ronkonkoma moraine westward
from the Manhasset–Lake Success pivot, fades from sight
underwater in Orient Point, the north fluke. The younger
moraine, which accounts for the Narrows, derives its name from
its highest elevation on Long Island—Harbor Hill (391 feet) near
Roslyn.

The Harbor Hill moraine extends southwest across Staten

Island as far as Perth Amboy, New Jersey, which pinpoints the southernmost reach of the glaciers in the eastern United States. All during the last retreat of the ice, the moraine remained a solid obstruction across the Narrows, which presumably had been part of the preglacial outlet route of the Hudson into the Atlantic. Consequently the moraine was a high earthen dam holding back a glacial lake whose immensity has only lately come to be realized.

The existence of Lake Albany, flooding much of the upper Hudson and lower Mohawk valleys, has long been recognized, but the location of the obstacle that created it has not been as certain. For want of a better theory, geologists surmised that the blockage was an impacted plug of ice and debris remaining in the deep gorge of the Hudson Highlands long after the withdrawal of the main ice front. Only within recent years has it dawned upon earth scientists that the Harbor Hill moraine across the Narrows may itself have been the dam impounding Lake Albany. Field studies of high-level beach lines both north and south of the Highlands strongly suggest an uninterrupted lake stretching from New York Bay northward almost to the Adirondack foothills. If such were the case, the hypothetical plug in the Hudson Highlands was perhaps either gone or underwater. The highest beach lines of Lake Albany north of the Highlands accord nicely with what would have been the crest line of the Harbor Hill moraine at the Narrows.

Granting, then, a tremendously larger Lake Albany than had ever been conceived, a problem remains as to the location of its spillway into the Atlantic. One good possibility is the Arthur Kill, around the west side of Staten Island, which slices through the moraine between Tottenville, Staten Island, and Perth Amboy, New Jersey. Another is the upper East River into Long Island Sound, which would perhaps explain the Hell Gate channel (almost a gorge) between Ward's Island and Astoria Park, crossed by the Triborough Bridge. By the latter escape, the water would have swollen Long Island Sound (at first a lake) to help it breach the Harbor Hill moraine east of Orient Point. More likely, both vents were used at different times or simultaneously.

Partially sheltered beneath the Staten Island exit ramps of the

Verrazano-Narrows Bridge is Fort Wadsworth. The fort begun by the Dutch was continued during colonial and Revolutionary times, and was quickly recaptured by the British in 1776. In the War of 1812, when a reinvasion by the British was momentarily feared, Fort Hamilton was built on the Brooklyn point of the Narrows to provide a cross fire on this all-important passage. As of this writing, Fort Hamilton is U.S. Army Headquarters for the New York Area Command. Fort Wadsworth is under its jurisdiction. Fort Hamilton does not qualify as a place for tourist visitation or a scenic view, but Fort Wadsworth does.

After passing scrutiny by the guard at the gate, visitors to Fort Wadsworth are free to roam the grounds landscaped on the blunt end of the moraine, and to enjoy the outlook across the Narrows from the underside of the great bridge. The fort maintains a good military museum depicting the history of the United States Army. This museum is open for group tours to be arranged by appointment.

The Verrazano-Narrows Bridge is reached from the Long Island side via the Brooklyn-Queens Expressway (U.S. Route 278). From lower Manhattan, the Brooklyn-Battery Tunnel ties into this expressway. From the New Jersey and Staten Island side, the approach is the Staten Island Expressway (also part of U.S. Route 278).

A vista of the Long Meadow in Brooklyn's Prospect Park, which spreads over the area of the Harbor Hill moraine where the Battle of Long Island was fought.

PROSPECT PARK
Glacial Heights of Brooklyn

Beyond the East River, some six miles on a diagonal from Central
Park, lies the strikingly different landscape of Brooklyn's Prospect
Park. In this case the scene is gentler and purely glacial, clothed
in green grass. The park spreads over 516 acres of the Harbor Hill
moraine four miles northeast of Fort Hamilton at the Narrows.
Prospect Park was directly inspired by the example of Central
Park and was laid out by the same two men—Frederick Law
Olmsted and Calvert Vaux.

Brooklyn was a chartered city in its own right, with a
population near 139,000, and was feeling its oats, with no
intention of taking a back seat for its overgrown neighbor.
(Brooklyn remained a city until 1898, when it became a borough
of New York City.) Moreover, Brooklyn was endowed with a
large open space near its heart which, with undulating
knob-and-kettle topography, was more readily adaptable to
recreational uses than the unkempt rocks and ledges of Central
Park had been at the outset. This tract, historically memorable as
the site of the Battle of Long Island, was then known as Prospect
Hill.

A Brooklyn Park Commission was created and the state
legislature of 1860 authorized it to purchase the land, but the Civil
War intruded. Landscaping and construction work on the park
did not begin until 1866. Olmsted and Vaux were not obliged to
compete for its design. They accepted the contract even before
they were finished with Central Park. To them its rounded and
dimpled terrain offered a refreshing challenge after their
experience with the rugged old Manhattan bedrock. Olmsted
observed that "the natural configuration of the surface is the

basis of the intended improvements. The hills, the valleys, and
the streams are nature's pencilling on the surface of the earth. . . .
To alter them would be desecration, to erase them would be folly.
. . . The goal is that every turn of one's head may reveal some new
feature, while an air of harmony pervades the whole and no
discordant contrasts offend the eye."

The park engineer for the Commission had already drawn a
tentative plan, which Olmsted and Vaux promptly discarded
because it would have had Flatbush Avenue cutting across the
northeast section of the park area. Flatbush Avenue is the
well-known thoroughfare that makes a beeline from the
Manhattan Bridge to the Brooklyn district of Flatbush, on the
level outwash plain extending seaward beyond the morainal
bluff. Olmsted would have no part of a busy street rumbling with
heavy traffic through his park. Because of this alteration in plan,
the city acquired additional park acreage on the flat south of the
moraine, which the architects then used for a parade ground and
a man-made Prospect Park Lake, an especially popular feature of
the park today.

The major portion of the park was tastefully adapted to the
glacial landscape. The attractive parkways curve around the
contoured slopes of the higher kame knolls, and dip through the
vales, making a complete inside perimeter road connected by two
crossovers. The park is two miles long on the north–south axis,
including the Grand Army Plaza at the main entrance which
emphasizes that it was developed in the lingering shadow of the
Civil War. An especially charming vista is the Long Meadow, a
mile in length. Erratic boulders are scattered about, a few of
which are put to use as the bearers of historic tablets.

After driving the British out of Boston in 1776, George
Washington transferred his Continental Army to New York,
rightly anticipating that this was the next place Lord Howe's fleet
would strike. Howe landed his composite army of British regulars
and Hessian mercenaries on Staten Island. The Brooklyn Heights
of the Harbor Hill moraine, if they fell into enemy hands, would
make defense of the city virtually impossible, as New York would
then be a helpless target for artillery fire. To guard against such

an event, Washington fortified those heights on the theory that
Howe, if he decided to cross the Narrows, would attack from the
south against the steep moraine front. From above, the Yankee
sharpshooters could then devastate the attackers, as they had done
at Bunker Hill. But Howe outfoxed Washington. While feigning
the frontal assault Washington expected, he sent a strong
detachment around the east flank of the American position by
way of the Jamaica Road pass, incredibly left unprotected. With
sunrise, the continentals were dismayed to find that the enemy
had crept in behind them. Total disaster was averted only by a
masterful withdrawal of Washington's entrapped main army
across the East River under cover of darkness and a providential
dense fog.

The Battle of Long Island, as this unfortunate encounter is
known, was the first open pitched battle of the Revolution. It was
also the first battle fought by the United States after becoming a
nation with the Declaration of Independence.

A number of monuments and plaques in Prospect Park
commemorate significant locations of that combat. Among these
is a tall shaft on Lookout Hill, the high point of the park, erected
to the memory of "Maryland's Four Hundred," a regiment of
fresh recruits who gallantly held a ravine under fierce assault to
give the rest of the army time to escape. Lookout Hill was briefly
used as a signal station during the battle. Beside the East Drive of
the park, the Battle Pass Tablet marks Valley Grove, which was
the outer line of defense.

The Grand Army Plaza, the principal entrance to Prospect Park
at the north, is rather spectacular, with its Soldiers' and Sailors'
Memorial Arch and heroic bronze groupings by Frederick
MacMonnies, an eminent Brooklyn-born sculptor. A sheer
bravado of beauty went into his modeling of "The Wild Horses"
and "The Horse Tamers."

Prospect Park is shielded from its surrounding streets and
sidewalks by a wall of stone masonry, which is pierced at intervals
by nine entrances. The street boundaries, besides Flatbush
Avenue, are Prospect Park West, Prospect Park Southwest, and
Parkside Avenue.

Olmsted's cavalier dismissal of the northeast triangle of the available park property because of teeming Flatbush Avenue was to the distinct advantage of the Brooklyn Institute of Arts and Sciences. The area was taken over for the later development of the Brooklyn Botanic Gardens, which many visitors find more enticing than Prospect Park itself. Situated along the very rim of the moraine escarpment, it makes the most of the glacial features, including a considerable collection of erratic boulders.

The Botanic Gardens are widely famed for their abundance of flowers and plants from all corners of the world, and in particular for the exquisite Japanese Garden. A humanistic novelty is a small, separate, walled garden for blind visitors, who have a chance to identify flowers and other horticulture by the senses of smell and touch. The plants are chosen especially for the enjoyment of such qualities by the blind.

The Botanic Gardens are right adjacent to the Brooklyn Museum of Arts and Sciences, at a corner of Eastern Parkway.

From Manhattan, subways are the rapid way to get to Prospect Park. Take IRT trains, on either the Lexington or Seventh Avenue lines, to Prospect Park station. Independent Eighth Avenue trains stop for the Grand Army Plaza. For autoists, the simple route is via the Manhattan Bridge and straight out Flatbush Avenue. A car is desirable for circling the parkways.

THE GREAT SAND BARRIERS
Jones Beach and Fire Island

After James II fled the throne of England in 1688, he took refuge in France at the court of Louis XIV. In the ensuing war with Britain and Holland, the French majesty backed the exiled James to create a second front in Ireland in a futile attempt to regain his throne. In the invading army was a Welsh soldier of fortune named Major Thomas Jones, who fought with outstanding valor in the Battle of the Boyne, at which the French and Irish allies were repulsed by an army of England's new king, William III. Back in France, James II rewarded Jones with a commission as a privateer (in effect, a wartime pirate) to seize and plunder enemy ships. The British navy finally cornered Jones' ship in the West Indies, but he escaped and made his way to Long Island, where he began a fresh career.

Thomas Jones won colonial offices, including that of county sheriff, and married a local beauty named Freelove Townsend, whose father gave her a large tract of land bordering Great South Bay as a wedding present. On the ocean side of the bay stretched a long, narrow sand reef that Jones added to his domain by purchasing it from the Indians "for a barrel of good cider." In 1696, Thomas and Freelove built a sturdy home that was half fortress on what later became known as Fort Neck, at the north edge of South Oyster Bay.

When Thomas Jones died in 1713, he was laid to rest on the barrier beach, and, by his wish, these words were carved on his gravestone: "This Seat He Chose, and Here He Fixed His Name."

No doubt Major Jones would have been pleased to know how indelibly and famously he had "fixed his name." Jones Beach

Jones Beach State Park from the air. The myriad specks on the sand are people. At upper left of the picture are crammed parking lots, and beyond them is Zach's Bay.

today is probably justified in its claim of being the largest, most complex seashore park in the world. In a recent season it drew a total of 13,500,000 visitors, and had one peak day of 240,000. Such statistics mean that Jones Beach is the most frequented of all New York state parks. The main reason is its proximity to New York City's millions, and many of the visitors counted are "repeaters." By the nearest express route, it is only 35 miles from midtown Manhattan. (To be fair, of Niagara's 10,000,000 a year, few are repeaters.)

Jones Beach State Park proper is laved by six unbroken miles of surf rolling in from the Atlantic, but it also offers a half-mile of still-water beach on Zach's Bay inside the sand barrier. The entire Jones Beach Island, however, is 17 miles long, including several other beach segments to the eastward, among them the Tobay Beach Bird and Game Sanctuary; Gilgo State Park, which is undeveloped and reserved mainly for fishermen; and some township and private beaches.

For many upstaters, it is surprising to know that New York State has an overall length of 450 miles, owing to the fact that Long Island juts 125 miles into the ocean. The offshore barrier-beach islands, separated intermittently by inlets, extend almost the full length of the southern coast, from Coney Island to Southampton Beach. Hemmed in behind them are the sheltered bays, spanned here and there by bridges, causeways, or ferries. Next in line to the east of Jones Beach is Fire Island, longest of all with its 32 miles. Enclosed behind these two is Great South Bay, famed for its oysters and clams, and for the clannish "baymen" who harvest them.

Early settlers were quick to note the resemblance of Long Island's shape to a giant fish or whale, its nose nibbling at Sandy Hook, its tail branching into two flukes—Montauk Point and Orient Point. The words of Walt Whitman, the island's poet laureate, reflects the illusion: "Starting from fish shape Paumanok where I was born. . ." Paumanok was an Indian name for Long Island.

Before the ice invasion, Long Island was part of the Connecticut land mass, and its now submerged outer margin extends a considerable distance to seaward. The inshore water is proportionately shallow. The mechanics of making a barrier beach are simple. Waves marching in meet friction with the shallow bottom far out, which puts an early brake on their velocity. Water crowding in from behind causes the wave crest to build up and break over, long before reaching shore. The advancing water has scooped up sand and pebbles with its impetus, and this burden is dropped along the breaker line, washing backward a little with the ebb. The space between the new bar and the old shore then became a lagoon.

Recurrent ice sheets bulldozed the Long Island shelf of Connecticut, depositing great heaps of end moraine at their frontal stands, that is, where melting balanced advance. Vast outwash aprons were spread forth beyond the melting front, accounting for the sandy levels such as the Hempstead plains and the Flatbush section of Brooklyn. Since the ocean level at that period was some 300 feet lower than it is today (because of the great amount of water locked up in the glaciers), the outwash material was swept much further south on the rock ledge than the present shoreline. After the normal sea level was restored, much of this debris was given back to Long Island by the surf, so that it now comprises a good portion of the barrier beaches. But the more recent and current substance of these beaches comes from another source. Where the bluffs of the southern (Ronkonkoma) moraine confront the ocean in the Montauk peninsula, their loose material is constantly being eaten away by storm waves. Since the "set" of the ocean is prevailingly west, the morainal rubble is slowly washed along in that direction, ground ever finer as it moves, until it is finally added to the barrier beaches nearer the city.

The name of another man than Thomas Jones is closely interwoven with Jones Beach State Park. That individual was Robert Moses, long-time president of the Long Island State Park Commission as well as of the State Council of Parks. More than any other person, Robert Moses was responsible for the creation not only of Jones Beach but of the entire Long Island system of parks and parkways, as well as most of New York City's complex of highspeed expressways and modern bridges. As a youthful idealist, Moses was impressed with the urgent need of the city's hordes for recreational areas and ways to reach them. He roamed the sparsely peopled regions of Long Island, formulating a visionary network of public parks and of parkways to make them attainable by people who owned cars. By coming into close association with Governor Alfred E. Smith during the 1920s, he gained the political power to make his grand dreams come true. As a product of the sidewalks of New York, Al Smith understood the need, and seized upon state parks as a political asset of wide popular appeal. By 1924, Governor Smith was able to press the legislature into creating a Long Island State Park Commission, then appointed Moses as its president. Other regional park commissions ensued, integrated through a State Council of Parks which chose Moses for its president. Thus the influence of Bob Moses and his visions spread statewide. One finds his name stamped as far afield as Niagara and the St. Lawrence Seaway.

Before 1927, Jones Beach was little known and rarely visited, occupied by only a few fishermen's shacks and cottages. It was almost inaccessible from the land side, even by boat, because of intervening grassy islands and choked channels. Given a state bond issue to work with, Moses set about turning Jones Beach into a recreational paradise. His biggest obstacle was getting title to the land, which was owned by the townships of Oyster Bay and Hempstead; but they were finally persuaded to turn over 2,245 acres for state development. Although the focal point of Moses's dream program was Jones Beach, his roving vision extended to other parts of the island, all the way to Montauk and Orient points and to the sacrosanct "Gold Coast" of the north shore.

In order for the masses of New Yorkers to enjoy the parks of his fancy, Moses knew there had to be through arteries of travel, bypassing villages and growing suburbia. Hence he began planning wide and beautiful parkways simultaneously with the parks. Principally, these were to be the Southern State Parkway and the Northern State Parkway. Spurs from the Southern State to Jones Beach, over causeways, became the Meadowbrook and the Wantagh State Parkways. The low, narrow strand had to be broadened and heightened to accommodate an Ocean Parkway

the full length of the bar as well as space for huge parking lots.
The sand and muck for this purpose were obtained by dredging
26 miles of boat channels through the marshes of South Oyster
Bay, the western arm of Great South Bay. The 17-mile Ocean
Parkway was then laid along the mounded fill, and at its eastern
end the Captree State Park was created, primarily as a marina
center for yachts and fishing boats.

Moses engaged good architects for all park structures,
beginning with two ornate bathhouses spaced 4,000 feet apart;
one had lockers for 10,000 bathers. The beach was fronted by a
boardwalk a mile-and-a-half long, lined by restaurant
concessions, food bars, beach shops, tennis courts, and such sports
facilities as archery ranges and shuffleboard. Beach grass was
transplanted from elsewhere to hold down the blowing sand. The
boardwalk is not merely a hot-weather promenade; many
wintertime visitors come for the sheer pleasure of watching gulls,
surf, and the drama of storms.

Zach's Bay was dredged out on the landward side of the barrier
for a still-water beach and a deep yacht basin. Just offshore in
this bay, Moses built a small island containing an elaborate
open-air theater stage. On shore, facing this stage, was erected a
semicircular grandstand which he named the Marine Stadium,
now known simply as the Jones Beach Theater. Moses introduced
the practice, still continued today, of bringing the company of
some Broadway musical show for open-air performances there
each summer. Guy Lombardo's Royal Canadians orchestra was
long a fixture of these shows.

Beneath its surface, Long Island is a vast reservoir of fresh
water. The glacial deposits piled on top of the bedrock shelf make
ideal aquifers. The depth and grade of the sloping rock, reaching
far out beneath the sea, prevent saltwater from seeping inland
(unless the fresh water should be foolishly overpumped). The
conspicuous landmark of Jones Beach is a handsomely designed
tower of brick and stone, 231 feet high, the pivot of the Central
Mall. This spire was patterned after the Campanile of St. Mark's
Cathedral in Venice, but the comparison ends there, without
bells. In reality, it is the park's water tower, storing 315,000

gallons. The limpid fresh water is pumped from three wells as deep as 980 feet—a figure that suggests the amount of glacial material lying atop the bedrock.

The east–west axis of Fire Island lies slightly south of the Jones Beach island and overlaps it by three miles, separated by the Fire Island Inlet. Fed by the steady accertion of sand from as far east as Montauk Point, Fire Island has grown westward more than six miles since 1670. When built in 1858, the Fire Island lighthouse stood at the western tip of the island; today it thrusts up its beacon four miles east of the tip.

The name Fire Island derives from the fact that a 1685 nautical chart labeled the barrier beach as "Five Islands" because it was, at that time, sliced into five segments by inlet channels. The word "Five" was poorly inscribed, so that later cartographers mistook it for "Fire." (Rival legends insist that it was named for the fires under the try-pots of whalers, which glowed weirdly by night; or that land pirates used to kindle fires on the beach to lure ships upon the shoals for plundering.)

When Robert Moses began his Long Island developments, the only state park on Long Island was a small one on the western end of Fire Island—the Fire Island State Park. After Moses resigned his state parks positions in 1962, the State Council of Parks renamed this park the Robert Moses State Park. It has since undergone improvements akin to those of Jones Beach. The Robert Moses Causeway was completed across Great South Bay to Captree State Park in 1964, and a Robert Moses Bridge was then flung across the Fire Island Inlet.

The bridge aroused keen anxiety among the summer frequenters of Fire Island, upon which no highway has ever encroached, save for a short service road in the Robert Moses State Park. The tradition of handcarts for deliveries to cottages is invincible. The fears of highway extension into the privately owned (and rented) sectors were allayed when the island was designated as the Fire Island National Seashore, preserving it henceforth in its natural state except for the man-made structures already there. Some 18 private-cottage communities are spaced along the barrier beach, served by ferry-boats across the bay.

These will not be condemned, but no future construction will be permitted. The ocean side is now named the Great South Beach.

Just one other bridge, besides the Robert Moses, taps Fire Island. This one is at the far east end of Great South Bay, bringing the William Floyd Parkway across from Smith Point to the Smith-Point County Park, reserved for residents of Suffolk County.

From the New York metropolitan area, beachbound motorists usually head for the Southern State Parkway. Direct exits to Jones Beach are the Meadowbrook State Parkway and the Wantagh State Parkway. For Captree State Park or Robert Moses State Park, the preferred exit is further east to the Robert Moses Causeway.

CAUMSETT STATE PARK
The Fabulous North Shore

The serrated region of the Necks, with its deep-set harbors and bays, bold gravel bluffs fronting Long Island Sound, and myriad yachts and sailboats, was dubbed the Gold Coast long before F. Scott Fitzgerald leased a mansion at Great Neck, drove his Rolls-Royce off a curve and into a pond "because it seemed more fun," and created that flamboyant character Jay Gatsby. The golden sheen of that exclusive shore was like a reflection of the vast wealth and giddy social status of its denizens, whose financial ties were mainly with Wall Street.

During the oligarchic era when Morgans, Astors, and Vanderbilts reigned over the North Shore like uncrowned royalty, it was almost literally impossible for a common citizen to set foot on the beaches of the Sound within the Gold Coast precincts, because he would be liable for trespass. Although changing times and the proliferation of suburbia have lowered the barriers to some extent, restrictions of private property still apply to the waterfront as a whole. The recent opening of Caumsett State Park is a real breakthrough for the general public to Long Island Sound in its western extent nearest "the city."

The further victory of Caumsett is the fact that it encompasses one of the most opulent of the former private estates, making up two-thirds of Lloyd Neck, which protrudes between Oyster Bay and Huntington Bay. In its halcyon epoch, this estate was the principality of Marshall Field III, who inherited the fortune of his grandfather, founder of the great Chicago department store empire. The place includes a score or more of the buildings that Field bestowed upon his domain, and some of these will

The beach front of Caumsett State Park on Long Island Sound. The shore is strewn with varicolored pebbles washed down from the bluffs of Manhasset moraine outwash material.

eventually be put in shape for park use. The central brick mansion is earmarked for the park administrative headquarters. Meanwhile the buildings are closed for lack of state funds to restore them. Among them are indoor tennis courts and horse stables.

For the time being, Caumsett is designated as an environmental park. This means that, although undeveloped, it is open to visitors for picnicking, hiking, use of the bridle trails, and nature-study programs. The pebbled beach can be attained only on foot down a steep incline, but it is decidedly worth the effort.

Lloyd Neck is a large headland—three-and-a-half miles wide by two miles deep—which is almost completely severed from the island by the narrow inlet of Lloyd Harbor. It hangs only by the thin shred of Lloyd Beach, across which the highway enters. The eastern portion of the Neck is occupied by a private residential community.

Lloyd Neck was historically an English manor. Governor Thomas Dongan, as colonial governor of New York under King James II, granted it to Henry Lloyd in 1685, anointing him as Lord of the manor of Queen's Village. Before that, the Indians had known the landmark as Caumsett, the name that Marshall Field revived for his lavish estate.

Long Island Sound was preglacially the valley of an east-flowing river when the island was a part of the New England coast. Tributaries to that river flowed north out of a modest Long Island upland, eroding the side valleys which are now exemplified in the North Shore bays. One such tributary originated the valley of what is now New York City's East River. The glaciers scooped out the larger depression now occupied by the Sound, and much of the rubbish was dumped on Long Island in the form of terminal moraines, chiefly the Ronkonkoma and the Harbor Hill deposits.

Oddly enough, the North Shore Necks, including Lloyd Neck, are not part of the Harbor Hill moraine. Instead, they are largely the product of a much earlier advance than the Wisconsin Ice Sheet which was responsible for both the Ronkonkoma and Harbor Hill terminals. This was the Manhasset Ice Sheet, dated around 300,000 years ago, which did not even reach Long Island. Perhaps 1,000 feet thick, the Manhasset ice front halted somewhere in the depression of the Sound. From that stand, its meltwaters spread a thick outwash apron of sand and gravel an unknown distance across what is now the island. The heaps that appear today in the North Shore bluffs of the Necks are remnants of that outwash material which have been eroded backward by the waters of the Sound. This erosion was probably aided by the action of the later Wisconsin Ice Sheet, which surmounted them to leave its moraines further south on the island. Although some of the bluffs range up to 300 feet above water, the high spots on Lloyd Neck are around 120 feet.

The Harbor Hill moraine, built by the last stand of the Wisconsin Ice Sheet, appears in prominent hills at the inland heads of all the North Shore embayments, as at Roslyn Heights, Cold Spring Harbor, Huntington, and Northport. It is the Harbor Hill ridge that makes the continuous wave-cut bluffs of the north shore from Port Jefferson eastward to Orient Point.

As a student at Eton and Cambridge, Marshall Field III developed a taste for the British manorial style of living and its solid Georgian architecture. After he became a New York financier, he combed Long Island for a place to build an estate along those lines, and found it on Lloyd Neck. He then laid out Caumsett as a nearly self-contained town, with ornate manor houses, guest and servant houses, dairy barns, horse stables, and various athletic facilities such as pools, a golf course, and the indoor tennis arena. The Field ménage kept 85 servants. Twenty-five miles of road twined over the premises. In a lagoon below were dockages for Field's palatial yacht, speedboats, and an amphibian plane that he personally flew for commuting to his Wall Street office. In World War II, he turned the yacht over to the Coast Guard and leased the estate to the Office of War Information for a dollar a year.

The lord of Caumsett died in 1956, leaving $160 million divided between his widow and the Marshall Field Foundation. The widow occupied the main Georgian mansion only part of each year, maintaining other homes elsewhere in the world. The Long

Island State Park Commission cast its eye upon Caumsett, but was discouraged by Mrs. Field's asking price of $8,500,000. When a bond issue for expansion of the state parks system was voted in 1960, the overture was revived, and Mrs. Field settled for $4,278,000. This was the highest price ever paid for one piece of property for park purposes in New York State, and it left no residue for development. Caretakers guard the buildings and keep the grounds in shape for future restoration.

A good view of Long Island Sound may be had from the top of the Lloyd Neck bluff. A pathway leads around and down to the beach, which is strewn with a rich and colorful variety of pebbles, a treasure trove for mineral collectors. The pebbles and larger rocks have dropped out of the glacial heap as it is worn down by waves and weather. The beach, and the water to some distance offshore, also contain many large erratic boulders from the same source.

Toward the base of the eroded bluff, a bed of light-colored clay can be observed, markedly contrasting with the overlying gravels. This is a deposit of Cretaceous age (100 to 120 million years ago) which has never been consolidated into rock. It was laid on top of the Long Island shelf during the final epoch of the Mesozoic Era (age of reptiles), and is the youngest deposit of prehistoric sea-bottom sedimentation known in New York State.

Caumsett State Park is reached by driving either the Long Island Expressway or the Northern State Parkway, taking the exit for New York Avenue (Route 110) north to Huntington. Thence, on West Neck Road, go around Lloyd Beach Road to the Lloyd Harbor Road veering east. The main gate for the park will be encountered along the Lloyd Harbor Road. An eventual parkway approach is envisioned.

Orient Point, the north fluke of the Long Island "whale." Beyond is the
tidal race of Plum Gut, separating the point from Plum Island.

ORIENT POINT
The North Fluke

The Harbor Hill moraine, glacial spine of the Long Island "whale," stretches from the jaws of the Narrows to the tail end of Orient Point. As earlier noted, it comprises the wave-eroded north shore escarpment eastward beyond Port Jefferson. To carry on the whale metaphor, Orient is the north fluke of the tail, opposite the south fluke of Montauk Point, 20 miles distant across Gardiner's Bay and Block Island Sound.

The Orient peninsula, narrowing to a harpoon tip as it stretches northeast 30 miles from Riverhead, makes a tempting goal for motorists, a magnet for curiosity merely from the way it lies on a map. As a practical travel route, the highway terminates at the ferry that crosses Long Island Sound to New London, Connecticut. As a tourist destination, the point offers Orient Beach State Park, with bathing on Gardiner's Bay, picnic grounds, and game fishing. This park also includes the singular hook of Long Beach, which is largely a nature preserve area.

Orient Point, as such, is not to be confused with Orient Beach State Park. As a matter of fact, the Point itself is not even public ground, and the final approach is through uninspiring farmland. In order to reach the gravelly spit without a half-mile's rural hike, a driver has no choice but to trespass on private dirt roads. As a scene, the Point is rather disappointing and not very photogenic. Instead of hurling defiance at Neptune with dramatic heights, as Montauk Point does, Orient dwindles off into a mere fingertip in the water. As someone has felicitously said, it is "a place where the land has not so much boldly stopped as just given up."

Still, there is a peculiar satisfaction about standing at the

N.Y. State Commerce Dept.

land's-end of New York State, as represented in Orient Point.
One reflects that the name means east, or to face toward the east,
and specifically the Far East; and that it must have originated
with seafaring men. Straight ahead, marking the submerged nose,
is the Orient Point lighthouse. Across a mile-and-a-half of
sinister-looking water arises Plum Island, strictly off limits to
visitors because it is occupied by the U.S. Department of
Agriculture for research in dangerous diseases of animals. The
strait between the Point and Plum Island is Plum Gut, the first
escape vent of Long Island Sound into the Atlantic, and through it
surges a tide of fierce power. The deepest sounding in this tidal
race is 190 feet. Plum Gut may possibly have been the place of
the original breakout of the imprisoned waters of the Sound when
it was still dammed by the Harbor Hill moraine as a glacial lake.

     This is the spot where one clearly sees that Orient Point is not
the actual eastern terminus of the moraine after all. The Harbor
Hill ridges continue on northeastward, diving beneath Plum Gut,
surfacing as Plum Island, submerging again to reappear in the
guise of the Gull Islands and Fishers Island, then joining the New
England mainland at Watch Hill, Rhode Island and extending on
to the elbow of Cape Cod.

     The entrance road for Orient Beach State Park turns south from
Route 25 about a mile before the ferry dock. The park embraces
Long Beach, a four-mile spit that loops backward, like a
fishhook, from the Point into Gardiner's Bay. The recreational
area of the park, with a fine sandy beach and appurtenances, is
two miles in from the entrance, and most visitors are content to
stop there. For that matter, driving further on Long Beach is out
of the question, unless by special service vehicles able to take the
stress. From there on, the hook, about two miles to the end,
consists of large, wave-tossed pebbles, cobblestones, even
boulders—moraine materials that have been washed out of Plum
Gut and transported around to westward by the tidal currents and
storm waves. The rough and treacherous surface makes walking
for any distance thoroughly disagreeable.

     The stony extension of Long Beach is one of the truly bizarre
spots in New York State, and park authorities are making sure

that it will be preserved that way. The only practical, as well as comfortable, means of inspecting the full length is by boat, landing at will. A striking and freakish feature encountered at intervals is a series of gravel wash-over deposits produced by violent storm action from the south, Tempestuous waves laden with coarse sand and gravel, leap as far as 200 feet across the rocky foreshore to fill up marshy places on the lee side. The resulting heaps are terraced and leveled off like tabletops.

The extreme western end of the Long Beach spit is a wildfowl sanctuary from which the public is excluded in favor of the birds.

The Long Island Expressway terminates in a "Y" four miles short of Riverhead. For Orient Point, take county road No. 58 left at the fork, then the Northville Turnpike which comes to a dead end at Sound Avenue. There turn east on county highway No. 27 through to Greenport where it runs into Route 25 for the rest of the way to Orient. This itinerary bypasses the towns along the old Route 25 and picks up good views of the Sound. For travelers wishing to visit both flukes of the island, there is a crossway, Route 114, using two ferries to traverse Shelter Island between Greenport and Sag Harbor.

The "walking dunes" of Hither Hills State Park. The fine sand here blankets hillocks of the Ronkonkoma glacial moraine, and constantly shifts position under the spur of ocean winds.

HITHER HILLS
The Walking Dunes

By "Hither Hills," pioneer Long Islanders meant "the hills this side of Montauk Point." For the most part a wind-sculptured wilderness of abnormally high sand knolls, the Hither Hills State Park bisects the waist of the slender peninsula like a cummerbund 10 miles before Montauk Point State Park. Its showcase is a magnificent beach on the seashore, but behind that rises a desolate upland of blown sand which has no counterpart elsewhere on the island.

The Hither Hills comprise all the northern portion of the park's width, which varies up to two miles, with water frontages on both Napeague Bay and Napeague Harbor. The Montauk Point State Parkway shuns the hilly terrain, passing between it and the bathing beach, which is continuous with the superb Napeague Beach on the west. These are not barrier beaches, as they are attached to the island's mainland. Hither Hills is the only state park on Long Island that has public campsites facing directly on the Atlantic Ocean.

The Napeague Beach conceals the location of a former open channel that connected the ocean with Napeague Bay on the north side of the peninsula, making a separate island of the Montauk end. As sand from the wave erosion of Montauk Point was wafted westward, it built a barrier beach across the entrance to this strait, finally closing it off. This accounts for the Napeague Harbor, which washes the base of the Hither Hills on their western flank.

The entire Montauk peninsula, some 40 miles long, is a seaward extension of the Ronkonkoma moraine. The frontal margin of the Wisconsin Ice Sheet, at maximum advance, stood on that line until perhaps 20,000 years ago. An interval of warmer climate ensued, causing a retreat of the ice at least into New England. When the ice sheet later readvanced, it came to a more northerly halt along the line of the Harbor Hill moraine. The two end moraines overlap toward the west, as previously explained, but they separate eastward like the blades of a pair of scissors, with their pivotal point at Lake Success near Manhasset.

The Ronkonkoma moraine takes its name from Lake Ronkonkoma, which, like Lake Success, occupies a large kettle-hole left by the melting out of a buried block of glacial ice. Lake Ronkonkoma nestles in the morainal hills near Smithtown and Hauppauge.

When the Long Island State Park Commission was created in 1924, the Hither Hills were the first property appropriated for park use under the right of eminent domain, probably owing to their uselessness for anything else. The mile-and-a-half of ideal beach, to be sure, was what made the property attractive, and most park visitors understandably cling to the waterfront.

Those who are inquisitive enough to explore the hills behind must face some difficulties. The grooves that make a pretense of being roads are, with the exception of two or three, so deep with fine sand as to be very discouraging for any but four-wheeled vehicles. At least one passable road does find its way through to the shore of Napeague Bay, on the western fringe of the park. Nobody gets acquainted with the Hither Hills, however, without some arduous footwork. It isn't so much the height, which is not great, as the yielding sand. For every foot gained, one slips backward six inches, and shoes become sand-logged. The expenditure of energy is more than justified by the rewarding view of the weird region, with the Atlantic Ocean rolling to infinity on one hand and Napeague Bay on the other.

These hills are more complex than mere giant sand dunes. Some rise over 100 feet high. Their core foundations are solid mounds of the Ronkonkoma moraine. The hillocks of glacial debris have been blanketed over, hidden, and heightened by wind-whipped sand. The so-called "walking dunes" are a grotesque phenomenon of the area. Blowing sand, like drifting snow, buries scrub-oak trees up to their crotches or beyond, so that the upper branches grow out almost parallel to the surface level, creating the illusion that the trees are trunkless. The sand keeps moving onward—or "walking"—uncovering the gaunt skeletons of dead trees in its wake. In some instances, the dunes have buried and smothered entire stands of oak woods. Still another oddity of the Hither Hills is seen in what are called "blowouts." On the western flanks of some larger hills, concavities of almost cavelike proportions occur. These have been scooped out by strong, dry west winds, in contrast to the moisture-laden winds that blow in from the adjacent sea.

From New York City, the most direct approach to the Montauk peninsula and Hither Hills is the Sunrise Highway (Route 27). This highway is, in effect, an eastward extension of the Southern State Parkway, which comes to an end at Heckscher State Park on Great South Bay. If one's main route east is the Long Island Expressway, veer onto Route 24 from Riverhead.

The Montauk lighthouse warns mariners off the easternmost tip of New York State. It stands on a portion of the Ronkonkoma glacial moraine, which is being inexorably eaten away by Atlantic storm waves.

MONTAUK POINT
The South Fluke

The state of New York, which sets forth placidly enough at the
western extreme near Ripley on Lake Erie, comes to an abrupt
and jolting halt where the eastern headland of Long Island is
eternally at war with the Atlantic Ocean. Here the state is losing
length at the rate of perhaps two feet a year. The famous
Montauk lighthouse will have to be moved before many more
years.

Montauk Point is no armor-plated Gibraltar, and its
vulnerability to the often savage assaults of the sea enhances the
drama of the spectacle. It ranks as the windiest spot on the
Atlantic coast. The Ronkonkoma moraine confronts the enemy
that is ruthlessly hacking it away, without so much as a small
offshore island to shield it. The debris of the battle is refined
down to the consistency of sugar, and distributed to all the
westerly beaches as far as Coney Island.

The south fluke of the Long Island "whale" juts into the open
Atlantic a good 10 miles farther than Orient Point does into the
Sound. Its exposed bluff of glacial gravel and silt rises 60 to 80
feet above the surf. Fortunately, the pace of erosion is retarded
by a surplus clay content in the mix, which serves as a binder.
Huge boulders, transported by ice from sources throughout New
England and even into Canada, have been arranged by park
engineers around the base of the point like stolid sentinels as a
semiprotective breakwater.

Surely the most photographed object on Long Island is the
Montauk lighthouse. An octagonal tower 108 feet tall, it flashes a
powerful rotating beam of light far out to sea. Mariners have

always had ample need for that beacon. The waters off Montauk Point, where strong tidal currents emerging from Long Island Sound clash with the colder ocean tides, are notoriously treacherous, and the resultant turmoil is frequently whipped simultaneously by conflicting winds. This stretch of awesome water is known as the Rip, and was the cause of many a tragic shipwreck in old sailing days. Although celebrated for its game fishing, it is risky even for high-powered fishermen's craft. As recently as 1952 a large fishing schooner, the *Pelican*, capsized in the Rip and 45 of the 68 persons aboard were lost.

The original Montauk Light, constructed in 1795–1797, was the first coastal lighthouse to be financed by the U.S. Congress—that is, as distinct from the earlier colonial lighthouses that were confiscated at the time of the Revolution. At that time it stood 297 feet back from the brink of the bluff. The tower has since been rebuilt and enlarged more than once on the same site; today it stands a mere 50 feet or so from the brink.

In former years visitors were admitted to climb the spiral stairway and share the outlook with the keeper of the light, but their numbers increased so greatly that the Coast Guard had to suspend the privilege. A considerable area around the tower is enclosed by a high chain-link fence patrolled by armed guards. Only at certain weekend hours are the gates opened for the public to roam closer. The lawn is strikingly green and well groomed. The spume, the dense fogs, and storm lashings generally keep the grass of Montauk Point in the best of health. From colonial times, farmers of the eastern island region used to drive their herds and flocks out to the Point for summer grazing.

The landscape of the Montauk peninsula is of the typical glacial knob-and-kettle variety. It contains a number of kettle-ponds, among them Oyster Pond, Big Reed Pond, and Fort Pond, where blocks of buried ice melted out. The largest is Montauk Lake, which was until recently a freshwater pond; an artificial channel has been cut through to join it with Block Island Sound and create the Montauk Harbor, so useful to fishing boats. The Point itself was at one time a separate island, cut off from the remainder of the peninsula by a strait through Fort Pond to Fort Pond Bay.

The name of the Point is derived from the Montauk tribe of Indians, who inhabited most of Long Island. They were gradually subjugated by the fiercer Pequot Indians of Connecticut, against whom they maintained palisaded fortifications on Montauk Point. The Indian Fields, passed en route to the Point, were a favorite camping ground.

The Montauk Point State Parkway, eastward from the Hither Hills, is one of the truly memorable scenic roads in the state, with its blend of intriguing landscape and marvelous seascapes. The rolling hillocks of morainal origin have often been referred to as the Montauk Downs, in a comparison to the famed Sussex Downs of southeast England. (The difference is that the English Downs are higher and composed of chalk.)

Along the way, the remains of a grandiose scheme of the 1920s to transform the Montauk peninsula into a "Miami Beach of the North" make an incongruous sight. That was the brainstorm of Carl G. Fisher, a millionaire who had built the Indianapolis Speedway and developed Miami Beach. He and his associates obtained options on 10,000 acres of Montauk property to indulge the dream of a Florida-type boom—plush hotels, gambling casinos, yacht clubs, golf courses, polo fields, and of course lavish residences. Near Fort Pond, a Montauk Manor Hotel and a seven-story office building were actually constructed, and they still stand as relics of a busted bubble. The Long Island State Park Commission began appropriating land on the peninsula; then the Florida boom collapsed, the stock-market crash interposed, and Fisher never exercised his options.

As in the case of Orient Point, Montauk is not the veritable ending of the Ronkonkoma moraine. While the ocean level was some 300 feet lower than at present, with vast quantities of water locked up in the ice caps and glaciers of the world, the Ronkonkoma front reached many miles to the eastward on the sea floor. Outlying remnants of the moraine high enough to be showing above the restored water are strung along as Block Island, Martha's Vineyard, and Nantucket. Geologists estimate that the eastern coastline of Long Island has retreated 10,000 to 15,000 feet in the past 5,000 years.

The quintessential flavor of Montauk cannot be fully

appreciated without venturing along the narrow fringe of beach at the foot of the main bluff. This is no beach for swimming. It is carpeted with pebbles, cobblestones, and coarse grains of sand that have not yet been machined by very much wave treatment. In places the walking degenerates into splashy boulder-hopping. The rapidly eroding earthen wall of the bluff is the backdrop; the ever-pounding surf is the music.

Somehow the giant boulders that the park people have lined up around the base of the disintegrating escarpment bring to mind old King Canute seated on the shore of Britain, vainly forbidding the tide to come in.

The approach directions for the Hither Hills State Park apply similarly to Montauk Point, adding 10 miles of distance. The Sunrise Highway, Route 27, extends the full way from the Queens–Nassau County boundary to the Shinnecock Hills, at which point it merges into the Montauk State Parkway.

BYWAYS AND DETOURS

What follows is a roundup of additional places that, although not in the front rank of New York's natural attractions, merit visitation for certain scenic or geologic reasons. Some of these may hold special appeal for wanderers with a taste for the offbeat.

LOCKPORT'S CANAL LOCKS

The final hurdle to overcome before the Erie Canal could attain the level of Buffalo and Lake Erie was the escarpment of Lockport dolostone, the same thick stratum of Silurian age that makes Niagara Falls. In choosing the location for locks that would raise and lower canal traffic a matter of 60 feet, the engineers, in effect, founded the city of Lockport. Before the Niagara River settled on its present route, the drainage of Lake Erie fanned out helter-skelter over the plateau of lime-rock, on which the glacier had left irregular deposits. The water spilled over the cliff edge at random spots. One of these was at Lockport, where the falls were major enough that the spot nearly became the permanent location, and where the falls hewed the beginnings of not one but two gorges, 18 miles east of Lewiston. These made ready-cut notches in the dolostone for the canal locks, and the eastern one was adopted.

Twin sets of five locks each were built side by side to handle traffic in both directions, and were an engineering marvel of the time. First made of wood, they were later replaced with stone. Each lock in series provided a lift of 12 feet. It was their completion that permitted the triumphal procession of canalboats from Buffalo to New York in 1825. When the State Barge Canal superseded the Erie in this century, the number of locks was reduced to two giants, but one set of the old locks was preserved for history. Besides two observation decks and a Lock Walkway, the contemporary scene has a yet higher Canal Overlook.

A mile to the westward is the Gulf, a much larger incipient gorge, heavily wooded and preserved by the city as the Gulf Wilderness. Outwater Park, which affords a scenic view of the Gulf and the Lake Ontario plain, is reached via Transit Street, north to Outwater Drive. Lockport itself is approached from Exit 49 of the Thruway, taking Route 78 due north; or from Lewiston east on Route 104 (Ridge Road) to Wrights Corners, then south on Route 78.

CHAUTAUQUA LAKE

No place in Chautauqua County, it has been said, is more than a half-hour from open water. The lake by that name is the central feature, whereas Lake Erie forms the slanting northern boundary. Chautauqua Lake, 25 miles long on a diagonal bias, is celebrated for the Chautauqua Institution, hotbed of culture, on its northwest shore; and also for its muskellunge fishing. It is a congenial lake in a gently glaciated setting. In shape resembling a bag tied in the middle, it is freakishly narrow at Bemus Point where cars cross on a ferry, almost the last remaining in upstate. This ferry is doomed, as a bridge .9-mile long is scheduled for completion in 1982. The bridge will permit the extension of the Southern Tier Expressway (Route 17) straight on to the Pennsylvania border. The lake valley was probably two valleys preglacially, divided by a rock ridge at Bemus Point from which a stream flowed northwest into the Erian River. The glacier knocked out the divide and dammed off the valley at the north end, so that Chautauqua Lake now drains south into the Allegheny River at Warren, Pennsylvania. It made a favorite route for French explorers, shortening the portages between Lake Erie and the Ohio River system. Long Point, a needlelike cape jutting from the east shore above Bemus Point, is a state park with 1,700 feet of lake frontage. The lake can be reached from Exit 60 of the Thruway at Westfield. Pending completion of the bridge, Route 17 serves the east shore, and Route 394 out of Jamestown the west shore. Two overlooks on Route 17 (one for each lane) between Jamestown and Bemus Point provide good views of the lake.

SENECA OIL SPRING

The earliest discovery of petroleum in America on record was in a small pond near the present village of Cuba, in which oil rose through the water. Indians had found it long before any white man, and they jealously guarded it. To the Iroquois, this spot was a kind of shrine. They collected the oil by spreading blankets on the surface and wringing them out, and journeyed far to get it. They ascribed magical healing powers to the stuff, used it as a base for body paints, and poured it on tribal fires to make them flare. The first printed report of the Seneca oil spring was in a *Histoire de Canada* published in Paris in 1632. It quoted a letter written in 1627 by a Franciscan friar, who said that the Senecas had shown him "a good grade of oil which the Indians called Antonontons." Jesuit missionaries later described the pond as "a thick stagnant water which when lighted would burn like brandy." Under the Treaty of Big Tree, signed at Geneseo in 1797, one square mile around the pond was made, and still is, an Indian reservation, although no Indians ever dwelt there. The oil long since vanished from the water, as pumping of the Olean and Richburg oil fields depleted the underground source. The murky pond, some 20 feet in diameter, is the centerpiece of a vest-pocket park. Bronze tablets on a nearby monument relate the story. In 1927 the New York State Oil Producers Association dedicated the momument in observance of the 300th anniversary of the discovery of oil in America. Cuba is 15 miles northeast of Olean on the Southern Tier Expressway (Route 17). Two miles west of the village on Route 408, turn north one mile on the Cuba Lake road.

ALLEGANY OIL FIELD

Oil wells are an uncommon sight in New York State, but quite a
collection of them may be seen in Allegany County without
leaving the highway. Along a 10-mile stretch of Route 417
between Wellsville and Bolivar, about 1,000 wells are usually in
operation on the hillslopes, and the odor of petroleum hangs in
the narrow valley. The pumping involves secondary recovery of
oil by water flooding of the wells. Spiderlike black rods radiate
from central pumphouses to work the pumpjacks. Some wells are
active in dooryards beside the highway, and one is conspicuously
located at a church corner. Route 417 can be picked up east out
of Olean or west out of Wellsville. From the Southern Tier
Expressway (Route 17), Wellsville is reached via Route 19 south
from Belvidere.

PETROLIA

The first petroleum boomtown in Allegany County is now a
ghosttown, but its site and a few reminders are preserved at
Petrolia, a crossroads hamlet near Wellsville. Here the Allegany
Oil Field was tapped in 1879 by a well called the Triangle No. 1.
An imposing tablet telling the story of the strike is anchored in a
huge boulder standing at the Petrolia corners. It was erected by
the New York Oil Producers Association in 1929, the fiftieth
anniversary of the event. The capped casing of the well is in a
nearby field. Petrolia is found by driving three miles west from
Wellsville on Route 417, then south two miles on a blacktop road.

CORNELL UNIVERSITY CAMPUS

Cornell University at Ithaca is generally acknowledged to be the
most attractive college campus in New York State. Although it
has become cluttered with new buildings, the natural beauty of its
environment, framed by two picturesque gorges and giving a
superb vista of the glacially mounded Cayuga Inlet valley,
remains unaltered. The campus proper is sliced off on the north
by the Fall Creek gorge and on the south by Cascadilla gorge,

both amply bridged and viewable. Fall Creek is the largest of all
streams that drop from hanging valleys in the Finger Lakes
region. Its gorge is exceptionally deep where it borders the
campus. A suspension footbridge crossing it from the
fraternity-house neighborhood on Cayuga Heights is the prize
vantage point. A series of waterfalls and rapids bring Fall Creek
down 400 feet in less than a mile. The final plunge to the Cayuga
Lake level is Ithaca Falls, one of the truly superior Finger Lakes
cataracts when at full flow. These falls may be frontally viewed
from a bridge near Ithaca High School at the north end of the
city. At the head of the gorge, the Triphammer Falls amounts to
a dam impounding Beebe Lake, a small gem of a lake that
occupies a wider interglacial gorge section (that is, first eroded
during a prior withdrawal of the ice). At the opposite boundary
of the campus, the Cascadilla gorge is less spectacular but has
stairways and an enjoyable nature trail through its bottom.
Cayuga Lake itself is not within sight from the quadrangle, but
can be seen by climbing the Library Tower. The Baker
Laboratory of Chemistry stands on a high "fossil" delta that Fall
Creek built in glacial Lake Ithaca. Such steplike delta terraces are
common around the mouths of Finger Lakes gorges.

GENESEE GORGE AT ROCHESTER
The Genesee River has been doubly diligent since it was freed by
the ice. In addition to the grandeurs at Letchworth State Park, it
is the author of a surplus gorge through the midst of Rochester.
Like the Portage chasm at Letchworth, the latter plunges the
stream over three waterfalls, down to the level of Lake Ontario.
Unhappily, the rapid growth and industrialization of the city
permitted what should have been another fine spectacle to
degenerate and become largely closed off from view. Thanks to
the waterpower, Rochester became the first flour-milling capital
of America. The Genesee Falls (the upper), with a total 92-foot
descent, used to be a celebrated sight for which trains stopped to
let passengers look. In recent years a campaign has been
launched to restore the abused gorge to some of its pristine

splendor. The Upper Falls Terrace Park has been developed at midtown with an observation deck overlooking the Genesee Falls, whose beauty is still marred by a dam. By removing buildings, the Main Street bridge has been opened up. The lower falls is higher (105 feet), but disfigured by a power plant; a view is obtainable from the Driving Park Avenue bridge in the north part of town. There is no good viewpoint for the main gorge or the middle falls; Seneca Park comes nearest. St. Paul Street and Lake Avenue flank the gorge on either side, both giving access to the Driving Park Avenue bridge.

PINNACLE HILLS

Toward the southern fringes of Rochester rises a prominent east–west rank of steep glacial ridges known as the Pinnacle Hills. One of these is monopolized by the ornamentally flowered Highland Park, famed for its luxurious lilacs. Cobb's Hill Park claims another, with an oval municipal reservoir encircled by a pleasant parkway affording panoramic views over the cityscape. The central Pinnacle Hill is usurped by some private dwellings and a cluster of radio and television antennae. These hills belong to a kame-moraine range representing a temporary halt of the ice front in retreat after piling the lavish deposits of the Mendon Ponds Park. This recessional moraine was a key factor in blocking the Genesee River from regaining its preglacial route through the channel of Irondequoit Bay. The river was backed up into a lake behind the barrier for some time, finally breaking through west of Highland Park (about where the University of Rochester campus is today) to begin cutting the Rochester gorge to Lake Ontario. Highland Park is reached from downtown Rochester by Mt. Hope Avenue (Route 15). Monroe Avenue (Route 31) leads directly to Cobb's Hill Park. Highland Avenue, skirting the southern base of the Pinnacle group, is a link between those two streets.

TULLY VALLEY

Not all Finger Lakes valleys now contain lakes. The great Tully valley south of Syracuse is the most striking of several empty

valleys that formerly held high-level glacial lakes. It might have
been one of the major Finger Lakes if it had not been drained.
Onondaga Lake at Syracuse is a remnant of glacial Lake Tully in
a northerly extension of its valley. An ice tongue had sculptured
the valley with the typical U-shaped profile, leaving it dammed at
the south end by a thick loop of kame-moraine deposits below the
village of Tully (a highway now crosses that loop). The resulting
Lake Tully doomed itself by ferreting out a spillway at the north
across the series of rock ridges at Syracuse into the Mohawk
Valley (see the chapter on Clark Reservation). Today this
magnificent valley is drained only by the small Onondaga Creek.
The cross-state Route 20 swoops down into and out of it by stiff
grades. Interstate 81 parallels the east rim and, six miles out of
Syracuse in the southbound lanes, provides a turnout for an
overview. The lake-bottom floor of the valley may be driven on
Route 11-A between Cardiff and Tully.

CHITTENANGO FALLS

On its way to Oneida Lake, the Chittenango Creek descends the
north margin of the Allegheny Plateau through a narrow valley
which constricts into a gorge where the Chittenango Falls foams
down 134 feet over a series of resistant strata. The picturesque
cascade is the cynosure of a refreshing state park. It resulted from
a glacial diversion of the stream over a wide terrace of the
Onondaga limestone. Its evolution was more complicated than
would seem from what meets the eye. Three stages of gorge
development are identified in the park, the earlier two efforts
having been filled in by readvances of the ice. The oldest gorge
section, which branches off at nearly right angles below the falls,
was evidently eroded during an interglacial period of many
thousands of years. Whereas the recent gorge is barely 200 feet
long, the buried one extends more than eight times that length.
Some of the bouldery fill at its head has been reexcavated by the
postglacial stream, and material from it is used by the highway in
climbing up to the terrace level. Chittenango Falls is easily
accessible by a short detour from the Thruway, leaving at Exit 34
to Canastota; thence west on Route 5 to Chittenango, and south a
few miles on Route 13.

HERKIMER DIAMONDS

The countryside north of the Mohawk River between Little Falls and Herkimer is prospecting ground for the attractive quartz crystals known as Herkimer diamonds. There is nothing scenic about them, but they are an interesting geologic novelty. "Rock hounds" (hobbyists) from all over the nation come there to hack the Little Falls dolostone, and some ordinary tourists drop by to watch them, or perhaps have a hand at it themselves. These nondiamonds are hexagonal quartz prisms of amazing clarity, whose pyramidal facets resemble those of cut gemstones. Many collectors fancy them in jewelry settings. They are found in small rock cavities called vugs, where they crystallized from silicates held in solution by trickling water. The owners of several "diamond farms" keep the topsoil cleared from the parent dolostone and make a business of admitting amateur prospectors for a modest per-diem fee. Digging tools may be rented on the premises, and gem shops have choice "diamonds" for sale. The "farms" center around Middleville, on Route 28 some eight miles north of Thruway Exit 30, and continue east to near Fonda.

CANAJOHARIE POTHOLE

The Canajoharie Creek debouches into the village of Canajoharie directly out of a sizable gorge. In the lower reaches of this gorge, the village maintains Wintergreen Park, the key feature of which is a large pothole in the creek bed. Canajoharie takes special pride in this pothole for which the village was named. The Mohawks called it "Can-a-jo-harie," meaning "the pot that washes itself." The current from a low waterfall enters the cavity with a swirling motion so that gravel and sand perpetually scour its sides. The pothole is nearly a perfect circle, at 20 feet in diameter and over eight feet deep—one of the largest potholes in the state. The village keeps it clean of debris and children use it for a swimminghole.

Canajoharie (of Beechnut fame) is across the Mohawk River from Exit 29 of the Thruway. Drive straight through the business center, then left on Moyer Street. A short mile uphill turn right on Floral Avenue, which comes to a dead end just above the pothole. A little further on Moyer Street is the signed entrance to Wintergreen Park, a woodsy creekside haven for picnicking and camping. When the water is low, the pothole may be reached by walking down the creek bed.

GREAT SACANDAGA LAKE
The Sacandaga Reservoir, whose sluice gates were closed in 1930 for flood control of the Hudson River, is the largest man-made body of water wholly within New York State boundaries. In area it approximates Lake George. The state legislature of 1968 upgraded its public image with the name Great Sacandaga Lake. The reservoir is nearly an exact duplication of a previous lake left behind by the glacier—a lake that had since emptied itself.

Before the Ice Age the Sacandaga River, draining much of the southern Adirondacks, had flowed south into the Mohawk, and hence the Hudson. The glacier dumped a heavy complex of kames across its old route between Gloversville and Broadalbin. Thus blockaded, the postglacial river backed up into a vast, Y-shaped lake, at whose northeast prong the water found a spillway over a ridge at Conklingville into the upper Hudson. When the high waterfall there had slashed a narrow gorge through the divide, the lake drained out, leaving rich farmland and marshes. By that act, the Sacandaga River became the largest Adirondack tributary of the Hudson and the major cause of its devastating spring floods. To govern these deluges, the Hudson River Regulating District built the Conklingville Dam across the ready-made gorge. So closely did the resulting reservoir repeat the earlier lake that in some places its waves have lapped on the original glacial shoreline. The straight north-northeast trending escarpments bordering the lake are striking fault-line scarps.

In the total scale of Adirondack scenery, Great Sacandaga Lake is not a premium exhibit. Nevertheless, the drive around its perimeter roads with a crossing of the dam is pleasurable, especially in the fall foliage season. Its mountains are in the

foothill category. There is a good bathing beach at the
Northampton Beach State Campsite. From Thruway Exit 27 at
Amsterdam, take Route 30 north to Sacandaga, where a bridge to
Northville leads to the road encircling the lake.

McCAULEY MOUNTAIN

The Fulton Chain, a connected string of eight small lakes much
favored by canoeists, stretches from Old Forge to Raquette Lake
in the southwestern Adirondacks. These lakes occupy glacially
scoured basins chiseled out of a relatively weak strip of
meta-sedimentary rocks between ridges. They are named after
Robert Fulton of steamboat fame, who had made a study of
canals in France and England and was consequently appointed in
1811 to a State Canal Commission to help reconnoiter a route for
the proposed Erie Canal. Fulton took it upon himself to explore a
potential digression through the lower Adirondacks, investigating
the chain at that time known as the Middle Branch Moose Lakes.
Although he dismissed them in his report as "inexpedient" for the
canal, he wrote so glowing a description of these lakes that
newspapers dubbed them the Fulton Chain. A choice view of the
first four of the numbered lakes is available from the summit of
McCauley Mountain, attainable by a chair lift two-and-a-half
miles northeast of Old Forge on a town highway. The mountain
is a ski resort in winter, but its lift is operated in summer and fall
for the scene. The crest is 2,334 feet high, and the distant
silhouettes of Whiteface and Mount Marcy are visible under the
right atmospheric conditions.

THE NEWCOMB OUTLOOK

Main travel routes encircle the Adirondack High Peaks region like
a giant's lasso, but it is not easy to find comprehensive horizon
views from the highways. The finest such vista from the southern
side is afforded by a turnout maintained as a public service by the
Town of Newcomb beside Route 28-N about 15 miles east of
Long Lake. Twelve of the major summits are lined up in

sequence. The property for the outlook was donated to the
township for that purpose by the Finch-Pruyn Company, Inc.
(paper mills), and was developed as a picnic and rest area. A
large signboard duplicates the view in miniature, identifying the
names and altitudes of the peaks. The mountains seen include, in
order, Santanoni, Andrew, Henderson, MacNaughton, the
McIntyre Range (four summits), Colden, Skylight, Marcy, and
Haystack. Route 28-N was designated, by a recent act of the
legislature, as the Roosevelt-Marcy Memorial Highway. In 1901,
when it was a narrow, muddy wagon road, Theodore Roosevelt
became president while he was being driven along it through a
dark and rainy night to the Delaware & Hudson railhead at North
Creek. He had been summoned from a climb of Mount Marcy.
A stone monument at the roadside marks the approximate spot he
was passing at the moment when President McKinley died of an
assassin's bullet in Buffalo.

TAHAWUS AND TITANIUM

No other industry in New York State can claim so majestic a
scenic setting as the titanium mining operation of NL Industries,
Inc. Its open-pit mines and concentrating mill are an alien
enclave in the heartland of the Adirondack High Peaks. The
plant offices stare across the torn valley of the infant Hudson
River at Mount Santanoni. Mounts Marcy, Algonquin, and
Colden can be seen in glimpses from a company road along the
west bank of the river. This industry flourishes in the midst of the
Forest Preserve because the property was staked out by the
Adirondac Iron Works long before the "forever wild" clause was
grafted into the state constitution. It has remained in private
hands ever since. A primary reason for the decline of the iron
mining was that the ore contained an "impurity," titanium, a
metal for which no use was known at the time. Two miners'
villages, Tahawus and Adirondac, were deserted and huge heaps
of the waste titanium tailings lay forgotten. Uses for titanium,
and a method for its refining, were discovered in the present
century. It was urgently needed in World War II, (it was used in

paints, in smoke-screens, and in certain high-strength metals) and the National Lead Company acquired the property, running in a railroad line. A section of the Hudson River channel was since relocated westward because it was underlain by rich ore. Now, the iron content is the "impurity." (The National Lead Company has altered its name to NL Industries.)

Although visitors are not admitted to the plant, they can park in an adjacent plaza and, through a tall chain-link fence, watch mining operations in an awesomely deep quarry. Samples of the heavy ilmenite ore are free for the taking. From Route 28-N, roughly midway between North Creek and Long Lake, an eight-mile company highway branches north to the titanium workings.

LAKE PLACID

By an odd quirk, the famous resort village of Lake Placid is situated not on Lake Placid but on Mirror Lake. Lake Placid is over beyond Mirror Lake, separated by a narrow strand, and Mirror Lake is part of its outlet system. Lake Placid laves the southern base of Whiteface, from whose summit it appears in the shape of a ladder, with two rectangular islands down the middle between the rungs. These are Moose Island and Buck Island, which, at 300 feet above water, are the highest as well as largest islands in any Adirondack lake.

The sidepieces of the "ladder" are mapped as East Lake and West Lake; before glaciation they were parallel stream valleys parted by an unbroken ridge. A local glacier from the flank of Whiteface kept on operating after the main ice sheet withdrew, gouging these twin valleys abnormally deep (as much as 300 feet below the present water level). The crosspieces, or rungs, represent fault zones hacked out by erosion. The Whiteface glacier heaped moraine detritus at its forefront, making the knobby terrain on which the village and the Lake Placid Club are laid out. Mirror Lake is a kettle-pond left by the melting of a block of ice buried in the morainal stuff.

No road circles Lake Placid, as its sides are too steep. The only way to get around it handily is by tour boat; an interesting cruise takes off from Holiday Harbor. The shores of the lake are largely private and occupied by elegant summer mansions of the wealthy.

Route 73 passes through Lake Placid village. To find Holiday Harbor and the tour boat, follow the west shore drive beside Mirror Lake.

CROWN POINT

The Champlain Bridge to Vermont crosses one of the tightest squeezes of Lake Champlain, from Crown Point to Chimney Point, a scant half-mile. Beyond the bridge the lake broadens abruptly, presenting a superb waterscape as viewed from Crown Point. The geographic Crown Point is seven miles north of the village so named. The Crown Point Reservation is a National Historic Landmark—for good reason. The French were first to fortify the point, in 1731, with Fort St. Frederic. The British under Lord Jeffrey Amherst captured it in 1759 and erected a much larger Fort Amherst. The ruins of the latter, including several roofless stone barracks, are remarkably well preserved.

Crown Point is the north end of a large peninsula, with Bulwagga Bay indented on its west side. The slender part of the lake southward from the Champlain Bridge was presumably the course of a preglacial tributary to a master Champlain River flowing north into Canada. By sharp contrast, Bulwagga Bay is two miles wide and quite deep to its true rock bottom, and points due south toward Lake George. It seems that the ancient Ticonderoga River, draining the Lake George basin northward from the Narrows, eroded this valley to make the Champlain River. Bulwagga Bay shows signs of vigorous glaciation, indicating that the Champlain ice lobe adopted that route south, and in its retreat left morainal deposits southward across the valley that now confines the bay. Although a glacially dammed. Lake Champlain persisted at a higher level, its outflow apparently used the narrow southerly extension to Whitehall, creating the gorgelike characteristics that are seen today.

Exit 28 of the Adirondack Northway (I-87) taps into Route 74 eastward to Ticonderoga; there a north turn on Route 9-N leads to Crown Point.

STARK'S KNOB

Close to the west bank of the Hudson above Schuylerville there is a hump of blackish rock, 200 feet high, which is at once a geologic and a historic curiosity—nothing else. It bears the name Stark's Knob because General John Stark mounted cannon on its top to help entrap Burgoyne's army after the Battle of Saratoga. For years a state marker identified the thing as an "Extinct Volcano." The tablet was quietly removed after a fresh study proved otherwise. The stone is basalt, of volcanic origin indeed, but the eruption did not occur here. It is even remotely possible that it occurred in northwest Africa. Puzzled by the peculiar makeup of the mass, geologists formerly mistook it for the neck, or core, of a small volcano. It is typified by lumps, big and small, jammed together, and these were thought to be fireballs that had fallen back into the lava during eruption. The lumps have since been identified as pillow lava, a form taken by molten basalt cooling underwater, as in known flows on Hawaii that have run off into the sea. The material of Stark's Knob has no "roots"; it penetrates no more than 200 feet underground and is totally unrelated to the surrounding Hudson River slates. It is now interpreted as an erosion remnant of a much larger sheet of basalt spewed forth as a submarine lava flow in an Ordovician sea; and as part of the Taconic klippe, which avalanched off from the New England "Alps" during the last contact between the continent of Africa and North America. Could it be that some African rock was mingled in the mélange? Whatever the case, the knob was being quarried for road metal, making a great cavity in its eastern face, when the state intervened. To find it, leave the Northway (I-87) at Saratoga Springs, drive east on Route 29 to Schuylerville, then north one and one-tenth mile on Routes 4 and 32 to a gravel road turning sharply left. Park and walk in.

STONE CABBAGES

The most lavish natural display of fossils in the state is the Cryptozoon Ledge near Saratoga Springs. (Cryptozoon means "secret animal".) The fossils are seen at two locations a half-mile

apart on the same road. The largest and best is the Petrified Sea
Gardens, privately maintained, with an admission fee. The other
is Lester Park, state-owned and free. The fossils are laid out like
circular designs in a carpet, ranging in diameter from a few inches
to three feet, and spectators walk over them. At the Sea Gardens,
the area of open limestone ledge is over 20 acres. The fossils were
a lowly species of blue-green algae. These proliferated in the
intertidal zone of a warm, shallow sea, in colonies that gradually
enlarged into stocks or "heads" loosely resembling
cabbages—hence the term "stone cabbage." Concentric layers
were added annually. Spaces between layers were filled by sand
as storm waves washed over the colonies; finally the "heads" were
buried altogether by sand, and in time became calcified. As a
favor to science, the glacier planed down the ledge so that the
"heads" were cross-sectioned. The state-owned ledge, Lester
Park, was so named for Mrs. Willard Lester of Saratoga, who
donated the site to the State Museum in 1914. From Saratoga,
take Route 29 west three miles to a junction with the Greenfield
Center Road; turn north three-fourths of a mile to the Petrified
Gardens Road. Lester Park is a little further ahead.

VALE OF SPRINGS

Rarely has a city owed so much to a fault as Saratoga Springs.
The McGregor Fault (see the chapter on Mount McGregor)
supplied the fissure up which the celebrated naturally carbonated
mineral waters arose from the depths, making Saratoga the
"Queen of Spas" in the Victorian era. In this century the state
created the beautiful Saratoga Springs Reservation, now a state
park. The newest asset of this park is the Saratoga Performing
Arts Center, fitted into a natural amphitheater in the ravine of
Geyser Brook. A short stroll down this ravine may be found the
Vale of Springs, which nicely symbolizes the role of the waters in
Saratoga's life. The so-called geysers are more realistically called
spouters. The star performer is the Island Spouter, which throws
a steady plume 30 feet high from a rock pedestal in midstream.
Mingled with the spouters are simple flows of water out of the

banks. As the carbon dioxide escapes from the water, the high
mineral content precipitates as tufa in the form of cones, mounds,
and terraces with a spectrum of pastel shades.

In the north part of Saratoga, in High Rock Park along Spring
Avenue, the dry cone of High Rock Spring is kept in a kiosk-like
shrine. This was the original Saratoga geyser that attracted the
Indians and was visited by Sir William Johnson for treatment of
his ailments. Behind it is a wall of rock that is the upthrust side of
the McGregor Fault coming aboveground. The famous Old Red
Spring, still flowing, is a short distance beyond.

Leaving the Adirondack Northway (I-87) at Exit 13, follow
signs for the Saratoga Performing Arts Center. A turn-off inside
the Reservation leads to separate parking areas for the Vale of
Springs. An alternate approach is Route 50 north from
Schenectady to the Performing Arts Center parking lot.

WINDHAM GAP

Windham High Peak is a unit in the towering northern rampart of
the Catskill Mountains, high above the humbler Helderbergs. It
attains an elevation of 3,524 feet. The higher levels of the
Helderberg Plateau are on the order of 2,000 feet, and the Catskill
silhouette looms beyond like a misty blue backdrop, at once
beckoning and austere. About midway up the bastion is a narrow
notch, the Windham Gap, which serves as a side entrance to the
inner sanctum. It is noteworthy that only on the east and the
north do the Catskills present a bold, distinctive wall; on the south
and west they dwindle off into foothills.

Route 23 west from Catskill (Thruway Exit 21) passes through
Cairo and then climbs the mountain, entering the Catskills proper
through Windham Gap. Near the crest of the ascent is a turn-off,
Point Lookout, which offers a striking perspective over the
Helderbergs and down the valley of the Catskill Creek to the
Hudson River and the Taconic Range beyond. If one chooses to
come upon the lookout from within the mountains, Windham
Gap is reached via Route 23-A through Tannersville, veering
north on Route 296 just beyond Hunter, to Route 23.

MIANUS RIVER GORGE

Hardly known to upstaters, the Mianus River puts on a capricious performance in the extreme southeast corner of the state. A short stream as rivers go, it sets off northerly from a source near Middle Patent in Westchester County. When close to Bedford Village it abruptly changes course to due south, describing a hairpin turn, and misses by only a mile-and-a-half the extreme embarrassment of meeting itself coming back. After decorous behavior up to now, it all at once goes rampantly whitewater through a wild gorge, then quiets down again in a city reservoir (Stamford, Connecticut), after which it proceeds tamely across the Connecticut panhandle into Long Island Sound.

Mianus River seems originally to have been a tributary to some north-flowing stream in New York State. The glacier changed the rules of the game, first by trapping an icy lake in the Bedford locality which drained into the Sound by creating a waterfall across a rock ridge in its way. The falls slashed a gorge straight through the ridge, a distance of less than two miles. The glacier then left behind mounded deposits that blocked off the previous northerly route of the river, forcing the Mianus to turn south and adopt the ready-made gorge to reach saltwater.

Through private subscriptions from nearby residents, the Mianus River Gorge has become a Wildlife Refuge and Botanical Preserve, and is registered as a Natural History Landmark. It was the first such preserve acquired with direct aid from the Nature Conservancy. Free to the public, the gorge is a naturalist's delight for its variety of fauna and flora, including a climax forest of tall hemlocks up to 300 years old. It is also the only place visited during field trips for this book that has trail signs warning against snakes—in this case, copperheads. Although they tend to mind their own business unless disturbed, it is well to watch one's step and keep to the trail. The latter is primarily a nature walk, and it does not follow the river after the start; the defile is so narrow that this would entail wading. Instead, it gradually mounts the west slope, permitting glimpses of cliffs and the galloping stream below.

Route 22 passes through Bedford Village. Bear south at the

village green on the Bedford-Stamford Road; turn right on
Miller's Hill Road, cross a bridge to the Mianus River Road, and
follow that to the entrance sign.

THE BEWILDERING BOULDER

Residents of the northeastern angle of Westchester County have
long known it as the Balanced Rock. It is an enormous boulder of
red granite estimated to weigh from 60 to 90 tons—a glacial erratic
ferried in from the north by creeping ice. It attracts a good deal of
passing notice in a grassy yard at the hub of North Salem, just
across the border from Danbury, Connecticut. The freakish thing
about this rock is the fact that it is perched about three feet off the
ground on five upright, tapered limestone "legs." To say the least,
it is a remarkable coincidence that the glacier would have let the
boulder down gently upon the tips of erect stones that nature had
thoughtfully arranged to receive it. Recently a claim that the
hand of man was involved has been drummed up by a clique of
amateur archeologists, but is dismissed as poppycock by the
professionals. The theorists are hammering the theme that this
elevated rock and other stone structures scattered in New England
were erected by Celtic pioneers who sailed the Atlantic as long as
2,000 years before the Christian era. The effort has come to a
head in a book, *America, B.C.*, by Barry Fell, a Harvard linguist,
who classes the North Salem rock as a dolmen—that is, an ancient
monument to some chieftain or to a historic event. He equates it
with known dolmens in Europe, which are usually flat slabs raised
on supports. The idea is that the Celtic invaders placed the
peg-stones, covered them with an earthen ramp on which they
jacked, or dragged, the great boulder into position, then removed
the earth. Dr. Robert W. Funk, state archeologist, discounts the
guesses about pre-Viking white settlers in America, saying there is
not a shred of hard evidence. Nonetheless, the activities of Fell
and his group have triggered a flurry of media publicity, and as a
result the Balanced Rock has become an even greater curiosity
than before. The North Salem Historical Society has placed a
"landmark" sign at the roadside.

North Salem can be found via Interstate 84 from Newburgh, veering south at Brewster on Route 684, leaving at Exit 8, following Hardscrabble Road and Baxter Road east. The village center is at the junction of Routes 116 and 121. From the metropolitan area, take Route 684 north from the Cross-Westchester Expressway (U.S. 287) to Exit 7, at Purdys, thence east on Route 116 (the Titicus Road).

FOREST PARK

As Brooklyn took advantage of the Harbor Hill moraine for its Prospect Park, so the Borough of Queens has used the same belt of glacial hillocks for its pleasing Forest Park, six miles further east. A mature oak woodland, laced with footpaths, shades a good portion of this tract, accounting for its name and that of the nearby community of Forest Hills. The west segment of the park is given over to the Forest Park Golf Course. This unit of the New York City parks system excels Prospect Park in the abundance of glacial kettle-holes, several of which contain ponds, and these have been tastefully merged into the landscaping. Erratic boulders are plentiful. The crest line of the moraine rises steeply 100 feet above the populous outwash plain, of which occasional vistas are glimpsed spreading southward to Jamaica Bay.

Forest Park is attainable via a number of heavily trafficked expressways. If driving direct from Prospect Park, follow Eastern Parkway (Route 27), taking a slight jog on Atlantic Avenue onto the Interborough Parkway, which passes through the north margin of Forest Park. Woodhaven Boulevard, south from the Long Island Expressway, bisects the park.

LAKE RONKONKOMA

Long Island has two glacial kettle-ponds of exceptional size: Lake Success and Lake Ronkonkoma. The former, just south of Manhasset, has been cited earlier as marking the pivot where the Harbor Hill and the Ronkonkoma moraines diverge like scissors blades. The adjacent village of Lake Success will be recalled as the original meeting place of the United Nations while its permanent home was under construction in Manhattan. The lake as such is not accessible to the general public, being incorporated in a golf course belonging to the village and thereby restricted to its residents. The village offices overlook the lake.

Lake Ronkonkoma, much the larger of the two, is nestled in the Ronkonkoma moraine about midway through the island. It is roughly a half-mile in diameter and 55 feet deep at maximum. Obviously, the block of ice that was left buried here and later melted out was monstrous. The basin is bowl-shaped and the lake has no visible outlet, its level varying with the subterranean water table. The lake is not especially scenic; it is almost entirely surrounded by cottages and a few restricted private and township beaches. Although it may be driven around, the only public access to the water is through two commercial approaches—the Lakeview and the Lighthouse Beaches.

Lake Ronkonkoma is reached from Exit 60 of the Long Island Expressway, north on Pond Road, then west on Smithtown Boulevard.

INDEX